ON RACE AND RACISM IN AMERICA

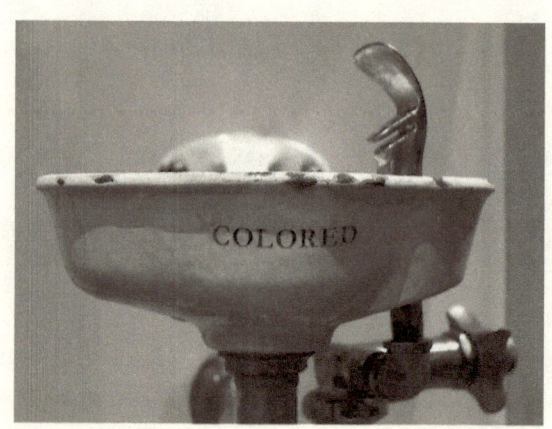

ON RACE AND RACISM IN AMERICA
Confessions in Philosophy

Edited by
ROY MARTINEZ

The Pennsylvania State University Press
University Park, Pennsylvania

Chapter 6 © David Couzens Hoy, 2008

Library of Congress Cataloging-in-Publication Data

On race and racism in America : confessions in philosophy / edited by Roy Martinez.
p.   cm.
Summary: "Essays by eight philosophers, working in the Continental and American pragmatist philosophical traditions, that address the issue of race, its social construction and myth, and the problems it raises on a daily basis"—Provided by publisher.
Includes bibliographical references and index.
ISBN 978-0-271-03639-7 (cloth : alk. paper)
1. Race awareness—United States.
2. Racism—United States.
3. United States—Race relations.
I. Martinez, Roy, 1947–2009.

E185.8.O52 2010
305.800973—dc22
2009032392

Copyright © 2010 The Pennsylvania State University
All rights reserved
Printed in the United States of America
Published by The Pennsylvania State University Press,
University Park, PA 16802-1003

The Pennsylvania State University Press is a member of the Association of American University Presses.

It is the policy of The Pennsylvania State University Press to use acid-free paper. Publications on uncoated stock satisfy the minimum requirements of American National Standard for Information Sciences—Permanence of Paper for Printed Library Material, ANSI Z39.48–1992.

This book is printed on Natures Natural, which contains 50% post-consumer waste.

In memory of

my sister,
Alice,
friend and confidante;

and my brother,
Mike,
my schoolboy model,
because of his intelligence
and
academic achievements.

CONTENTS

Preface and Acknowledgments   ix

Introduction   xi
Roy Martinez

PART ONE

1 Virtually Invisible:
On Seeing in the Dark   3
John D. Caputo

2 Personal Reflections on Racism in America   29
Joseph Margolis

3 The Dangers of Confession:
White Contributions to a Continental Philosophy of Race   38
Shannon Sullivan

4 Racism and Biopower   55
Ladelle McWhorter

PART TWO

5 Social Minimalism in a Liberal Culture
and the Problem of Racial Hubris   89
Cynthia Willett

6 Theorizing Difference:
Phenomenology Versus Post-structuralism   99
David Couzens Hoy

7 Continental Philosophy and the Concept of Race   114
Georgia Warnke

8 Philosophy in Chains   132
John Ladd

List of Contributors   147
Index   151

PREFACE AND ACKNOWLEDGMENTS

The genesis of this project is serendipitous. One afternoon while in my study enjoying a respite from something I was reading, my gaze strayed to one of the bookshelves and chanced on *The Invention of Race: Black Culture and the Politics of Representation* by Tommy Lott. Without exclaiming, "Eureka!" I nonetheless felt the impulse to do just that. Hold on, I said to myself. Whenever I attended the American Philosophical Association annual conference and look up the session on race, it seemed to me that for the most part the same African Americans composed the panel of presenters: Howard McGary, Lucius Outlaw, Bill Lawson, Leonard Harris, and Tommy Lott. Then the mighty absence came home to me in full force: where are they—the white philosophers who can also make a difference? Surely, said I, concern for justice and interrogating the questionable social practices that infest this country cannot be the bailiwick or even the preserve of African Americans alone! For heaven's sake, I mused, did not Aristotle write on the Constitution of Athens?

I have always been aware of two white philosophers who have relentlessly pursued the question of race and racism: David Theo Goldberg and Robert Bernasconi. They, however, are more the exception than the rule. In fact, it might be fair to hazard that their excursions into this field—professionally risky as it was for them—have enabled, if not encouraged, younger white philosophers to do the same. But it is worth noting that both of these philosophers were born outside the United States: Goldberg is from South Africa and Bernasconi from England. Therefore it remains to be asked why homegrown white philosophers have systematically avoided the issue. As soon as the idea crystallized and the project assumed a more definite form, I prepared a list of thinkers who, based on their prominence and membership in the continental tradition, I felt certain would be willing to participate. And surely enough they all accepted. But shortly thereafter reality sank in: of the twelve who at the outset expressed their desire to contribute to the volume, only eight had the courage to weather the storm. After all, there is no denying the touchiness of the topic of race in this country. But now that the question has been raised, we can no longer bury our heads in the sand. That is why I have attempted to deal squarely with this question in an intellectually stimulating discussion in the introduction.

I would like to thank Cindy, David, Georgia, Jack, Joe, John, Ladelle, and Shannon for their Job-like patience in bearing with me throughout a long and difficult period of inactivity on my part due to sudden illness. I am certain that there were moments when they considered alternative uses for the work they had so painstakingly put together to support the cause I had presented to them. Their trust in me is greatly appreciated.

To Alicia Smash I extend my warmest gratitude for proofreading certain texts and, more important, for her frequent assistance in solving computer-related problems. Without doubt, her kindness and understanding contributed to my morale during those trying times.

I also want to thank Dr. Johnnella Butler, provost of Spelman College, for encouraging me in my scholarly endeavors. Her firm belief in the life of mind serves as a catalyst for intellectual activity among faculty.

Roy Martinez
1947–2009

INTRODUCTION

Roy Martinez

I

The attack on the United States on September 11, 2001, that destroyed the twin towers of the World Trade Center and damaged parts of the Pentagon took the nation by surprise and forever changed the way Americans perceived themselves. They were forthwith compelled to see their country in a new light: the unique position of being the sole superpower yet no longer conferred the special privilege of invulnerability. They came to the bitter realization that they were not, after all, untouchable. There is more. It is crucial to bear in mind that this historic event severely wounded the nation's pride. Indeed, the unspoken pique that rankled and roiled the nation's soul is the fact that the foreign enemy that violated her on her own soil, the unseemly other that dared to aggress her and succeeded in outmaneuvering the global reach of her unparalleled intelligence, was not the legitimate military power of a sovereign state, but rather a small organization of *racially and religiously different* men. The telling feature of this muted rancor is that an act so singular and devastating, whose ferocious indecency reverberated worldwide, was perpetrated by a group of nonwhite men from the Middle East. It is not difficult to imagine how searing and challenging this experience must be for a country as racially charged as the United States. That is why the country, stunned and saddened, found itself deeply traumatized by the sheer insolence of the assault and felt instantly coerced to engage in a mode of painful soul-searching. In fact, since the United States takes such inordinate pride in its European heritage and the corresponding sentiment of racial purity and superiority, it is safe to surmise that its supreme self-confidence was seriously impaired, if not shattered. In a word, 9/11 marked a critical moment in U.S. history. Little wonder that the reaction of practically every American was heartfelt and visceral. No one escaped the ordeal unscathed. Irrespective of one's bent of mind—philosophical and ideological differences notwithstanding—the inhabitants of this erstwhile-inviolable land felt forced to reappraise their various attitudes toward one another and reassess their understanding of their own social reality.

The notion of social reality brings us face to face with the question that organizes this anthology: given the racial complexity of the United States—not to mention the persistent racism of its foundation—why is it that the most influential white philosophers have not addressed the issue of race, its social construction and myth, and the problems it raises on a daily basis?

It is clear from the outset that a simple and single rejoinder will not suffice. Nor is such an easy way out the aim of our inquiry. In fact, instead of parrying or otherwise burking the question with learned galimatias or gaseous disquisitions, we have attempted to treat our subject matter with intellectual honesty in the mode of *confession*, without, *pace* Saint Augustine, any religious undertone. For even if an act that considers itself a confession must be accompanied by a penitential strain, these chapters are not primarily motivated by a sense of remorse or offense. They tend, instead, to examine and analyze the problem in the dispassionate and reserved manner of philosophy. Further, the absence of a negative sentiment in this regard—if that is what it is—might merely mean that when many perpetrate an act, it is humanly difficult to assume personal blame. Or, even if culpability were in fact involved—that is, guilt was fervently felt—it nevertheless could have been so adroitly managed that repentance subtilized itself into a triumphant state of serene repose under the guise of insouciance. Given the intricate niceties of the heart, we would, in such a case, be better inspired by the observation made by Rémi Brague: "One must confront the past without letting a paralyzing guilt, which would prevent even the repair of what can be repaired, contaminate repentance."[1] Be that as it may, one thing is certain: a confession always attempts to come to terms with a consequential moment in a person's life. Our authors' participation in this project serves as an example of this claim. The question is direct and earnest, but its impulse is not, for that reason, accusatory. It intends neither to condemn nor blame. In spite of its interrogative form, its basic thrust does not mean to intimidate but to challenge and engage. Indeed, it hardly harbors the pretense that the truth lies buried beneath a murky mound of evidence that simply needs to be teased out or extracted "by any means necessary," to borrow the current parlance of politics. Philosophy, we trust, is infinitely friendlier than that; dialogue and discussion, not intimidation and coercion, should remain its animating principle or distinguishing trait. For although the chapters in this volume purport to "confess" their response to our question, they by no means do so in the Procrustean bed of "the dark twins."² No doubt the authors are confronted with the difficulty of telling the truth about an issue that is both personally and culturally sensitive. But they have undertaken the task with the plausive determination that accompanies what, in Foucault's lexicon, is named *parrhesia* or fearless speech.³

Even if the question is not accusatory, however, it is still not conciliatory, nor is it irenically rhetorical. It arises, after all, out of the troubling realization that something untoward, if not sinister, has been surreptitiously taking place in the profession. Its occurrence, we maintain, is not fortuitous. The assumption is that the silence concerning the issue of race is *willed*. It is an evasion. Further, this reticence seems to be supported by the axiom *quieta non movere*. In less esoteric language, so long as the current state of affairs suits one's purpose or sustains one's designs—however nefarious or crass—there is no urgency or need to upset the equilibrium. So let sleeping dogs lie. But in a racialized society such as ours, the situation is always one of human degradation, so that the silence surrounding it amounts to an indifference that is in essence virulent and vile. For indifference is not, as it might at first seem, an innocent and passive attitude that demurely awaits acquiescence. On the contrary, insofar as it disregards the suffering and daily humiliation of fellow human beings, indifference eo ipso assumes the rebarbative characteristics of contempt. How? As far as we know, "contempt constitutes the other as decidedly inferior, if not as some subhuman creature unworthy of human consideration. It is an attitude of extreme superiority on one's own part, which, as always, should make us suspect a certain defensiveness as well."⁴

In light of our study, the key term here is "a certain defensiveness." For it intimates, or rather indicates, that a person who shows contempt for another furtively protects something fragile in herself, something that threatens to disintegrate at the very moment of discovery. Let's be honest: we speak of the fear of self-discovery. What is being anxiously guarded in remaining mum about race and racism is a sense of vulnerability that refuses the risk of exploration and exposure. One reason for this defensive gesture might be that ancestral memory is at play, that the harsh, intolerable conditions that drove people from Europe in search of a decent life and a brighter future in this part of the world—conditions such as "poverty, prison, social ostracism, and not infrequently, death"⁵—continue to exert subterranean influence on the behavior of their descendants.

Hence, by the volatile quirks of self-preservation and survival, and with the aid of a cautionary calculus of *ne obliviscaris*, these descendants perversely, however inadvertently, ensure that a relapse to their previous ignominious lot will not occur. More interestingly, as if the erection of such a psychic fortress were not enough, they find it therapeutically fitting, with the device of race construction, to subject others to the same abject ways of living from which they themselves have been fortunately released. It is likewise curious that by a quaint logic of self-supporting superfluity this same creature, formerly forlorn, now has the gumption and guile to construe himself, in the revealing words of Tocqueville, "as the first who attracts the eye, the first in enlightenment, in power, in happiness." And here is the kicker: he projects himself as "man par excellence."[6] Serious stuff, this. Imagine popping up in your field of vision a peacockish pixilated popinjay. Behold the man indeed!

It is no matter for surprise, then, that a guarded silence reigns. After all, more than any other group of intellectuals, philosophers are conceptually attuned to the dynamics of dialectics, and are thus sensitively leery that questioning this issue may open up a Pandora's box, that it can always induce a shift in the focus of critical attention away from the hapless victims of racism to its cunning perpetrators. In other words, a great deal has certainly been written and said about the deleterious effects of racism on its intended victims, but hardly enough about the pathology that festers in the hearts and minds of those who practice it and profit from the debasement it fosters.

After all, the question must be asked: "Will we know one day? Will more extensive excavations enable us to understand the mystery of the birth of the classes? We confess we do not see how archeological finds will enable us to *understand* that, starting at a certain 'moment,' people saw one another and acted with respect to one another not as allies to help one another, rivals to surpass, enemies to exterminate or even to eat, but as *objects to possess*."[7] The question is rife with difficulties because of the contradiction or recalcitrance inherent in the very idea that a person, eminently endowed with subjectivity, is capable of considering another person as bereft of it. More intriguing is the fact that the *subject turned object* is treated not exclusively as the one or the other, but as a hybrid distillate of both, but more as object than as subject.

For try as one may, it is simply impossible to disregard the human element in the person one reprehensibly tries to render into a mere thing. That is why, among other reasons, the *slave*—considered as property, not as a *person*, much less a *citizen*—was regarded as "divested of two-fifths of the *man*."[8] Think, for a moment, of what might be going on in a mind that busies itself with determining the *worth*, not the *value*, of a human being in quintessentially quantitative terms. Think too of the motives, not just the intentions, behind such contrivances. Note well that while our intentions usually collaborate with our will, and are for that reason transparent, our motives tend to conceal themselves from fear of recognizing the full force of our actions and, by the same token, who we really are. They therefore incline to obscure, dissemble, or disguise themselves. In this way it is easy to appease our conscience when our deeds are degenerate or morally blameworthy. We can then rationalize, for example, that:

> in all social systems there must be a class to do the menial duties, to perform the drudgery of life. That is, a class requiring but a low order of intellect and but little skill. Its requisites are vigor, docility, fidelity. Such a class you must have or you would not have that other class which leads to progress, civilization, refinement. It constitutes the very mud-sill of society and of political government; and you might as well attempt to build a house in the air, as to build either the one or the other, except on this mud-sill. Fortunately for the South, she found a race adapted to the purpose of her hand. . . . We use them for our purpose and call them slaves.[9]

So wrote Governor James Hammond of South Carolina. Baffling, how progress, civilization, and refinement are gingerly associated with human degradation. Is it not worth our while to inquire into so vitiated a bent? The good governor had no problem identifying the qualities of his slaves: physical strength, malleability, subservience, and deficiency in intellect. But we now wonder what qualities the governor would have attributed to himself had he fortitude enough to examine himself *in foro conscientiae*. Could he have thought that the unflattering qualities he saw in the slaves are those of which he sought to divest himself? Might that not be one reason for constructing the notion of a *class*, a *race*: to compile the qualities in oneself that one deems detestable, and attribute them instead to the class, the race, to which one putatively does not belong?

Put in slightly different terms, if the collective consciousness is imbued with the sacred tenet that all men are created equal, then the illative is unerring that the *need to be superior* to others—this insalubrious gesture of serpentine pride—is directly proportional to the *inferiority one painfully feels* with respect to them. Again, it may very well be that the abortive effort to differentiate oneself from the ontological parity that defines human beings as a species is the sorry expression of a person desperately struggling to escape the self-induced horrors—perhaps the sense of a baleful foundation of nothingness—she confronts in the unbearable confines of her own singularity.

In a different manner, this process of rationalization is also discernible in Daniel Webster's March 7, 1850, speech, in which he descanted on the fugitive slave laws:

> But I will allude to the other complaints of the South, and especially to one which has in my opinion just foundation; and that is, that there has been found at the North, among individuals and among legislators, a disinclination to perform fully their constitutional duties in regard to the return of persons bound to service who have escaped into the free States. In that respect, the South, in my judgment, is right, and the North is wrong. Every member of every Northern legislature is bound by oath, like every other officer in the country, to support the Constitution of the United States that they shall deliver up fugitives from service is as binding in honor and conscience as any other article.[10]

Never for a moment did Webster pause, during his mellifluent and unctuous delivery, to think that the people who were fleeing from the South were desperately pursuing the full exercise of their subjectivity, the very freedom he himself was in fact abusing by mounting an argument so specious and self-righteous, so seemingly venal, as to draw tears from animals and stones. For employing the fig leaf of legality to disguise political ambition and craftiness, personal caprice and whatever else, cannot in truth justify a Constitution whose determined end is to transform human beings into beasts of burden. "No forms," says Emerson, "neither constitutions, nor laws, nor covenants, nor churches, nor bibles, are of any use in themselves. The Devil nestles comfortably into them all. There is no help but in the head and heart and hamstrings of a man."[11] There is no excuse, Emerson implies, for any human beings to empty themselves—in the manner of a vulgar kenosis, as it were—of the very principle that constitutes them as human beings, *dignity*, by daring to treat another as if she had none. What is more, no amount of casuistry, or sophistry, or solipsism, or any form of contrived self-deception, can ever succeed in undermining the moral substance of an individual. For to abuse one's sovereign freedom by dishonoring the person of another—as the torturer does to his powerless and unarmed victim—eventuates only in debasing oneself: "Then they eased him down, the noose tightened gradually, and Witzleben began to strangle even as they slid his pants off once the clogs had dropped. The camera missed none of this, although it could not smell the soiled pants from the last wearers, or what began pooling under him as he twisted, unable even to gasp. Face dark as liver. Froth. Penis like the iron crotch struts that jutted out, with metal foreskin flared, from the burning stakes of the Inquisition."[12] Is the torturer pleased with himself? Does he think that he is now more *exalted* than he was before perpetrating such sepulchral, heinous acts? The answer remains elusive if for no other reason than that the mind is nimble and wily enough to tell itself, "Evil is what my enemy does; it is 'never' what I do myself."[13] We say *exalted* because many a time, torturers, especially when employed by a government, will *execute* their lugubrious task with full confidence, unwavering conviction, and good conscience since their cause, *patriotism* or *national security*, is so noble! In the scene of execution cited above (from Paul West's historical novel *The Very Rich Hours of Count von Stauffenberg*), the torturers were acting on behalf of der Führer and the Reich. But if it is impossible to answer whether the executioner feels exalted, is it possible that in this case there is "a dilapidation of the soul"?[14] Let us move on. Now we come closer to home, following Ralph Ellison's story "A Party Down at the Square":

> I was trying to back away when Jed reached down and brought up a can of gasoline and threw it in the fire on the nigger.... The fire had burned the ropes they had tied him with, and he started jumping and kicking about like he was blind, and you could smell his skin burning. He kicked so hard that the platform, which was burning too, fell in, and he rolled out of the fire at my feet. I jumped back so he wouldn't get at me. I'll never forget it. Every time I eat barbecue I'll remember that nigger. His back was just like a barbecued hog.[15]

Admittedly, raising the question of race may signal some degree of danger or discomfort to the ego. But burying one's head in the sand is not in this case an option. For now that the question is on the table, intellectual integrity, together with social responsibility, demands an answer. Perhaps, when the prince is finally caught without his splendid raiments on, when his naked backside is deliciously or disappointingly exposed, he himself may come to realize or even admit the total destitution of the substance and heft he had hitherto feigned to possess. Another apt way of phrasing this is to say with Emerson, quoting Montesquieu: "It will not do to say that negroes are men, lest it turn out that whites are not."[16]

II

Why the Contributors Did Not Answer the Question Directly

The contributors, to be sure, wanted to reflect on race, but not necessarily in a way that would directly answer the question I raised. In fact, it appears as though in their own minds they answered the question by actually participating in the project. But the deeper question remains: why had they not hitherto addressed the issue? In my view, it would not be remiss to surmise that part of the reason for the demur should be sought in the practice of tradition. Since the founders or fathers of American philosophy—Jonathan Edwards, Charles Sanders Peirce, William James, Josiah Royce, George Santayana, John Dewey, and so forth—deliberately burked or made short shrift of the subject of race, their less illustrious successors followed suit by feeling justified in fostering so appalling a practice of silence, however socially irresponsible it may prove to be. Of course, the venerable founders themselves cannot escape the charge. After all, other intellectual lights—Henry David Thoreau, Ralph Waldo Emerson, and a visiting Alexis de Tocqueville, for example—had the subject on their agenda. Indeed, is it not interesting that in our own day, two compatriots of Tocqueville—Jean-Paul Sartre and Paul Ricoeur—after visiting or residing in the United States, deemed it pertinent to engage in some form of reflection on race in this country?[17] So, the question persists: why not American philosophers of comparable stature?

With respect to this eminent silence or neglect, another possibility worth pondering is that, in keeping with characteristic philosophical hauteur, our colleagues may consider the subject of race quite beneath their hallowed dignity. Perhaps, in short, the reality of race and racism is too sordid and squalid, too philistine and picayune, to deserve their serious attention, the royal splendor of their ponderous Apollonian gaze. This position, however, holds no water. Social and political philosophy, ethics, theodicy, and the treatment of any aspect or form of evil remain securely within the bounds of philosophical reflection, and the problem of race and racism is clearly not an exception.

To recapitulate: the contributors have chosen to answer the question according to their own lights. They were encouraged to proceed in the path of such independence, given the touchiness of the topic, to maximize the ease of creative flow and to produce a piece that would be sincere in both content and tone. The upshot of their earnest endeavor toward this end is that we have a volume containing a rich variety of views and styles, especially since of the eight authors, four are men and four are women. All of them, however different in age, title, or rank, are well-known or prominent members of the American continental tradition in philosophy. The strength of the volume is also supported by the fact that each of these studies is original and has not appeared elsewhere. As it turned out, four of the chapters have a more personal resonance than the others. Hence, in concert with the optative strain of our project, we've placed them as the first part mainly to set the tone for the remaining four, which are less personally imbued and more esoteric in focus and formulation.

On the Use of "Confessions"

Finally, what inspired us to borrow the word "confession" from Saint Augustine is not the religious raison d'être of his work, not the portrait of a man over whose very soul the sword of Damocles seems to suspend, not the narrator's personal quest for wholesome rest and repose in an "eternally ambient truth."[18] Nor is it, more precisely, the fact that the *Confessions* remains a living document of consummate self-analysis—to boot, the telling story of an unsettled soul fervently beset by the errors of its ways and thereof assailed by abysmal grief, struggling, despite all odds, to recover its pristine condition and regain the clarity, confidence, and composure of mental equilibrium. It was, rather, the fact that its verbal effulgence and overflow stand in stark contrast to the embarrassing silence—the verbal dearth—that gave rise to our project. Hence, in approaching the matter with an ironic twist, we contend that if there can be a confession in the form of a profuse outpouring of words, there may likewise be an occasion for a confession induced by challenging a disquieting and calculated silence. That, in brief, is the sole reason for using Augustine's work as a *sursum corda*.

Summaries of the Chapters

Caputo makes no apologies for having neglected to focus thematically on "race" as an item of interest in his professional writing. Nevertheless, he is emphatic in showing that ever since he presented "radical hermeneutics" on the intellectual landscape in the 1980s, his work has continued to underscore the plight of the disadvantaged, the disinherited, the social outcast, the marginalized, the rejected—those who are systematically excluded, the helpless who have been arbitrarily subjected to silence. Relying on his consummate skill as a phenomenologist—a critical analyst of Husserl and Heidegger, and an astute and sympathetic reader of Levinas and Derrida—Caputo examines the underside of key claims and pretensions of Western thought and finds them suspect in their motive and wanting in their morals. Here, for example, is a glaring instance of phenomenology hoist with its own petard: "The so-called pure ego is not only implicitly the 'man of reason,' but is also a Euro-white man, as if white were not itself one more color and Europe not just one more place on the map. The 'neutralization' in virtue of which the *epochē* allows the pure ego to appear ends up meaning to whiten out, to make something pure white." Impelled by the full force of sheer intellectual integrity, Caputo drives home his point: "Husserl's attempt to elevate 'Europe' into a spiritual essence, to essentialize Europe, was also an essentialization of white. . . . Pure reason is pure white." Perhaps because in the canonical thinking of the West whiteness—purity—is identified with the highest reaches of reason, which in turn becomes synonymous with light, truth, life itself, Caputo chose darkness as his theme, the very darkness with which Paul Simon fraternizes in his song "The Sounds of Silence." The relevance of darkness in this regard pertains to a vigilance against a kind of thinking that would situate the subject in the light, ergo the right. Caputo is convinced that there is no privileged human being, no one entrusted with a special message, no one given a secret, and that since this is the case, we are all together in this thing called life, all huddled together in darkness. Hence darkness can be used as a metaphor—our common ignorance about life—and also as a target of our prejudice: the other, the *tout autre*, that challenges our sense of complacence and in the same breath provokes our suspicion, fear, and hatred. Caputo's reference to Conrad's *Heart of Darkness* is an example of what we mean: "Here, in the United States—where Europeans of many nations, seeking freedom and a new world, forged a country on the basis both of the political ideals of the European Enlightenment and of the slaughter of both the native population and the African slave population—all of this together, not one without the other—we do not lack the occasion for such hospitality." In Caputo's lexicon, "hospitality" means the recognition in oneself of an "egological agon" that is resolved by coming to terms with one's own shortcomings, and in the end accepting someone who is totally different in her complete otherness.

In a refreshing piece of personal history—a remarkable departure from the taxing prose of his more theoretical work—Margolis presents a rare glimpse of his encounter with the sinister practice of racism. He recounts, with striking candor and sincerity, his painful experience of betrayal by neighbors, friends, and colleagues in academia when he dared to take a stand in the name of justice. On his accounting, one would have thought that, like Milton's Lucifer, Margolis had toyed with the sacrilegiously subversive idea of making a heaven of hell and a hell of heaven. Yet the gesture that incurred such vehemence and ire consisted of simply publishing a brief article on segregation—in the 1950s, granted—in the *AAUP Bulletin*. It was then that all hell broke loose: "My university contract was not renewed. The local and national AAUP never came to my defense or to the defense of free speech. And no one that I knew in the whole city of Columbia [South Carolina]—in government, university, town, media, circle of friends, acquaintances of every kind—ever came to my defense. Everyone shunned me like a leper." But as often happens in such crucial moments, a decisive individual comes forth. So, Margolis continues, "except for one white colleague who taught at a black college in Columbia, a splendid man, a neighbor in fact, who, together with his wife and children, was so terribly marginalized that he could make no possible difference," nobody supported him. There is much more in these rare down-to-earth reflections by Margolis that warrants the reader's attention. Although on the basis of his scholarly work he comes across as a philosopher's philosopher and as the principal proponent of "robust relativism," Margolis is, for all that, a man whose feet are solidly planted on the ground. Here is an example: "Suppose . . . that the West begins to imagine that it must equal the religious zeal that it perceives among suicide bombers of the Middle East. I don't believe that this is happening or is about to happen. But I do see how easy it would be to move in that direction, and I mistrust its allure." The point here is that Margolis *knows* what is taking place in the present world order and *understands* the reasons for it. The question that takes center stage, however, pertains to racism: can it be defeated? Margolis has his own ideas about it.

Whether by inadvertence or by design, Sullivan's personal and professional experience as a white woman informs the tenor and tone of her reflections. It follows that the chapter she contributes to this volume is unambiguously animated by a feminist voice. Sullivan spells out several salient reasons why, in her view, white philosophers for the most part shy away from the topic of race and racism. Initiating her inquiry with reference to her own situation, she writes: "I began to concentrate on race and white privilege because of sexism. I did not want to be perceived as 'complaining' about oppression, a perception that feminist but not antiracist struggle risked in my case." With rare candor and intellectual honesty, Sullivan discloses the inner turmoil she experiences both as an individual involved in the "possessive investment in whiteness," to borrow an apt phrase, and as a woman compelled to struggle against the sexism of male domination. Probing deeper into the sources of this state of uneasiness common to many women colleagues, Sullivan shares the following confidence: "For a white woman to philosophically reflect on sexism generally is for her to be 'in the right,' a position that often is more psychologically comfortable for her (even though she is rightly wary of the danger that this position will be reduced to that of wronged victim) than a position that puts her 'in the wrong,' as reflection on racism tends to do." In other words, a white woman feels morally justified and socially vindicated in fighting a system that faults her on the basis of gender alone, as opposed to taking up the cause against racism that would in effect attempt to subvert the racialized hierarchies that constitute the actual social order. The implication here is that on a subliminal level these women support the system of white domination that grants them the privilege they verily take for granted. Besides the Augustinian strain of self-analysis that marks Sullivan's captivating piece, other key factors are given equal consideration. She treats, for example, the questionable intellectual dependence of some American philosophers on thinkers from Europe; the effects of racist practices in the United States on the skepticism entertained by some white philosophers about the intellectual capabilities in philosophy of nonwhite individuals; the continued impact of the "recapitulation theory" on the population as a whole; Julia Kristeva's theory of foreignness; and more. Sullivan concludes her chapter by suggesting feasible ways by which the question of race may be fruitfully included in the academic practice of philosophy.

McWhorter begins by avowing her lifelong confusion about racism, "even while encountering and experiencing it daily." To help her gain some clarity on the issue, she reverts to Omi and Winnant's *Racial Formation in the United States from the 1960s to the 1990s*. In this work she discovers, much to her dismay, that the civil rights movement did not succeed in dispelling the ambiguity and perplexity of what racism means to most Americans. What had apparently aggravated the issue is the realization that a theoretical shift had taken place: racist practices were less discernible in individual behavior and more manifest in institutional structures. In view of this "overall crisis of meaning"—that racism hovers somewhere in limbo between the individual psyche and a collective consciousness embedded in social structures—the conclusion is drawn that there is no "commonsense" agreement on what racism means. For this reason, since the very meaning of the word "racism" has been obscured, the effort to challenge the practice becomes even more herculean. But the absence of a commonsense understanding of what racism means should not—indeed, cannot—deter philosophical reflection or discourage social engagement. Hence, while acknowledging the difficulty of "philosophizing about something if you don't know what it is, . . . with the professional risks of venturing into a relatively uncharted philosophical terrain," McWhorter contends that we are nevertheless morally bound to try. Further, she adduces a more visceral reason why she considers writing about racism both difficult and daunting: "the emotional risks of closely examining phenomena that have shaped and scarred us all since early life." In fact, this odyssey into the deeper recesses of our scheme of things is one that very few of us are honest and courageous enough to attempt. That is why, according to McWhorter's musings, few white philosophers venture to write about race. Another reason has a more professional basis, even though this too is no excuse for avoiding the issue at hand. On McWhorter's accounting, continental philosophers allow their reflections to be determined, for the most part, by texts "authored by someone with either a French or a German last name." It is therefore not surprising that the very philosophers who profess commitment to social problems within the discipline find themselves "stuck discussing the topics" those European thinkers "thought were important." While acknowledging some input from Sartre, Horkheimer, and Adorno, it is in Foucault's work—which investigates the concrete genealogies of cultural realities—that McWhorter finds the kind of relevance she needs to develop a genealogical account of modern racism in the United States.

Willett identifies herself as belonging to, and so situates her discourse within, the liberal philosophical tradition. But although she subscribes wholeheartedly to its principles of individual freedom and equality, she takes issue with its undue emphasis on the autonomy of the individual at the expense of what, in Hegel's lexicon, is called *sittlichkeit*, the primary ethical substance that constitutes the social practices, the concrete life, of a people. In effect, Willett's dismay with the disregard for the material and cultural conditions of existence displayed by the liberal outlook led her to African American writers and their treatment of race. The consequence of race in this context emerges in connection with the question of identity, and the relevance of identity is established by its unmediated link with self-reflection. On Willett's telling, philosophical thought itself, insofar as it seeks to develop our capacities for self-understanding, begins with reflections we conduct about ourselves. The problem, however, is that today "white philosophers typically do not think of ourselves as having significant racial or social identities, and so categories such as race do not often play a role in our philosophical reflection." Willett is alluding to the deep-seated conviction on the part of many a white person that in establishing one's identity, reference to whiteness is simply unnecessary. The fact that our bodies manifest themselves in different perceptible forms should not oblige us, Willett argues, to subject those who look least like us to abjection, humiliation, or death. That is why working toward a color-blind and race-free society remains a worthwhile endeavor, even though, or perhaps precisely because, the obstacles to its realization are persistent, nefarious, and legion. In her efforts to articulate a response to the issues of racism in America, Willett deploys her ample acquaintance with the works of Hegel, Merleau-Ponty, Bourdieu, Patricia Hill Collins, Du Bois, Frederick Douglass, and Toni Morrison. The upshot of Willett's inquiry is that the tendency of liberal philosophers to downplay "the social drama of the family, its entangled connection with community and history," must be renounced if the urgent problem of race is to be given serious consideration.

While agreeing on the timeliness of race as a social issue, Hoy indicates that philosophers have disregarded the question of race because of first philosophy's ingrained pretension to treat only the universal and timeless features of human existence. The mishap of Thales—his notorious artesian dip due to inordinate astral musings—is the legendary case frequently adduced to illustrate the perils of paying scant attention to the ways of the world. But Hoy points out that efforts have been made by some philosophers—Sartre and Foucault, for example—to focus less on universal essence and more on difference and particularity. Hence, to offset the structural shortcomings of first philosophy (or foundationalism, as it is also called), Hoy reverts to the methodologies of critical theory and the reflexive sociology of Bourdieu. "Briefly," writes Hoy, "whereas traditional theory assumes a timeless standpoint for its pronouncements, critical theory recognizes that the need for theory arises only in a certain situation and that it can illuminate only that situation. Thus when race is the topic, even if one does not think that race is real under ideal circumstances, one can think that in present society race has real effects." Under this rubric, race would be an apt and viable topic for analysis. The insight in Bourdieu that has a singular appeal to Hoy is the conception of a "field" and the "habitus" that come into play. Hoy's concern pertains to the likelihood that there is indeed something about the field of philosophy that has blinded philosophers from seeing what should be so obvious: issues about race. He explains: "The habitus is made up of dispositions that have been built into the bodily hexis throughout the formative years and that are shared by all who belong to a given social group. The field is the background that makes the moves of the habitus intelligible. If the field is the game, the habitus is the feel for the game." He then remarks on the two possible ways of construing the relation of the field and the habitus: (1) causal, where the individual's actions are determined by the habitus; and (2) as a grid of intelligibility, where some actions may seem appropriate and others inappropriate. Hoy subscribes to the second option because it enables philosophy to reinterpret itself to overcome its empyreal aloofness and immediate social evils. According to Hoy, Sartre and Foucault are good examples of thinkers who have owned up to their social responsibilities in treating, however tentatively or programmatically, the problems engendered by the construction of race. He supports his claim by a close reading of Sartre's "Portrait of the Anti-Semite," for example, and by examining the notion of biopower in Foucault's *"Society Must Be Defended."*

For Warnke, the conundrum of racism consists in its overriding insistence on a totalizing tendency. Given the plurality of human characteristics and the variety of social markers people employ in calling attention to themselves, why do they incline toward singling out a particular feature or trait to claim adamantly, to establish conclusively, who they are? Phrased in a different way, by what moot measure, from what misguided motive, in the name of what perverse affectation does one opt to confer on oneself so perilous a reduction of being? Warnke, who initiates her inquiry with a close reading of a study on race by Kwame Anthony Appiah, shares his contention that a partial solution to the problem of race and racism is to assert and affirm one's nonracial identities. Thus, "if we remember that we are not only 'blacks' or 'whites,' but also brothers and sisters, members of different or no religions, chess lovers and baseball players, we can take up a set of crosscutting and interlocking identities. . . . In this way we reduce the tendency of our racial identities to exhaust the options for who we are." An idea in Appiah that appeals greatly to Warnke is the distinction made between racial identities that purport to be "recreational." When one is construed to belong to a separate "race" in the United States, as was the case with the Irish and the Italians, for example, the difference is taken to be *fundamental*. But when "whiteness" was transmuted into the defining characteristic of a race, whiteness itself became basic, and being "Irish" or "Italian" transposed into an exercise of optional identification. In this sense, persons can choose to disclose their ethnic identities and display their cultural affiliations on days of national celebrations and other occasions of group gatherings. The snag here, of course, is that under this state of affairs only persons categorized as white are granted the privilege to assume recreational identities. The good thing about recreational identity—its salutary feature—is that it is freely chosen. More, the individual does not feel constrained to remain straitjacketed in it. That is why Warnke wonders about the possibility of attaining the freedom of recreational identities without presupposing the inflexibility of a more fundamental racial identity. How will she treat the issue? What tack will she pursue? She responds: "I think the insights of hermeneutics, and particularly of Gadamer's philosophical hermeneutics, can help in this endeavor." Why? "To identify individuals as black, white, Hispanic, or Asian is to understand them in a certain way. To this extent race is an interpretation, and our inquiry into it might begin by looking at the elements that philosophical hermeneutics identifies in our interpretations of texts."

In a discussion designed to be open-ended and thought provoking rather than conclusive, Ladd demonstrates how the experiential basis of philosophy has been stultified and hedged by the arbitrary constraints of Anglo-American practice. The fact that the chapter is admittedly programmatic in form should not belie the significance of the problems it treats, the gravity of the claims it makes, and the solutions it proposes. By the term "philosophy in chains" Ladd means "that the dominant ethos of today's mainstream Anglo-American philosophy imposes restrictions on the right aims of doing philosophy, on the proper sorts of problems to be explored, and on the right ways of dealing with them. As a result it closes off areas of philosophical exploration that an open inquiring philosopher might want to develop." The question that immediately arises is this: what would motivate a discipline, whose reason for being consists in exploring whatever pertains to human development, to stifle or impair its own nisus by such self-imposed constraints? The answer offered in this piece is as clear as it is complex: cultural imperialism. In Ladd's view, to summarily dismiss as "primitive" the social practices of others without exerting any effort to understand their *sittlich* bases, "is not only theoretically (and empirically) absurd but also immoral and politically dangerous." This observation, banal as it may seem because of its truism, is nonetheless apt to inspire, for example, a critical self-assessment on the part of those whose lives have been affected by 9/11. In other words, arrogating "rational" privilege to our own entrenched ways of being, and in the same breath ascribing primitivism, decadence, and barbarism to other societies, can no longer be assumed as grounds for a solution. On the contrary, that way of thinking contributes eminently to the problem. Ladd also considers the question of personal identity, regarded by mainstream philosophy as purely metaphysical and, in his view, treated with corresponding detachment or indifference. Inspired by

Eric Erickson's theory of "identity crises," Ladd proffers that "the concept of identity used by people of color belongs to an entirely different category from that of the concept used in mainline philosophical circles.... The kinds of problem that involve this psychosocial concept of identity are questions like: 'Who am I?' 'Where do I fit in a multiracial and multiethnic world?' 'Where do I belong?' and so on." It is worth noting that Ladd's reflections on these issues remain consistent with his efforts long ago to broaden the scope of philosophy as far back as 1957, when he published his groundbreaking study *The Structure of a Moral Code: A Philosophical Analysis of Ethical Discourse Applied to the Ethics of the Navaho Indians.*

In sum, the distinctive feature of this anthology—the mark that sets it quite apart—lies in the fact that of the myriad studies that focus on race matters in this country, it alone dares to ask distinguished white philosophers why they have not hitherto addressed publicly the urgent issue of race and racism. Thus the question that guides our work, which is as direct as it is unflinching, compels the individual contributor to engage in an unusual and critical self-analysis that, by virtue of its sheer personal tenor, is certain to draw the attention of faculty and students in various academic disciplines.

NOTES

1. Rémi Brague, *Eccentric Culture: A Theory of Western Civilization,* trans. Samuel Lester (South Bend, Ind.: St. Augustine's Press, 2002), 139.
2. Regarding "the dark twins," Michel Foucault writes, "Greek law had already coupled torture and confession, at least where slaves were concerned, and Imperial Roman law had widened the practice." *The History of Sexuality,* vol. 1, *An Introduction,* trans. Robert Hurley (New York: Vintage Books, 1980), 59n1.
3. Michel Foucault, *Fearless Speech,* ed. Joseph Pearson (Los Angeles: Semiotext[e], 2001), 13.
4. Robert C. Solomon, *The Passions: Emotions and the Meaning of Life* (Indianapolis: Hackett, 1993), 233.
5. Toni Morrison, *Playing in the Dark: Whiteness and the Literary Imagination* (New York: Vintage Books, 1993), 34.
6. Alexis de Tocqueville, *Democracy in America,* trans. and ed. Harvey C. Mansfield and Delba Winthrop (Chicago: University of Chicago Press, 2000), 303.
7. Cornelius Castoriadis, *The Imaginary Institution of Society,* trans. Kathleen Blamey (Cambridge, Mass.: MIT Press, 1998), 154.
8. Alexander Hamilton, James Madison, and John Jay, *The Federalist; or, The New Constitution* (New York: Dutton, 1961), no. 54, p. 280.
9. Quoted in Jean-Paul Sartre, *Notebooks for an Ethics,* trans. David Pellauer (Chicago: University of Chicago Press, 1992), 568.
10. Daniel Webster, "The Seventh of March Speech" (March 7, 1850), http://www.dartmouth.edu/~dwebster/speeches/seventh-march.html.
11. *The Portable Emerson,* ed. Carl Bode (New York: Viking Penguin, 1981), 551.

12. Paul West, *The Very Rich Hours of Count von Stauffenberg* (Woodstock, N.Y.: Overlook Press, 1989), 298.

13. Jean-Paul Sartre, *Saint Genet: Actor and Martyr*, trans. Bernard Frechtman (New York: Pantheon Books, 1963), 151.

14. West, *Count von Stauffenberg*, 7.

15. Ralph Ellison, "A Party Down at the Square," in *Flying Home, and Other Stories*, ed. John F. Callahan (New York: Random House, 1996), 9.

16. *Portable Emerson*, 553.

17. Jean-Paul Sartre, "The Oppression of Blacks in the United States," in *Notebooks for an Ethics*; Paul Ricoeur, *Critique and Conviction: Conversations with François Azouvi and Marc de Launay*, trans. Kathleen Blamey (New York: Columbia University Press, 1998), 47.

18. William C. Spengemann, *The Forms of Autobiography: Episodes in the History of a Literary Genre* (New Haven: Yale University Press, 1980), 1.

PART ONE

1

VIRTUALLY INVISIBLE: ON SEEING IN THE DARK

John D. Caputo

> Hello, darkness, my old friend,
> I've come to talk with you again.
> —*Paul Simon, "The Sounds of Silence"*

On the Verge of Having Very Nearly Seen It

Here I am, *me voici*, on the spot, having been summoned before the law by Roy Martinez, put in the accusative by his inquisitorial question, about my failure to raise the question of race.

Here I am, guilty as sin, trying to explain myself. I, who have always been a question to myself long before I read Augustine or Heidegger, now have another question keeping me up at night. How am I to understand what is not there, to explain something that did not happen? It is like exhuming an empty grave, or hoping to recall a past that was never present—or looking for an invisible man.

Martinez is right. Except for certain marginal or passing references, certain asides or remarks in apposition, certain discussions occasioned by the context, I have never really raised the question of race. Not *as such*. I have never really thematized it, made it an explicit object of analysis, never subjected it to a sustained inquiry or examination, never made the question completely *visible*.

I want here at the start to acknowledge the invaluable assistance given to me in the preparation of this chapter by my graduate assistant, Leigh Johnson. By her incisive and careful critique of my argument she saved me from myself more times than I can count. Further, she not only improved the body of the text substantially, but by her exhaustive knowledge of the field of race studies she supplied all the crucial endnotes—the interesting and informative ones are hers!—that refer the reader to the appropriate literature and relate my views on the ongoing debates in the field.

The jury is back and I am a convicted man. All that I can do now is plead for mercy at the sentencing. Here is my plea, my poor excuse for an explanation, although my attorneys advise me against it. It has clearly been on the tip of my tongue, or in the back of my mind, and everything indicated that I was on the verge of having very nearly said it, of having very nearly seen it. It was virtually visible, *in virtute*, by the power of a certain presence (which, being strictly virtual, is also a very telling absence). It was present every time I sang a song with Derrida to the democracy to come, a democracy all the way down, in which we give hope a chance, and every time I sang a song with Amos to let justice flow like water over the land. It was there every time I cited and recited with Levinas the biblical string "the widow, the orphan, and the stranger." Surely everyone knows that such a list is not meant to be an exhaustive inventory but rather a kind of metonymic sampler of all the world's misery, of the suffering born not only of untimely death and uprooting, but of all of the suffering of everyone in every corner of the world who suffers for whatever reason. The widows, orphans, strangers—*and so on and so forth.* There it is, as clear as day, in the "and so on and so forth." What more could Martinez, could anyone, want of me?

Alas, the attorneys are right. I should just confess and ask for forgiveness and let it go at that. I know as well as anyone how lame an argument this is, to have gotten as about as far as the "and so on and so forth." If the question of race is only virtually visible in my texts, that means it is actually invisible. I am convicting myself and only making things worse. That is the old problem of Ralph Ellison's "invisible man."[1] I have walked right into it and Martinez has called me on it. The faces of the jury have grown sterner and I am breaking out into a sweat.

Here I am, a guilty man. I do not deny it. I am just trying to avoid a lengthy sentence and so I ask the court at least to enter this much into the record, to include it in my allocution, so that my grandchildren will not think the less of me. Whenever I spoke about the democracy to come, or the widow, the orphan, and the stranger, race was on my mind as well, or at least in the back of my mind. Somehow or other it was staring me in the face. It was clearly included in *On Religion* when I was talking about "true religion": "True religion, genuine religiousness, means loving God, which means a restlessness with the real that involves risking your neck; it means serving the widow, the orphan, and the stranger in the worst streets of the most dangerous neighborhoods."[2] By the "worst neighborhoods" everyone will certainly understand that I meant the ghettoes of American cities, which are populated disproportionately by the raced "and so and so forth," these citadels of shame to the distance between what is called democracy and what democracy calls for, the democracy to come. By the "widow, the orphan, and the stranger" I was clearly talking about the great-great-grandchildren of slaves who populate the most desperate and deprived spaces in this land of excess. Indeed, what makes more sense than to add the slave to this list?[3]

Moreover, when I was defending the idea of the democracy to come against the charge that it might lead to despair, I said that the slightest injustice is intolerable and that we cannot tell "those poor, ill-housed children in North Philadelphia, going to some of the worst schools in the nation, [that they] are moments in the progress of free-market capitalism towards the City on the Hill, so relax, they will get by . . . justice is to come, it is not here, not now, not in the Bronx or North Philadelphia, not in Manhattan's skyscrapers or Silicon Valley."[4]

Again, in another place in the same text, explaining the fruitfulness of the "concrete messianisms," as opposed to the abstract messianic, I got down to naming names, to real people who instantiated what I, as a faithful follower of the prophet Amos, meant by true religion, even when they are nameless: "That is why it has always been possible, and this is its finest hour, for a given messianism [like Christianity] to nourish and bring forth the likes of Dietrich Bonhoeffer, Martin Luther King, and Dorothy Day, and beyond them countless other peacemakers, in parish basements and crime infested neighborhoods everywhere, who do not make headlines but who do make peace and justice flow like water across the land, which is the best flow of all."[5]

I beg the court's indulgence to allow me to add one thing before sentence is passed. Everything, and I mean *everything*, that I found objectionable about Heidegger in *Demythologizing Heidegger* and *Against Ethics* had to do then, and still has to do now, with the extent to which his hymn to the Greco-Greeks was at one and the same time the stuff of a despicable politics that invidiously celebrated *Volk*, race, blood and soil, and a higher transcription of that politics into a spiritual form.[6] Heidegger not only wanted the streets of Germany to be *Judenfrei*, but that is also how he envisaged his mythical history of Being. In a famous interview, Heidegger said, evidently with a perfectly straight face (I was not there), that the only way the truth of Being could be poetically thought and experienced was in Greek, and that the German language was the spiritual cousin or son of—you can be sure that it was some kind of blood relation to—Greek. Heidegger was not speculating idly about this. He had proof of it: some of his best French friends assured him that when they wanted to think—as opposed, perhaps, to selecting a good wine or making love—they had to switch to German; they could not make it in their own language. As Derrida said, this would be wildly funny were it not wildly dangerous.[7] Everything about those two books turned on a satire—Heidegger's position is beneath contempt, beneath argument—both of this racist non-sense and of a new phenomenology of suffering "jew-greek" flesh, an expression meant to fuse Derrida's Joyceanism and Lyotard's *les juifs* to give concretion to Levinas's *tout autre*.[8]

So the "widow, the orphan, and the stranger" covers a lot more than widows, orphans, and strangers. When I speak about religion I do not have in mind a priestly but a prophetic performance, a call for justice in the streets. By religious people I do not mean career diplomats at the Vatican but wild-eyed prophets like Amos giving holy hell to the Israelite powers that be. As Johannes Climacus quipped, what religion needs today (by which he meant 1844, but it was ever thus) is not a new hymnal, but a will to convert the currency of religious talk into the coin of a *deed*. Climacus said we need to bring religion into the living room, which is perfectly true, but I would add that we also need to bring it into the streets, the worst streets in the worst neighborhoods![9]

Protesting Too Much

So, then, we can all sleep easily tonight, and I especially have earned a good night's sleep, ever the reward of the sound-snoring somnolence of a drowsy good conscience.

Alas, would that it were so and that I could get some rest. Poor wretch of a fellow that I am, I am protesting too much, and with each word out of my mouth the jury forms a more unfavorable opinion of me. I should simply face my sentence like a man, which is what the attorneys advise. For the fact remains that the issue of race has never been thematized, not *as such*! The fate of black Americans in particular, as such, as black, as African American, as a diasporic *race*, has never been raised *as such*. The streets of the "worst neighborhoods"—which is an economic category—are also populated by white people, too, who can be just as desperately poor as the next guy. By the same token, *les juifs*, while it can be made to stand for all the others, all the other others, does not explicitly name the African or the Asian or the Arab—not *as such*. While there is much to be said for maintaining, as does Lyotard, that today *les juifs*—uncapitalized, the others who suffer from their alterity—are actually the Palestinians, it would be asking too much to let things stand with that irony and settle for calling the Palestinians the new Jews. That, after all, is what we mean by being invisible.

While it is true—I at least believe, even if no one else does—that I did have race in the back of my mind, what is exposed by the merciless white light of Martinez's interrogation is why I was never moved to make it explicitly visible, to put it down in black and white (if I may say so). As best I can explain this to myself, it is because the category that interested me all along was the wider category of "innocent suffering," in which racial injustice is included as the particular included in the universal. Well, to be a little more honest, not "all along," but since the mid-1980s. Like a born-again Christian, I can almost identify the day and the hour: it was the point at which I decided that *Radical Hermeneutics* was not concluded with the completion of the seventh chapter, which is where it was supposed to end; that moment when I sat there looking at those seven chapters with the gnawing feeling that the book was not over and that I needed to add something "in my own voice." So I opened my mouth and out came three chapters, on rationality, on ethics, and on religion, that forged my "research program" for the rest of my life (although I did not realize that at the time). I had, in my mid-forties, finally begun to get around to ethics and politics. "Religion," which hitherto had mostly meant mysticism to me, began to mean prophetic religion, which means the summons to address the victims of innocent suffering. By that I meant, among other things, the suffering of the other who suffers in and from his or her alterity. The cases, the casualties of alterity, who pressed themselves on me at the time were homosexuals, women, and the victims of economic oppression, which reflected the concerns of both the new left and the old left, the evils of both humiliation and poverty, but without favoring one over the other. While Rorty has made a point of distinguishing them,[10] to single out the distance that the academic left has put between itself and the real political left, I never felt any impulse to have to choose between them. Why not take over the English department *and* form more and stronger labor unions?

My friendship with Drucilla Cornell drove home the arguments of feminist theory to me in a way that made perfect sense, and I made them my own. When I read the feminists I realized that I had all along, always and already, long before I had thought about or read feminist theory, taken the side of what feminists called an alternate epistemology. I realized that right from the start, from my earliest studies, I too was in search of an alternative to the "man of reason."[11] I have been looking for a way of thinking separate from Enlightenment rationality before I even knew much about the Enlightenment.

By the same token, homosexuality too was a perfect example for my ironic stand "against ethics," a perfect illustration of "inventing the good," of the plurivocity, polyphony, and polymorphism of the good, of making love not war, as we used to say in the '60s, as opposed to the monotony of evil that always comes back to innocent suffering. Defending homosexual rights offended the reactionary sensibilities of the Christian right wing and forced a critical rereading of the relevant scriptural texts, which gave me great delight. I was sure it passed the "WWJD?" test—it is exactly the sort of thing that Jesus would have done and, as Dostoevsky predicts, the Christian churches would have made Jesus pay dearly for it! The gap between Jesus and the "churches" seems to me to be irreducible. The issue of homosexuality had taken on a biblical tonality. The victims of AIDS—at that time, in the early and mid-1990s, AIDS was primarily a homosexual problem—were treated like the biblical lepers, victims of a terrifying and incurable disease, from whom everyone feared contamination. The religious right—God bless them, you can always count on them to say something profoundly stupid and deeply offensive—pronounced AIDS a just punishment from God for the unnatural sin of homosexual love![12] We watched brilliant artists and gifted thinkers—we American continentalists all knew that Reiner Schürmann and Michel Foucault were dying—succumb to it. Today in the United States and western Europe, of course, the drugs that are necessary to control AIDS are available, so that it has become not a homosexual but an African disease,[13] a "black" disease, where fully a third of the population of Africa, a land of abject poverty, over thirty million people,[14] have been infected and the resources to control it are unavailable because they are so costly.

Heart of Darkness

If Martinez is right, if the question of *race*, race *as such*, never managed to become the subject of an explicit analysis for me, what do I have to say now that I am asked to raise the question explicitly? How can I graft this question into my work, or better, expose my work to this question? To answer that, I will take darkness as my theme, addressing darkness our old friend, as Paul Simon says. What follows will be an essay on darkness and on things that are visible and invisible in the night.

As a start in that direction, allow me to revisit my debate with my dear friend Bill Richardson about Heidegger and the interpretation of Joseph Conrad's *Heart of Darkness*. I was in that text very explicit about the black faces that in my view are erased by a Heideggerian reading of Conrad, according to which Kurtz's corruption was a matter of the errancy of Being itself, *die Irre*. Against this I protested that it did not have to do with Being, but on the contrary: "it had to do with *faces*, with his [Kurtz's] utter nullification of the face of the other.... Those black faces around him in the jungle were not faces that faced Kurtz down, that commanded his respect, but instruments of Kurtz's 'plans' or obstacles to be removed."[15] So I introduced Levinas to counter this Heideggerianism. I continued: "When he went out into that dark world, that wilderness that was devoid of the trappings of European civility, of its laws and institutions, Kurtz made himself into a kind of white god and a law unto himself.... It was Kurtz himself who had become the savage among these hapless people who were thoroughly terrified by this magnificent European specimen, half English and half French.... Kurtz was out to save them, to bring them Being's word from the West." Kurtz might well have approved of Heidegger's story about how the sun of Being had settled over white Europe but not the Dark Continent. I went on:

> The darkness here is not the darkness of Being but the darkness of dark skins and of faces from which the light of humanity had been extinguished, of black men who are not us, not Greco-European, who are not capable of *Dichten* and *Denken*, and the darkness of a heart which cannot see a human face looking back at him from behind these blackened skins, which is invulnerable to the violence of severed heads. It was not his unmindfulness of Being's gleam that had darkened Kurtz's heart. It was his oblivion of the Law inscribed in those faces, the darkness of a heart that saw nothing human, nothing worthy of respect, looking back at him from those black faces, that indeed saw no face at all in this land where anything is possible, where you could do anything.

I take this up not as a further plea for mercy, for it is clear that even here what is at stake was the interpretation of Heidegger, not the question of the Congo. Be that as it may, I return to it because, having been confronted with the question of race by Roy Martinez, this piece has been my most explicit treatment of race, where the approach I took was Levinasian.

In Levinas, the face is—and, in this context, this now seems striking— precisely "invisible," a word that, in the context of race, is so politically charged. But taken in its own context, Levinas is distinguishing between a visible physical surface and an invisible moral depth. The face is not merely a visible surface, not because it is less than visible, but because it is more than visible, because the sphere of visible phenomenality does not reach as far as the true face. It is not that the face fails to be visible, but that visibility fails to reach as far as the true face. The true face of the other is not the visually given face—eyes, lips, a nose, and so forth—first, because it is the entirety of the incarnate flesh of the other, not just a part. More important, the true face is not simply the visible body but also the invisible moral command that is issued from that body, which is paradigmatically or metonymically centered on the face or the eyes of the other. The face of the other for Levinas issues the first word, the archi-imperative "thou shalt not kill," like the blood of Abel crying from the ground. This command comes to us from beyond visibility, beyond being, with the power and the impotence of a face, which has no armies.

Levinas is clearly a postholocaust thinker and his ethics, or meta-ethics, has clearly been born of the Jewish experience of the deportations and the camps, where the only defense against a merciless murder was face of the other, of the Jewish other, from whose helpless eyes issued the cry of Abel, "Thou shalt not kill." Levinas said that this analysis was not in any way limited to Jews but had to do with everyone. *Otherwise Than Being* is dedicated, in this order, to: those who were closest to him—and at the bottom of the dedication page he identifies in Hebrew his mother and father, his brothers, his mother-in-law and father-in-law—to the six million Jews killed in the Holocaust, and to everyone else who was murdered by the Nazis.[16] They were all victims of "the same hatred of the other man," which he describes as "the same anti-semitism," without capital letters, where the "Semites," the "Jews," stand in, metonymically, for every human being who is unjustly persecuted, a usage that prompted Lyotard later on to speak of *les juifs*, without capital letters, as a metonym for every innocent victim. What Levinas is saying is entirely justified by the context. But it is of course not without risk, for the danger is that one would be lulled by this usage into forgetting the suffering of everyone who is not Jewish, like the sufferings of the Palestinians. Exemplarism is risky business, like saying "fraternity" when what you mean is the communal bonds that unite both men and women, or "phallus" when you do not mean anything merely anatomically masculine.

One understands Levinas's motives for stressing the invisibility of the other person; they are Husserlian, coming as a re-inscription of the primarily epistemic or cognitive analysis of the Fifth Cartesian Meditation into an ethical context.[17] In Husserl the alterity of the other is constituted precisely by the inaccessibility of the other, the radical and in principle *non*-givenness of the *Erlebnisse* of the other ego. That inaccessibility is not a privation or defect but an affirmative mark of excellence, the positive excess of the other beyond the reach of our intentional stream. The impossibility of being phenomenally given as a part of our intentional stream constitutes in an affirmative way the very phenomenality or ultra-phenomenality of the other person, the eminence of the other. Levinas's motives are also Kantian, as he is re-inscribing a Kantian motif about the noumenal self into a phenomenological context. The categorical command to treat the other as the object of an absolute respect comes to me indeed from beyond the phenomenal order, not as a noumenal command issued by an abstract "reason," but concretely in the face of the one before me, the one whose claim on me is not exhausted or contained by his or her visible presence. Against Kant, this ethical command is concrete, not a dictate of pure reason; against Husserl, this ultra-phenomenality occurs in an asymmetric ethical field, not on the level plane of cognitive analogy and reciprocity. The face is constituted not by its visible surface, but by its distance, which always already recedes from vision like a shore that we can never reach.

We cannot be grateful enough for the profundity of Levinas's analysis: it is not too much to say that it spearheaded a deeply ethical turn in continental thought in the last twenty-five years. But the difficulty with it is that, however concrete it means to be, it is not concrete enough. Levinas changed the grammatical case of the self from a pure transcendental epistemic "I," in the nominative, to a pure ethical subject, "me," in the accusative. He changed the *case* of the "I" but not the *space*, for this was a change that took place more in pure transcendental—or metaphysical—space than in concretely situated space of factical life. To be sure, Levinas had made considerable headway in this direction when he complained, against Heidegger, that *Dasein* does not get hungry,[18] and insisted that philosophy should be interested in good soup and produced an analysis of the body that would have been worthy of Merleau-Ponty himself. But the work of concretization he undertook stopped short and resisted the analysis of the political, sociological, economic, and historical circumstances in which the ethical subject is always and already factically situated, in which questions of race and gender are lodged. In *Adieu to Emmanuel Levinas*, Derrida tried to nudge this largely ethical analysis in the direction of politics.

To employ a Heideggerian distinction that Levinas would reject, his analysis is conducted too much on an ontological level and is not adequately ontic. To use Levinas's own vocabulary, it is too exclusively or profoundly "metaphysical," too transcendent. It runs the risk run by everything that wants to be deep—a risk of which Heidegger regularly ran afoul—of obscuring what is superficial, of missing what is obvious "on its face," like the letter from the queen hanging on the mantel in Poe's "The Purloined Letter." What is more than visible runs the risk of becoming less than visible; what is more than being runs the risk of being less than being.

One way to view the limits of Levinas's analysis is to say that he allowed the *alterity* of the other to be taken up entirely by the *invisible distance* of the other—that is, by the infinity of moral or ethical eminence beyond the visible order—and not to have seen that alterity is also constituted by *visible differences*. To go back to a distinction I made in *Against Ethics*, alterity means both distance, which implies "heteronomy," the law of the other, something "holy" (*saint*); and difference, which implies "heteromorphism," the multiplication of polymorphic diversity, which is a little more "pagan."[19] The face of the other—the body, the flesh of the other—not only comes to us from a distance we can never reach, which undoubtedly insures its moral dignity, but it is also different, in this case, skin-deep different, in the space where we make contact. The face is always visibly black or white, masculine or feminine, fair or scarred, gruesome or comely, amicable or threatening (and so too, of course, is the face of the "same," a point to which I will return below). Gender and race are plainly written all over the face—and perhaps race more so than gender, although that may be a contextual issue—so that any analysis of the face that wants to be truly concrete cannot or should not miss it. Levinas, I think, slips into a kind of ethical essentialism by turning the ethical into a kind of archi-sphere of transcendence to which every other form of transcendence is subordinated, so that there is no room in his work for real aesthetic transcendence (which is basically Lyotard's complaint) or even for true religious transcendence (since religion is reduced to ethics). But he also situates ethical transcendence itself on too deep and metaphysical a level. He suffers a certain blindness about visible faces, such as about Palestinian faces—to which one responds, it seems, by building an army, not by taking the food out of my mouth—and about feminine faces—which he thinks belong to catlike beings whose patter about the house ought not to disturb the masculine master, who is presumably reading something serious in his study.

Now the task—a lifelong one, it turns out—of the "radical hermeneutics" that I posed for myself in the mid-1980s was to adhere ever more closely to the "difficulty of factical life," to "poor existing individuals," which meant swearing an oath of loyalty to the concreteness of life. By the "radical" in radical hermeneutics, and in even "more radical hermeneutics," I did not mean anything deep, like a very deep and hidden root, but the radical resolve to adhere as closely as possible to the concreteness of everyday life, to be scrupulously observant of the lumps and bumps of everyday things that are as plain as the nose on your factical face—like "race," whatever that is. Like Levinas, I too had not singled out race, not *as such*. Race is nothing deep, nothing deeply metaphysical beneath the visible physical surface, nothing transcendent beyond the range of ordinary perceptual experience. Even from the scientific point of view, the molecular biologist will tell you that there is nothing deep there, nothing scientifically in our genes or our blood or our organic constitution that corresponds to "race."[20] Race is all surface, face and surface, skin pigmentation and anatomy, and there are no agreed-on "racial" groups.[21] There is no secret to race, just a polymorphic, pluriform dissemination of colors and shades and sizes and shapes and local environmental adaptations that belong to the affirmative and infinite task of the invention of the other, the incoming of the wholly other. Humanity, the great human chorus or collectivity, is less a common essence with accidental variations than a constellation of differences that, taken as a whole, have the effect of a great and marvelous patch quilt.

Monsters

Getting race into view in a way that I had not done before means seeing that, if race is nothing scientifically or metaphysically deep, not in the order of things, it nonetheless produces sharp—and in that sense "deep"—ethical, social, and political effects, that it cuts deeply ingrained patterns of discrimination. It pretends to a depth of difference that serves as a pretense to justify deep hatred. Race is not deep, but racial hatred is. To be sure, I do not mean to sound so downbeat. I do not mean to reduce race to a negative category. I do not mean to deny that race forms the positive basis of bonds of familial and social community. I do not mean to downplay the positive polymorphism, the joyous celebration of differences, the marvelous, multiform, patch-quilt effect that belongs to what Derrida calls, in the context of gender, our dream of innumerable differences, which surely include innumerable colors.[22] I have no more desire to do away with the category of "race" than to do away with the category of gender. I mean only to single out how powerful a platform race provides for what Levinas calls the "hatred of the other man."

Ironically, we are helped to understand all this by none other than old father Husserl, whose preoccupations were so strongly cognitivist, and who succumbed entirely to a European prejudice that elevated "Europe" from a merely geographical classification into a higher spiritual type (as opposed to Eskimos, who evidently spent too much time shivering in the cold to practice the *Wesensanschauung*). The affirmation of the *tout autre* in the Fifth Cartesian Meditation turns on an act of analogical apperception. That is, paradoxically, the affirmation of the irreducible alterity of the alter ego, of the irreducible distance of a conscious life whose *Erlebnisstrom* is and never can be experienced as such, begins with a perceptual recognition that takes place on the level of *visible appearances*, an act of "pairing," which is an instance of the association of ideas in which we match like with like. When eyes meet eyes, one sees oneself seen; when hand meets hand, one feels oneself felt. The more visibly alike the like are, the more instantaneous and unimpaired the pairing, whereas the more unlike the like are, the more the pairing is impeded. That is why Husserl wisely did not let things rest with pairing, but went on to include two other operations within the scope of analogical apperception: (1) the course of subsequent experience, of confirming and disconfirming "fulfillment" of the first take we had; and (2) those acts of free variation in which I imagine what it would be like for my body "here" to be over "there." These further acts correct for the limits of pairing in the total act of affirming (he called it "constituting") the other, and allow the course of experience to right itself when it is made tipsy by something unexpected.

Husserl is more or less right about all that, but with one massive and immense proviso that changes everything—that his cognitivism prevented him from seeing that these are not merely epistemic issues but ethical, social, political, psychological, and religious matters. There is, in particular, something profoundly—and here is where I locate talk about "deep" things—shocking or traumatizing about the encounter with racial difference. Irigaray says as much about the primordiality of sexual difference rather than race. That is also true, but it would be a mistake to get into a contest about which difference is more primordial, which sets off a war among contenders for the crown of "first philosophy," like the little war that Levinas waged on Heidegger. Because I don't believe in the secret, I do not think that sex or race or the desire for my mommy is the secret. The only secret is that there is no secret.[23]

The shock visited on each other by different skins, mine among them (I will come back to that), and not just skins but facial and bodily anatomies, gestures, cultures, languages—the whole gestalt of difference—is considerable: to take an example that is not simply an example, the shock that the white European (especially as you head toward the northern latitudes) and the sub-Saharan African deliver to each other echoes across the centuries, across the continents, around the globe, giving birth to the infamous slave trade, to Europe and Euro-America's eternal shame, and to its ignominious aftermath even long after emancipation. The other is not simply a perceptual incongruity but a fearful thing—perceptually, socially, ethically—a *mysterium tremens et fascinans*. We are not sure whether the other is a god or a monster, especially not the first time we meet. Indeed, as Derrida likes to point out, the *tout autre* actually is a "monster," structurally speaking, from *monstrare*, meaning one whose appearance puts on quite a "show" (*monstratio*), who shows up with a quite a bang, whose "incoming" (*invention*) knocks us off our pins. The fear and the trembling, the repulsion, and also the awe—both the *tremens* and the *fascinans*, both the antipathy and the sympathy—are very ancient movements of the spirit. Infants cry when confronted with the faces of someone other than their parents; toddlers cling to their parents when they meet someone new whom they look on with profound apprehension. We are all afraid of the other, to some degree, even as we are fascinated. Perhaps such responses even have evolutionary, selective value, and perhaps they are nascent forms of hatred. *Je ne sais pas le secret*.

But the monster indeed, the monster in truth, is not the monster without, not the traumatizing monstration of the other, but the monster or the monstrosity *within*; not the phenomenal monstration of the stranger, the shock of the other, but the moral monster that I am, the monstrosity of my autonomy, which is what Levinas calls the murderousness of my freedom. I must always worry over my own autarchic power to assert and enhance my place in the sun at the first appearance of the other. What Levinas calls ethics concerns the problem of the "hatred of the other." For the appearance of the alterity of the other can all too easily become an opening, an opportunity, an occasion, a pretense to assault the other—physically, politically, psychologically, and to deprive them of their dignity, their freedom, or their life. When that happens, the alterity of the other is erased and I find myself "alone," in an ethical solipsism more frightening than the cognitive one that Husserl is concerned to lay to rest, one that from a racial point of view is deeply charged.[24]

Allow me to introduce the following hypothesis. What we philosophers *mean* by "modernity," by the advent of seventeenth- and eighteenth-century theories of consciousness, freedom, and autonomy, is nothing transcendentally neutral but in fact *colored white*, the evidence for which is found in the simultaneous advent of both colonialism and the pseudo-science of race.[25] What Martinez's Grand Inquisitor has made me realize is that the transcendental *epochē* is not a neutralizing operation but an operation of color, a transcendental *whitening* that while purporting to neutralize every natural property leaves one bit of nature still standing, the color white. We should see that included in the *mondialisation* that Derrida worries about, the sweeping of the globe by Euro-Christian culture, is what we might call a global blanching or blanchification, which makes everything white or other-than-white. I have spent a professional lifetime trying to enumerate all the reasons why the *epochē* cannot be carried off, trying to itemize all the factical limits that still cling to the surface of "pure" consciousness—like historicity, language, and gender—even after the *epochē* has been earnestly enacted. But now I see that the pure rational, transcendental ego was not only implicitly or invisibly *male* or Euro-male, but it is also invisibly *white* or *Euro-white*. In just the way that Derrida says we have been misled by the "invisibility" of air to miss the work of *différance* in speech, so we have mistaken white as pure colorless spirit. Blanche, blanc, blank, a pure neutral stuff. We have to do here with another "white mythology," where the color white passes itself off as uncolored transcendentality. The so-called pure ego is not only implicitly the "man of reason," but is also a Euro-white man, as if white were not itself one more color and Europe not just one more place on the map. The "neutralization" in virtue of which the *epochē* allows the pure ego to appear ends up meaning to whiten out, to make something pure white. Husserl's attempt to elevate "Europe" into a spiritual essence, to essentialize Europe, was also an essentialization of white. White maleness becomes the default universal. Pure reason is pure white. Levinas noticed that *Dasein* does not get hungry, but not that *Dasein* is white, just as the truth of Being is Being's whitened clearing. One is blinded in this discourse by the light of the pure sun of Plato's Good, by the white ecstasy of all this white light.

To depict the peril of this frightening white freedom is the genius of Conrad's tale, where the heart of darkness was not the darkness of the faces in the Congo, the trauma of the monstration of the black man or the jungle, but the darkness of Kurtz's monstrous heart, hard, blackened heart. Kurtz is Abraham—the ethical law has been suspended—but without God or any other telos, without faith, without restraint, an utterly cruel man who had so annulled the other as to find himself alone, a moral *solus ipse*, untrammeled, unimpeded by any "thou shalt not kill" when it came to "niggers." The trauma of the wilderness without was not itself the monster, but rather the occasion for unleashing the monster within, awakening the memory of "monstrous passions," Conrad writes.[26] If I may be permitted to cite again from what I wrote in my critique of Richardson's Heidegger:

> He [Kurtz] had gone out into the wilderness and gone mad, not with the madness of a dark power that overtaken him and led him astray,

poor thing, but with the madness of a man who had come to believe that he was alone, that all human restraints had been lifted from him in that wilderness, that he was worthy of supernatural honors, that he had power over life and death.... [Conrad writes:] "I [Marlowe] had to deal with a being [Kurtz] to whom I could not appeal in the name of anything high or low. There was nothing either above or below him, and I knew it. He had kicked himself loose of the earth.... He was alone. I saw the inconceivable mystery of a soul that knew no restraint, no faith, and no fear, yet struggling blindly with itself."[27]

His was the solitude of a man for whom there were no other faces, nothing above him, nothing to come to him from on high.... Kurtz's house was landscaped with the heads of his victims ... whose severed heads were propped on poles and plunged into the ground around his house.... Only one face greets the visitor, which Charlie Marlow spies through his binoculars: "... there it was, black, dried, sunken, with closed eyelids—a head that seem to sleep at the top of that pole, and, with the shrunken dry lips showing a narrow white line of the teeth, was smiling, too, smiling continuously at some endless and jocose dream of that eternal slumber."[28]

There was "no restraint" in Kurtz's soul, Marlow says. Kurtz was alone; there was no Other, no Law of the Other, which he respected.[29]

The heart of darkness is the darkness of Kurtz's heart. Conrad concentrates the monstrosity of Kurtz in the monstrous image of the severed heads whose black faces smile with some eerie and eternal irony at the visitor to Kurtz's island. Here, the face, which is the seat of the "thou shalt not kill," which proclaims the moral impossibility of murder, is precisely what announces wholesale and unchecked murder, the banality of physical murder, made as commonplace as the shrubbery and trees. These black faces stun the approaching visitor with their majesty defiled, infinity profaned. They look but do not see, greeting the visitor with dead eyes, violated faces that also announce the prohibition of violence, a prohibition that even Kurtz in his heartless heart was not able to extinguish. He tried to annul the face of the native, the non-European, to reduce the "primitive" to nothing, or something from another world, belonging to another species.[30] The *difference* of the Congolese faces was allowed to extinguish their *distance*, their transcendence, their moral eminence from whose ethical height the prohibition of murder is issued. "The horror, the horror," were Kurtz's dying words, which Marlowe says "pronounced a judgment upon the adventures of his soul on this earth."³¹ For all his murderousness, Kurtz failed finally to silence the word of condemnation spoken by those dead lips, whose deathly smile testified to the moral impossibility of murder, like the ghost who haunts Macbeth. Like the eyes of Abel staring back at Cain from the grave, their lifeless stare bore witness to the infinite distance of the other, which cannot be extinguished by the sword. Finally, in the end, those black faces faced him down into the pits of hell.

Seeing the Other in the Dark

I have seen the other and the other is I myself.

I have seen the monster and the monster is I myself.

Here I am, *me voici*, the other and the monster.

This brings me back to my theme of darkness, our old friend.

I have been arguing that the face of the other is visible *and* invisible, marked by difference *and* distance, that it is both heteromorphic and heteronomic, not like two different substances but in an intertwined and chiasmic interlacing. For the face or flesh is, with all its ethical distance, always and already a face of color, of some color or other, of some gender, race, and ethnicity, even as the language the other speaks not only bears witness to his or her infinity but is always and already some natural language or other, with accents and inflections that betray a region, social standing, education, and so forth. The infinite and invisible other is always and already finite and visible, factically situated in a way that is literally as plain as the nose on his or her face, and we radical hermeneuts are called on to respond no less to one than to the other, to the finite no less than to the infinite. There is no colorless norm, no un-raced, un-colored people, which makes "people of color" colored variations on a norm, even as there is no neutral normative language of which every other language is a dialect, accent, or inflection. There is nothing neutral, *ne uter*, neither this nor that. There are only singularities.

But then all that goes for me, too, for the self, for the same, for the "I," for this Euro-white male that I am who is sometimes given to masquerading as the pure transcendental I or as what Climacus liked to call the absolute professor. For I am not myself un-raced, un-colored, and I do not speak a standard uninflected, unaccented language of which every other language is a variation.³²

In addition to the others, *I too* am the other. I am myself an other, one more other, one among many others. I am always already within or among others even as the other is within me. The other is I myself. I am as much (and no less) the other as is anyone else. If I am the "same," I am *the other, too*, not just the "same," not some absolute null point or neutral standard, some fixed center around which everything different is arranged. I am one of the other others, another patch, a part of another patch, in the quilt. That is easily demonstrated. The I is constituted by its egological or monological perspective. The I is a perspective, a ray of attention or regard emanating from a null point, yet it is but one perspective, one more perspective among many, so it is only a relative null point. Hence the I must resist the transcendental illusion by which it is regularly seduced and peculiarly pulled, the perspectival illusion that the I represents an absolute point of view, a notion that is in fact incoherent, implying as it does the view from nowhere, which means no view at all. The spell of this illusion is broken in the interplay of "reciprocity" between the self and the other in which I readily recognize that I am the other's other, that were I there, where the body of the other is, then the other one there would be a "here," for which my body here would be a "there." That is reciprocity, the real truth of relationality, not relativism. Ergo, I too am the other. From this serenely Husserlian demonstration there follows a monstrous conclusion.

I too am the monster, the white monstration, the monstrous monstration of whiteness, an appalling show of albescent alterity whose blanched paleness from the point of view of the other-than-white shocks and traumatizes. I am the pale monster—in the pre-ethical and purely structural sense of a phenomenal manifestation or monstration of alterity that, according to the principle of reciprocity, is as traumatizing to the nonwhite other as black is to white. But I am also Euro-white, Euro-American-white, an instrument of global blanching or blanchification, the monster in the Levinasian sense, in the nonreciprocal sense, of the monstrousness of my freedom, of the autarchic, colonizing, proprietary power, the power that is engendered by absolutizing the pseudo-neutrality of what I call "transcendental consciousness," "pure reason," which is the disguise worn by my whiteness, by my white point of view, my white privilege. By a kind of racial *epochē*, I make my pure, whitened-out ego the pure transcendental norm of which everything else is derivative variation. That is the bias of the white—of white reason and white consciousness, of white men, of a world ruled over unilaterally nowadays by an aptly named and very albescent "White House."

So the truth is out, the hard truth that this monstrous show of blanched rationality is a pretense. I do not have a transcendental passport that allows me entry into any country. I am but another bit of clay and earth, colored and gendered (and who knows what else). I have spent a lifetime trying in vain to keep up with what Kierkegaard meant by a poor existing individual, but I find I am no match for this fellow. I do not know who I am, and I have no right to show others the way, to point out the transcendental path, and no right to some privileged place in the sun, no more than the next fellow. The hard truth is that whiteness is a mask behind which a very troubled and divided fellow hides, wringing his hands and hoping he is not exposed by some merciless inquisitor like Martinez. I am, alas, not myself, not identical with myself, and so I do not have the wherewithal to carry off this pretense; I have no stomach for this violence.

Then who am I, I who have once again become a question to myself? What am I to do and where I can find help? If I may be permitted to try the reader's patience by again referring to *Against Ethics*, I remind you that I keep a painting of a Dionysian rabbi over my mantle, a chap who serves as a symbol or emblem of my favorite notion of a heteromorphic heteronomy. This painting portrays a shifty fellow, a dancer, a riddler and prankster, who is also draped in a prayer shawl, a gravely serious fellow who is at the same time strangely whimsical and given to levity. Best of all, for present purposes, this impish figure is adorned in a multicolored outfit, wearing as many colors as Joseph, every color under the sun, covering the whole breadth of the spectrum, from black to white and everything in between. So if de Silentio's knight of faith looked like a tax collector, mine looks like a tax-evading jokester. Such polymorphic, polytheistic, parti-colored plurivocity is my idea in the Kantian sense, my regulative ideal that I have spent a lifetime trying asymptotically to approximate.

Whenever I get in serious trouble, as I am now, having been summoned before Martinez's merciless Inquisition, I have always consulted my Dionysian rabbi, who has ever been a constant source of wise and prudent counsel. So as I contemplate this splendid painting, noting the benign smile on the fellow's face (all the while the sweat beads on my brow and I squirm beneath the white light of Martinez's inquiry), I see again—it is not the first time— that inscribed at the top of the scroll he is holding is the word "hospitality." This, I am reminded, is the first, last, and constant principle preached by this highly unpredictable prankster prophet. It is the watchword for us heteronomists with heteromorphic tendencies. As I meditate on the bust, well, on the painting, of my Dionysian rabbi, however, it occurs to me that hospitality is more complicated and difficult than I have hitherto realized. But as someone who made a lot of noise—white noise, no doubt—in the past about something called "radical hermeneutics," by which I loudly announced that I meant embracing the original difficulty of life, before philosophy makes everything look easy, I can hardly complain about that, although I must confess that these are words that I now regret because they have made my life difficult just at the time of life when I thought things would have started to get easy. The difficulty is this: that hospitality is a dual operation, for it is a quality that I must cultivate both as regards myself and as regards the other, which is a matter of some difficulty.

First off, I must learn to welcome the other in me, the other who is me, who is even a hostage, held hostage as I am by the wall of "white" and the trap of "male." It is extremely difficult to be self-welcoming, to welcome the other within me. It is a task of no small proportions to welcome myself as but a bit of colored clay, raced, gendered, and not quite so transcendental, a poor existing individual of an entirely particular color, kind, and shape, one among many, capable of setting off a monstrous monstration of albescence. It is the work of a lifetime to circumfess that I am not a soaring *aigle* of transcendental proportions, but a bit of gendered, colored factical life down below on the surface of the ground. It is an infinite task of Husserlian dimensions to learn to live within the limits of factical life, to confess the monstrousness of my monstrations.

But it is no less difficult to welcome the other. Indeed, I would hazard the opinion—let this be the hypothesis of the present chapter, my insignificant contribution to this debate, which I propose only here, at the conclusion, not out of any cunning strategy but only because I just thought of it—that self-welcoming, which is very difficult, is the condition of possibility of welcoming the other, which is at least as hard. If I am not tolerant with myself, where at least I have some say, I will be even less so with the other, who can't help himself. I begin with a hospitality that welcomes myself within my own factical limits, as one more bit of colored clay, and not just one, but a dangerous one, with a long history of very inhospitable behavior and blanchifying terror. That auto-hospitality opens the door to a hospitality of another kind, this time directed not to the other within me but to the others who are not me (but among whom I too am to be found). Hospitality of this sort, which means the welcoming affirmation of the other, is a rather rare commodity. What is commonly available on the market, what passes itself off for hospitality, is a cheap substitute. What commonly goes under the name of hospitality is almost always a matter of welcoming someone whom we have invited, someone who has made an exclusive short list of our friends, or of influential people whom we want to cultivate. But that is hardly hospitality, or at least not a very hard or hardy hospitality. For that is the welcoming of the same and not of the other; it is a guarded and conditional welcoming of those who are already welcome, of the well-guarded circle of those who like us and who are like us, where we are careful not to let others, the other others, whom we are excluding, know about the invitation. True hospitality, which is the really hard thing, happens only when we welcome the unwelcome, welcoming unconditionally the uninvited one who shows up at our door—or sits down at "our" lunch table, or attends "our" school, or rides "our" bus. Hospitality occurs when we welcome the one who is not like us, or who does not like us, someone whom we did not invite and were not expecting—in short someone who is not welcome. Hospitality is what Derrida calls an "event," which Kierkegaard would describe as a "deed," which finds a rightful place in the catalog of difficult things to do. Guess who's coming to dinner? Here, in the United States—where Europeans of many nations, seeking freedom and a new world, forged a country on the basis both of the political ideals of the European Enlightenment and of the slaughter of both the native population and the African slave population—all of this together, not one without the other—we do not lack the occasion for such hospitality.[33] Here like and unlike find themselves thrown together by a history of free immigration and violent importation, of the highest ideals and the meanest cruelty.

Now on my hypothesis, hospitality is not unlike a certain compassion, that is, a sense of a shared or common fate, for we are all siblings of the same dark night, all a little lost, all equi-destinerrant, and none of us knows the way.[34] Night is "our" element—*all* of us, white and black, north and south, however our patch-quilt species is cut up, with no transcendental exceptions. So I come back to still a third sense of darkness in this essay on invisibility and darkness: not the darkness of Heidegger's mythical *Irre*, nor Kurtz's dark heart, but the dark night of compassion. Whenever I pray for light, night is my answer. Life can be very difficult—I am not complaining—not because there is no one to show the way, but because there are too many people showing us too many ways and it is all very confusing. To discriminate against the other—black or white, male or female, straight or gay, east or west, Protestant or Catholic, Christian or non-Christian, religious or non-religious—amounts to a kind of hubris, a pretense, a failure to recognize that we are all poor existing individuals. It is to behave as if we actually did pull off the transcendental *epochē*, as if we knew the way, as if someone knows some secret thing that the other doesn't, as if someone has privileged access to a truth that has been denied to others. Who is the host? Who is the hostage? Whose home is this anyway? What if hospitality turned on *not knowing* the answer to these questions? For the truth is, there is no capitalized Truth, no Secret, and we do not know who we are. We do not know what Race is, or Gender, or Sexuality, or Ethics, or God, or Whatever-It-Is-You-Are-Inclined-to-Capitalize. Once again, I am not complaining, for I regard this nonknowing as a gift, as a marvelous open-endedness that gives these words a future (*l'avenir*), opening the way for something to come (*à venir*). The darkness of this nonknowing protects whatever is being named by these names from the harsh and withering light of knowledge and the rigid rule of essence, giving them an unforeseeable future, which is, if you think about it, the only kind of future worth having. What I do complain about is the capitals. For when someone starts capitalizing this or that, that means that the world is getting divided up into essential regions—like the ones that used to be marked by Jim Crow signs reading "Colored" and "White" (as if white were not a color)—and that those of us who do not live in the Right (White) region are going to be in trouble. I myself am against boundaries and favor lenient immigration laws. Compassion is a kind of de-capitalized companionship we offer one another on a starless desert night.

On my little hypothesis, auto-hospitality is the condition of possibility of hetero-hospitality; that is, welcoming the other within me, the other who is "me," is the condition of welcoming the other without. Were I able to tolerate my own colored particularity and destinerrance, acknowledge the extent to which I am myself one more colored guy wandering about in the dark, contingently situated here when I could as easily have landed there, of many minds and dubious about the way, the truth, or the light, would that not stay my hand? Would it not check my inclination to assert my own way, my own truth, my own type or kind or race or gender, my own *Geschlecht* (a remarkable German word that captures all these things at once), which altogether would amount to checking the monster within me, what Levinas called the murderousness of my own freedom? If I practiced a kind of sincere unknowing about my own way and my own kind, and about who owns what, what is proper to whom, whose property it is, would I not be more welcoming of the way of the other, who is as least as likely to be on to something as I am? If I were sensitive to the monster that I am, if I forced myself to suffer my own hospitality, might I not make a better show of hospitality, might I not make a better host?

Darkness is our element. We are all children of the darkness, our old friend, with whom, as Paul Simon says, we've come to talk again—both dark and light, black and white, male and female, every stripe and kind. We are all hostages of one thing or another, and in this darkness we must depend on the hospitality of others, on unpredictable hosts, even when we do not see them as such. We are all wayfarers, all strangers on the earth, depending on one another's good will, offering one another solace and hospitality on a hard road that leads who knows where.

Darkness is our element. It is the medium in which we see that we are at bottom fellow travelers, all a little lost, bound together by a common destinerrance, companions on an uncharted path. Darkness is the only medium in which to see the other, the stranger, the wayfarer, the only way these figures become visible, and the only way to see ourselves, for we too are the other. Only in the darkness of nonknowing does the invisible man or woman, the invisible self and other, become visibly, palpably present. In the dark, we can only touch. As Ralph Ellison suggested, it is a matter of the construction of "inner eyes," which, as Derrida suggests, go hand in hand with a kind of deeply deconstructive "blindness," that opens up the future.

In the darkness, eyes blinded by tears pray and weep for justice lying beyond being and beyond visibility, a justice in which they can only have faith.

In the darkness and the nonknowing, this compassion grows, offering hospitality in the night. Compassion is the heart of this hospitable darkness, the instruction given us by this friendly night, this black wisdom, the wisdom of this black Athena.[35]

Hello, darkness, my old friend, I've come to talk with you again.[36]

NOTES

1. In his seminal work *Invisible Man* (1952; New York: Vintage Books, 1955), Ralph Ellison writes, "I am invisible, understand, simply because people refuse to see me . . . because of a peculiar disposition of the eyes of those with whom I come in contact. A matter of the construction of their *inner* eyes" (3).

2. John D. Caputo, *On Religion* (New York: Routledge, 2001), 113.

3. Nothing would make more sense, and surely the Israelites, who learned a thing or two about slavery from the Egyptians, the Babylonians, and the Assyrians, might have been motivated to include it in their inventory of evils, as indeed they did from time to time: "Remember that you were a slave in the land of Egypt, and the Lord your God brought you out from there with a mighty hand and an outstretched arm" (Deut. 5:15). Nothing could be more obvious than the fact that the slave belongs in this biblical inventory. Nothing could be more obvious, more "phenomenally manifest," than that in a land significantly populated by the descendants of the slaves brought here violently from Africa by white Europeans, whose visible presence is everywhere to be seen, the Levinasian question of the face of the other should

above all concern the face of the black other. By the same token, offering hospitality to the stranger, even to these same Egyptians, headed up the list of ancient virtues. So if those same Egyptians should decide later to bring a gift to the Messiah, the Messiah should resist his impulse to reject it, for he should remember that the Egyptians first took in the children of Israel as guests, although the place of hospitality soon became a place of slavery (Ps. 68). See Emmanuel Levinas, *In the Time of the Nations*, trans. Michael B. Smith (Bloomington: Indiana University Press, 1994), 97; Jacques Derrida, *Adieu to Emmanuel Levinas*, trans. Pascale-Anne Brault and Michael Naas (Stanford: Stanford University Press, 1999), 71–72. "One belongs to the Messianic order when one has been able to admit others among one's own," Levinas writes. "That a people should accept those who come and settle among them—even though they are foreigners with their way of speaking, their smell—that a people should give them an *akhsaniah* [accommodations], such as a place at the inn, and the wherewithal to breathe and to live—is a song to the glory of the God of Israel" (*In the Time of the Nations*, 98).

4. John D. Caputo, "Hoping in Hope, Hoping Against Hope: A Response," in *Religion With/out Religion: The Prayers and Tears of John D. Caputo*, ed. James H. Olthuis (New York: Routledge, 2001), 124.

5. Ibid., 128.

6. John D. Caputo, *Against Ethics: Contributions to a Poetics of Obligation with Constant Reference to Deconstruction* (Bloomington: Indiana University Press, 1993); *Demythologizing Heidegger* (Bloomington: Indiana University Press, 1993).

7. Jacques Derrida, *Of Spirit: Heidegger and the Question*, trans. Geoffrey Bennington and Rachel Bowlby (Chicago: University of Chicago Press, 1989), 68–69.

8. Caputo, "Jewgreek Bodies: An Anti-phenomenological Supplement to the Lyrical-Philosophical Discourses," in *Against Ethics*, 194–219.

9. I should say that this strain in my work is not so obscure and esoteric as to have gone unnoticed by my commentarists. It was singled out by Mark Dooley in a generous introduction to my work—see *A Passion for the Impossible: John D. Caputo in Focus*, ed. Mark Dooley (Albany: SUNY Press, 2003), xi–xxiii—which I only regard as a portrait of a Caputo to come, even as my good friend Michael Zimmerman called me an American liberal (I think that was a compliment!)—see "An American and a Liberal: John D. Caputo's Response to Michael Zimmerman," *Continental Philosophy Review* 31, no. 2 (1998): 215–20.

10. See Richard Rorty, *Achieving Our Country* (Cambridge: Harvard University Press, 1998); and my discussion of Rorty in *More Radical Hermeneutics* (Bloomington: Indiana University Press, 2001), chap. 4.

11. See Genevieve Lloyd, *The Man of Reason* (Minneapolis: University of Minnesota Press, 1984). Also, for an excellent discussion of alternative epistemologies with regard to race theory, see Charles W. Mills, "Non-Cartesian *Sums*: Philosophy and the African-American Experience," in *Blackness Visible: Essays on Philosophy and Race* (Ithaca: Cornell University Press, 1998), 1–20.

12. "[Homosexuals] want to come into churches and disrupt church services and throw blood all around and try to give people AIDS and spit in the face of ministers" (Pat Robertson, *700 Club*, January 18, 1995); "When you see the rise of blatant open homosexuality and lesbianism, what you also know is God has given a society up . . . and we're at the mercy of the elements, the mercy of war, the mercy of economic disaster" (Pat Robertson, *700 Club*, April 26, 1993).

13. President George W. Bush said, "We spent a lot of time talking about Africa, as we should. Africa is a nation [sic] that suffers from incredible disease" (Gothenburg, Sweden, June 14, 2001).

14. See Geoffrey Cowley, "Hope for Africa," *Newsweek*, July 14, 2003, 24–28.

15. John D. Caputo, "Dark Hearts: Heidegger, Richardson, and Evil," in *From Phenomenology to Thought, Errancy, and Desire*, ed. Babette Babich (Dordrecht: Kluwer, 1996), 269–70; Joseph Conrad, *"Heart of Darkness" and "The Secret Sharer"* (1950; repr., New York: Penguin, Signet Classics, 1978).

16. Emmanuel Levinas, *Otherwise Than Being or: Beyond Essence*, trans. Alphonso Lingis (The Hague: Martinus Nijhoff, 1981).

17. See Edmund Husserl's *Cartesian Meditations: An Introduction to Phenomenology*, trans. Dorion Cairns (The Hague: Martinus Nijhoff, 1970).

18. In *Totality and Infinity*, trans. Alphonso Lingis (Pittsburgh: Duquesne University Press, 1969), 134, Levinas claims, "Dasein in Heidegger is never hungry."

19. See Caputo, *Against Ethics*, 42–62, 113–17.

20. For reasons that should be evident in this chapter, I do not propose to cast a vote to settle, finally, the internal debate of contemporary race theory regarding the "reality" of race, or what kind of "reality" it is, *if* it "is," a fact of which no one is sure. But the claim that race is not a legitimate *biological* category was put forth as early as 1911, most influentially by W. E. B. Du Bois, citing the *Papers in Inter-racial Problems Communicated to the First Universal Race Congress Held at the University of London, July 26–29, 1911* (London: P. S. King and Son, 1911). Du Bois's "Races," in *Writings in Periodicals Edited by W. E. B. Du Bois*, vol. 1, *1911–1925*, ed. Herbert Aptheker (Millwood, N.Y.: Kraus-Thompson, 1983), summarizes two claims from the Universal Race Congress: "1. (a) It is not legitimate to argue from differences in physical characteristics to differences in mental characteristics. . . . 2. The civilization of a . . . race at any particular moment of time offers no index to its innate or inherited capacities" (13). A more contemporary account, offered by Paul Hoffman, in "The Science of Race," *Discover*, November 1994, reports: "On average there's 0.2 percent difference in genetic material between any two randomly chosen people on Earth. Of that diversity, 85 percent will be found within any local group of people—say, between you and your neighbor. More than half (9 percent) of the remaining 15 percent will be represented by differences between ethnic and linguistic groups within a given race (for example, between Italians and French). Only 6 percent represents differences between races (for example, between Europeans and Asians). And remember that's 6 percent of 0.2 percent. In other words, race accounts for only a minuscule 0.012 percent of difference in our genetic material" (4). For similar statistical evidence, and genetic research, see the entire November 1994 *Discover*, a special issue dedicated to the science of race and used by many contemporary philosophers in the debate over race's scientific reality.

21. Of course, the scientific view is only one perspective on the "reality" of race. As Kwame Anthony Appiah argued in "The Uncompleted Argument," *Critical Inquiry* 12, no. 1 (1985): 21–37, inaugurating the ongoing debate concerning whether race is "real": "The truth is that there are no races: there is nothing in the world that can do all that we ask 'race' to do for us" (35). Lucius Outlaw, on the other hand, responded to Appiah with a sociopolitical challenge to the scientific rejection of the reality of race by claiming, in *On Race and Philosophy* (New York: Routledge, 1996), "As we struggle to realize social justice with harmony in America, given this nations history of race relations, we are unable to do away with the notion of 'race'" (157). On the third of many hands in this debate, Charles W. Mills grants a bit to both sides when he writes, in *Blackness Visible*, "Room has to be made for race as both real and unreal: that race can be ontological without being biological, metaphysical without being physical, existential without being essential, shaping one's being without being one's shape" (xiii). For an excellent historical account of the "invention" of the category of race, see Robert Bernasconi, "Who Invented the Concept of Race?" in *Race*, ed. Robert Bernasconi (Malden, Mass.: Blackwell, 2001), 11–36; and Emmanuel Chukwudi Eze, "The Color of Reason: The Idea of 'Race' in Kant's Anthropology," in *Anthropology and the German Enlightenment: Perspectives on Humanity*, ed. Katherine M. Faull (Lewisberg: Bucknell University Press, 1995), 200–241. For Appiah's later contributions to the debate, and his response to the growing number of social constructivist objections, see "Race, Culture, Identity: Misunderstood Connections," in K. Anthony Appiah and Amy Gutmann, *Color Conscious: The Political Morality of Race* (Princeton: Princeton University Press, 1996), 30–105. For yet another voice, which somewhat precedes the Appiah-Outlaw debate but discusses the notion of "race" more closely to my own idiom of deconstruction and religion, see Cornel West, *Prophesy Deliverance! An Afro-American Revolutionary Christianity* (Philadelphia: Westminster Press, 1982).

22. For a discussion, see Caputo, *More Radical Hermeneutics*, chap. 5.

23. See Caputo, "Hermeneutics and the Secret," in *More Radical Hermeneutics*, 1–13.

24. One might consider the "ethical solipsism" described here as a kind of psychopathological condition. In the racially charged context of colonialism, for example, the impulse to absolutize or universalize the ego, and thus to exert an autarchic power over the other, is tantamount to the "psychopathology of the colonizer." But assigning such a psychopathology to the racially neutral category of "colonizer" may just be another form of apologia. Dominique O. Mannoni famously conjectured that certain psychopathologies, such as the inferiority complex of colonized peoples, antedate colonialism; that is, there is the latent "germ" of an inferiority complex already present in the black, for example, which is exacerbated by the situation of colonialism. See Mannoni's *Prospero and Caliban: The Psychology of Colonization* (New York: Praeger, 1964). Arguing against Mannoni, however, Frantz Fanon emphatically insisted on identifying the racism at work in the psychopathologies that colonialism produces. The "so-called dependency complex of colonized peoples," as Fanon calls it, is not a latent racial inheritance actualized by colonialism, but instead the effect of systemic racial, and racist, exploitation. See Fanon's "The So-Called Dependency of Colonized Peoples," in *Black Skin, White Masks*, trans. Charles Lam Markmann (New York: Grove Press, 1967), 83–108. Hence Fanon's disagreement with Mannoni is meant to demonstrate that it is, in fact, the construction of a certain *white* psychology—which "European civilization and its best representatives are responsible for"—that underscores the psychopathologies of colonialism racism. As I will argue below, ethical solipsism, the "murderousness of my own freedom," has historically been a transcendental operation of color, a *white* psychopathology, reserved for and exemplified in a kind of un-self-conscious *white* psychology. See also Albert Memmi, *The Colonizer and the Colonized* (Boston: Beacon Press, 1965).

25. See Hannah Arendt, "Race and Bureaucracy," in *The Origins of Totalitarianism* (New York: Harcourt, Brace, 1951); Leon Poliakov, "Racism from the Enlightenment to the Age of Imperialism," in *Racism and Colonialism*, ed. Robert Ross (The Hague: Leiden University Press, 1982); Bernasconi, "Who Invented the Concept of Race?"; and West, *Prophesy Deliverance!* For an excellent collection of primary texts from both scientists and philosophers of this period (including François Bernier, J. F. Blumenbach, Arthur de Gobineau, and Charles Darwin, as well as Voltaire, Hegel, Herder, Kant, and Boas), see Robert Bernasconi and Tommy Lott, eds., *The Idea of Race* (Indianapolis: Hackett, 2000).

26. Conrad, *Heart of Darkness*, 136.

27. Ibid., 143–44.

28. Ibid., 132–33.

29. Caputo, "Dark Hearts," 268.

30. Conrad writes of the African natives: "The prehistoric man was cursing us, praying to us, welcoming us—who could tell? We were cut off from the comprehension of our surroundings; we glided past like phantoms, wondering and secretly appalled, as sane men would be, before an enthusiastic outbreak in a madhouse.... The earth seemed unearthly... and the men... No, they were not inhuman. Well, you know, that was the worst of it—this suspicion of their not being human. It would come slowly to one. They howled and leaped, and spun, and made horrid faces; but what thrilled you was the thought of their humanity—like yours—the thought of your remote kinship with this wild and passionate uproar" (*Heart of Darkness*, 105).

31. Ibid., 147–48.

32. "The accent indicates a hand-to-hand combat with language in general; it says more than accentuating.... If I have always trembled before what I could say, it was fundamentally [*au fond*] because of the tone, and not the substance [*non au fond*].... And even earlier still, in what gives its tone to the tone, a rhythm. I think that all in all, it is upon rhythm that I stake everything." Jacques Derrida, *Monolingualism of the Other or: The Prosthesis of Origin*, trans. Patrick Mensah (Stanford: Stanford University Press, 1998), 46–48.

33. "Buffalo Bill" is something of an exemplar of this. Heralded as the symbol of American rugged individualism and as an American hero, William Cody earned his name by the wanton, senseless slaughter of thousands of buffalo whose only fault was to get within his rifle range.

34. In describing the African *Ubuntu* philosophy, archbishop Desmond Tutu explains: "In the African *Weltanschauung*, a person is not basically an independent, solitary entity. A person is human precisely in being enveloped in the community of other human beings, in being caught up in the bundle of life. To be . . . is to participate." Quoted in Antjie Krog, *Country of My Skull: Guilt, Sorrow, and the Limits of Forgiveness in the New South Africa* (New York: Three Rivers Press, 1998), 143.

35. See Martin Bernal, *Black Athena: The Afroasiatic Roots of Classical Civilization*, vol. 1, *The Fabrication of Ancient Greece, 1785–1985* (New Brunswick: Rutgers University Press, 1989).

36. Since writing this article three things of note have happened. My "graduate assistant" is now Professor Leigh Johnson (Rhodes College, Memphis); the very white White House to which I referred has now been graced by our first African American president; my old friend Roy Martinez, whom I addressed throughout this essay, has died, and I wish to dedicate this piece to him, with gratitude for his provocation and in fond memory.

2

PERSONAL REFLECTIONS ON RACISM IN AMERICA

Joseph Margolis

If ever I betrayed another, I would have to give an accounting acceptable to me. I would make a start though I had no idea where its true beginning was. Asked now to say exactly how the race issue in America bears on my own life, how it has altered or affected it, I admit I find it difficult to answer, though I mean no betrayal by that. I note the symptom, of course: it must be explained, though I sense no urgency there. It may indeed be part of a benign inertia, barely aware of a larger source of assurance that allows good fortune to be acknowledged and used without invented guilt. I find myself bombarded by too many bits of memory, too many thoughts, pieces of theory, loyalties I should admit, too much that I would want to set aside to be sufficiently transparent for the occasion. It seems that I'm not particularly inclined to hurry to defend my personal history. Conviction, I suppose, gradually finds its subterranean thread in some apt confessional way. One must be patient. I begin, therefore, with what is near and ordinary, the evidence of uneventful events that have no program of their own, no zeal or doctrine, no more than the fluency of a daily routine read far more carefully in retrospect than in its initiating acts, colored, I would hope, by a civility that hardly ever chooses its minor deeds by strenuous principle, but operates instead by automatic habits it finds no reason to change.

I live in a racially mixed neighborhood—as people say (that is, my wife and I)—a neighborhood that has itself changed a great deal over thirty years. When we first moved in, we moved into a kind of urban frontier, a run of streets in full decline, blighted but not severely, problematic but recoverable; we were poor but had a canny sense of the market, of adventure really, of a new beginning—as well as a new marriage and new university posts for both of us.

I hardly felt the presence at the time of an actual neighborhood—that is, the presence of a spread of families bound together by something of an intimate, common, palpable history. There were too many empty houses in the area and I was much too single-minded. But there *was* a neighborhood and we found it soon enough. Our first house was renovated on pure spec, no doubt anticipating the chance interest of someone as headlong as me from another world. I flew in to Philadelphia from Cincinnati just to make the purchase—a house meant to be within my means. To be sure, I knew I'd made no more than a small move in a much larger venture to gentrify an extensive part of South Philadelphia, to piggyback the enormously successful, admired, and very glossy reclamation of Society Hill, which had moved out all its former residents, chiefly black, who couldn't keep up with a steeply rising economy. My realtor assured me that this new site, named Queen Village for whatever snob appeal it could muster, would never displace its older residents. It hasn't altogether failed, but it hasn't quite succeeded either. It was an appealing impossibility from the start. And, of course, once having moved in, we began to find the neighborhood that was always there for years, a black community known largely to itself despite its accelerating disarray, penetrated by a few white residents who probably had less in common with one another than with any black families along the street.

We moved again after less than ten years—I'm not quite sure how many—barely a few houses away. I remember the realtor's satisfaction—a decent man—on closing the sale of our second house. We were apparently the first whites to cross the line at Fifth Street, just beyond the zone we left. The house we bought was last an abandoned black church—whose congregation had moved to another neighborhood a few years back, presumably to where its members had drifted—a landmark building perhaps too difficult to sell or buy. We restored the façade to its early nineteenth-century beauty. It was a splendid house and we caught a little of its grandeur. That seems to have pleased the neighboring families—I think the work was admired and its intention accepted—though it spelled an inevitable and irreversible change in the street's fortunes.

As far as I can make out, unemployment among the original residents along Fifth Street was never less than 50 percent of the working population, and is hardly less than that today, except for the self-recruitment (above Fifth Street) of a number of rising black professionals who moved in after we did—partly because we did. In any case, though we couldn't have known, our effort to restore the house (in effect, the church) also signaled that, visually at least, the area remained congenially linked to its remembered past. One young man, who lived as a boy along the street, who's been essentially unemployed for years but hustles heroically for a living, told me (with obvious delight) that our house looked exactly as it had when he was young. (By chance, we even restored the same iron fence that had once gone the length of the entire house.)

Nearly all the older working-class residents had acquired a family home by the time we arrived, but very little more in the way of an improved income. The empty houses are now all occupied. Our own purchase seems to have released a small surge of confidence going well beyond the realty matter, though it has, of course, meant a substantial increase in price in the eventual sale of the houses of the older residents. A few buildings are now moderately successful rental properties. I find no sense of betrayal there, only an alert eye to the comings and goings of new residents, black and white, who obviously never experienced prolonged unemployment themselves.

We crossed an invisible barrier and we changed the neighborhood forever. It's now very much a world of blacks and whites without noticeable tension, noticeably more white than it had been, but not a bad mix for all that. You must remember that South Philadelphia has had its fill of brutal history—still has its occasional violence, its declining gang skirmishes, its sale and use of drugs, its street crime and pockets of pure hate. But all that is subsiding in an unplanned way—still in accord, I would say, with a pleasant sense of black civility. Our neighbors and passersby, just about everyone, have always greeted us before we ever greeted them—did so from the start in a natural and unforced way, often calling from across the street, publicly, spontaneously, warmly, greetings sometimes belted out a little louder than my pinched habits would have preferred, ritually perhaps, but never in a false or unkind way.

Whites, you realize, are much more fragile and timid in the street, though they may seem not to be. They need some coaxing and reassurance. Their black neighbors haven't the slightest interest in invading their lives or stealing their goods. They're much more likely to test and strengthen everyone's civility by their cautious habit of continually enforcing mutual recognition—which confirms security as much as continued standing along the street. All this undoubtedly belongs to their history of imperiled survival as an actual neighborhood. They hold the community together in a way that casual white residents would never dream of supporting. I am a witness to all this, though I am aware that I cannot possibly change the immensely unequal and unjust division of benefits and hardships that I see every day.

Of course, no one asks me to, except, by indirection, an occasional ideologue from the university or the political world. But that speaks to what I have in mind regarding a certain well-intentioned, natural etiquette that I've learned to share with all my neighbors, which simply mediates every encounter along the street (and leaves the world unchanged). It exacts no tribute, and it has no deeper purpose. But it fills the air very nicely.

I'm told that newcomers in a Japanese community call, unbidden, on their established neighbors, bearing gifts. They appear suddenly as untested strangers who, however inadvertently, may by their sheer presence have put at serious risk the entire atmosphere of a carefully managed order. Accordingly, they petition—ritually it's true, and well after the fact—for recognition and acceptance from the others. On the whole, it seems much easier for whites to enter a confirmed black neighborhood than for blacks to settle easily into a white neighborhood. I should add that when we sold our home in Cincinnati (to come to Philadelphia), we tried to put the house up for sale in a way that was open to black bids as well as white. We couldn't hold the line. No white realtor was willing to agree to the idea even informally. White realtors, we discovered, have earned the right to be the custodians of choice neighborhoods. They succeed because they "can be counted on," come what may. We were obliged to accede, on pain of never being able to sell our property at all; we couldn't have managed the sale by ourselves. Here again, I've played the role of witness—which is more than nothing but not by much.

I also recall that when I taught in South Carolina—in the mid-1950s, when segregation was at its worst just after the Supreme Court's busing decision—I and a number of university folk met regularly with our black counterparts from the university world and the local churches in the basement of a supporting church at night to discuss the possibility of combating segregation effectively. We learned to our bewilderment that the YMCA in Columbia maintained strictly segregated buildings for white and black members. We were outraged, of course, and vowed to expose the fraud. But one rather discreet woman among our black colleagues pointed out, very quietly, that if we protested publicly, it would certainly make it impossible for us to meet together ever again. She urged us not to act, and she was right. I bore witness to that as well as to a thousand similar indignities.

In fact, I wrote a small piece on segregation at the time and published it in the *AAUP Bulletin*, for which I became politically non grata in the whole of Carolina. I've never been such a public figure before or since. I think I may say that I was distinctly courted in every possible way in town and gown society before the issue was picked up by a segregationist reporter who had access to nearly every radio, newspaper, and television outlet in the state and who accused me publicly and repeatedly of claiming that the South was insincere in insisting on the color line. It was a deliberate misinterpretation of what I'd actually written, but it hardly mattered. My university contract was not renewed. The local and national AAUP never came to my defense or to the defense of free speech. And no one that I knew in the whole city of Columbia—in government, university, town, media, circle of friends, acquaintances of every kind—ever came to my defense. Everyone shunned me like a leper, except for one white colleague who taught at a black college in Columbia, a splendid man, a neighbor in fact, who, together with his wife and children, was so terribly marginalized that he could make no possible difference.

Still, by the strange logic of the crazy country that we live in, I prospered precisely by losing my appointment. I was instantly invited to teach a visiting summer at Northwestern University and a year at Berkeley, and was then appointed to the philosophy faculty at the University of Cincinnati. There's no question in my mind that my career was successfully launched as a result of being fired. I owe racist zeal a debt of gratitude. But I have no confidence in such bits of luck or in the courage of the academy—or, indeed, in its essential probity regarding the slightest matters of honest inquiry and citizen responsibility. If anyone wished to enlist me, then or now, in a principled political campaign to correct the abuses of racism (or any similar cause: say, to end the starvation of the Igbo after the civil war in Nigeria or the recurrent plight of the Ethiopians or the slaughter of the Rwandans or slavery in the Sudan), I would have to say I don't believe that any such projects are really viable, as matters stand, or that there was any point to enlisting powerless individuals like myself—apart perhaps from merely exchanging information that might help me and others bear witness to such horrors or contribute small civilities where we could.

We do very poorly with the United Nations and similar bodies, you realize, worse with the initiatives of individual nations acting unilaterally, and quite hopelessly with the longings of individual persons. But if American politics cannot, after all these years, restrain racism and racist injustice at home, then I for one cannot see what more I personally can do, apart from not permitting racism to play any part in my own professional and personal life, or apart from refusing to count anyone a friend who does not conduct himself conformably. I remain, I'm afraid, something of an Old Testament man: if thine eye offend thee, I say, pluck it out. But that's hardly a solution.

Why do I go on this way? It must be a fascination with what might be called (too glibly) the play of political entropy in an affluent world, the plain contradiction that one cannot, in America, spark a large correction of such a deep disorder—an inexcusable injustice in our self-congratulatory democracy—by simply drawing attention to its intolerable presence among the ordinary civilities of everyday life. It needn't have been racism, of course. It could have been the inaccessibility of adequate medical care for tens of millions of people in a land of plenty. It's the near-total disorganization of effective political power that's so dispiriting. My sense is that if the civilities of neighborhood life, which I've indicated I admire, cannot, if multiplied and strengthened across the entire land, effect a reversal through existing political channels, then it's simply not reasonable to suppose that political activism can be counted on at all. I don't deny that we are hostage to the forces of activism; I say only that they are completely unreliable, in America, for matters that go as deep as racism. I despise the fact and the impotence it signifies. The original American compromise on black slavery, you remember, was built into the Constitution from the very start—that is, by the absence of any mention of intended relief. Every change from then till now has failed to erase racism's persistent presence—the evil of the clever forms of injustice it never fails to reinvent again and again. I'll have none of it, though I cannot change it.

There has never been a sustained effort, after the Civil War, to welcome America's black people into the space of actual equality. If you ask why blacks have barely succeeded on their own, compared with other "immigrant" populations, part of the answer is simply that there has been no other people admitted to the country who've been so completely deracinated, disorganized, and demoralized by the very people who now claim to champion their new freedom. America has never practiced capacitation, as Amartya Sen might say, though it prides itself on providing universal rights. How could the persistence of racism be otherwise than it now is? Effectively, the liberties of blacks are doled out by the guardians of modified racism.

Racism is a structural disorder; it won't yield to good intentions. It's not like being mugged, for instance, or cheated or offended in one's own neighborhood. I've been through all that. I've been mugged in front of my own house—by a pair of young black men. I've learned to be streetwise. But racism cannot be overcome by ordinary political means, by successful legislation for instance. It can't because its overthrow depends on the good intentions and goodwill of just those public champions who have entrenched its deepest practice. There's nothing that can be done along those lines that cannot be instantly converted into its opposite. Think of Reconstruction after the Civil War. What actually happens is that well-meaning citizens finally learn to fail to see just how cleverly racism morphs into invisibility.

My own conviction is that racial contempt and hatred, as well as the exploitation of those who can be used to advantage, may be too close to the themes of our deepest nature. It may be in our bones. Racism could conceivably release one population for another—if it could find another to prefer (not unlike the old German tale of the man caught in the bramble bush). Nevertheless, the old deceits still seem the best by far. A friend of mine who'd been a prisoner of war in Germany during World War II once told me—I've never forgotten—that no matter how close to starvation the prisoners were, someone always trotted out a crust of bread to hire another to do a perfectly menial and pointless bit of service that would be duly witnessed by all the others. If we must lower our expectations, we needn't debase our intelligence. It's crucial to the dignity of life that we bear witness to whatever we take to be an abiding evil in our world. Politics is the opportunism of opposed sensibilities, but it is hardly an instrument for changing those sensibilities directly or reliably for the better.

I myself have never worked at eliminating racism from my own soul. I'm simply not a racist at any level of spontaneous or reflective life, as far as I've been able to fathom. But I have perfectly ordinary dislikes and fears, and they apply to people of every stripe. I take it to be a good sign that I cordially dislike one or another black acquaintance as I certainly do a sizable number of whites. I'm not a racist about whites either. I may say that I'm regularly conned by a number of unemployed young black men along my street. They need a handout from time to time. I don't really mind that, if the game is not too expensive or too frequent or too intrusive. I've come to an acceptable stalemate in my own mind about most of this; there's a measure of dignity I mean to preserve on both sides. It fits the civility I know and require—all from a vantage of privileged strength, I confess. But I see no clear way to parlay any of that into a political temperament that could possibly be relied on in dealing with racism's structural disorder. I may be mistaken—I hope so, but I doubt it. Possibly, it can't be altered without a deeper change in sensibility affecting the whole of the country's convictions and habits of life and mind. I'm prepared to believe, for instance, that American Christianity would have to change profoundly to make the effective elimination of racism possible. Do you believe that that's in the cards? Again, I doubt it.

Here I must make a speculative leap. I would normally have argued on purely rational grounds. A country becomes unstable, we say, when (as Aristotle remarks, in his wisely pedestrian way) its inequalities adversely affect the interests of its middle class or prompt a sizable subpopulation to prefer anarchy or revolution. Racism is probably not potent enough as a source of perceived injustice (in the United States) to destabilize, by itself, the order of the entire country; whereas, joined to other evils—for instance, the deepening poverty of an increased part of the population at a time of increased sacrifice required in the service of dubious empire—one cannot be sure of what might yet be in the offing. (And, of course, the Civil War has taught us other possibilities.)

The entire fabric of democratic assurances seems to be at risk now. But even that is not the line of thinking I mean to pursue here. No, my thought is rather that one might hope to bring the deeper sources of fellow feeling into accord with some sort of compelling recognition of racism's evil beyond what a purely rational review of the facts have as yet generated. I believe it's possible to create such a bond, and that it may be necessary. But it's a profoundly risky undertaking, not well understood, paradoxical in the extreme, capable of worsening matters in the name of supposedly deeper concerns. Imagine, for example, as Samuel Huntington conjectures (though he finds the question premature—and enticing), that we are moving closer to some apocalyptic conflict between Western Christianity-cum-technologized-rationality and Islam, so that in some irresistible way we begin to subordinate the rational interests of a thoroughly terrestrial politics to the imperious demands of salvational loyalties. Suppose, in short, that the West begins to imagine that it must equal the religious zeal that it perceives among the suicide bombers of the Middle East. I don't believe that this is happening or is about to happen. But I do see how easy it would be to move in that direction, and I mistrust its allure. I see the untapped possibilities of irrational and nonrational power, and I'm afraid that the resources of Western religion are as ambivalent as are all our other energies.

In any case, that too is not my cause. What I have in mind is not anything of this sort—however promising such resources may be in their own right and however related they may prove to the matter before us. The problem I see is this. If what I've said about racism is reasonably convincing, then it may be that I'm also right in thinking that we shall never erase the worst excrescences of racism in our lifetime unless we can harness the humane sensibilities of the country's traditions, whether religious or mundane. I'm not certain that would do, but it's all we have.

We must remember that Christianity itself was compromised in the matter of slavery, just as apartheid was rationalized in South Africa. That means, quite frankly, that religion itself would have to be transformed, politically, into an instrumentality guided by a consensus favoring an end to racism. But that's completely unlikely, given no more than our own past history. I reluctantly conclude, therefore, that America's claim to be a democracy is at best only half true—and is itself in danger of slipping further from any progressive realization of equality. The argument against racism is simply that it simply is—unconditionally—utterly indefensible.

I must add a final qualification. I don't believe we can reduce or eliminate racism in America without admitting a benign use of the racial distinction itself. There is no way to increase justice between blacks and whites except by recognizing the "racially" disadvantaged population for what it is. The denial of racism on biological grounds is largely irrelevant in political affairs. Race is a socially entrenched distinction, not a biological claim at all. It is fashionable nowadays to claim (in America) that there is no racism in the country, because, for one thing, essential racial differences *are* biological fictions, and because current public policies *forbid* discrimination of any sort. Let me simply say that these triumphal counterclaims have nothing to do with the matter. On the argument under consideration, there is no reliable way to defeat racism that is not essentially centered in the kind of natural civility that I have found practiced in the neighborhood I entered some thirty years ago. And that was child's play to learn.

3

THE DANGERS OF CONFESSION:
WHITE CONTRIBUTIONS TO A CONTINENTAL PHILOSOPHY OF RACE

Shannon Sullivan

> "We aren't angels. But we, at least, feel some remorse."
> What a confession!
> —*Jean-Paul Sartre, quoting a "bourgeois colonialist" defending the West*

Why have white philosophers in the continental tradition generally ignored issues of race? An important part of the answer to this question is that not all of them have. Robert Bernasconi's recent work stands out for its examination of the role that race and racism have played in the thought of key figures in Western scholarship, especially that of Kant.[1] Feminist philosophers, in particular, have made substantial contributions to a continental philosophy of race. Along with feminists of color such as Linda Martín Alcoff, Ofelia Schutte, and Jacqueline Scott, white feminists such as Judith Butler, Tina Chanter, Ladelle McWhorter, Kelly Oliver, and Cynthia Willett have used phenomenology, genealogy, psychoanalytic theory, and other continental resources to explain the operations of racism, colonialism, and white domination.[2] Yet as important as this body of work is, it does not eliminate the loud silence emitted by continental philosophy on issues of race. Why is that silence not experienced as deafening by most white continental philosophers?

At least some of them probably do hear the silence but are reluctant to risk the pain and vulnerability that writing on race could cause them and their loved ones. This reluctance has been encountered, for example, in feminist work outside the continental tradition. Two feminist philosophers recently put together a collection of essays on whiteness, widely distributing a call for papers and inviting prominent feminists to contribute.[3] They explain in the book's preface that they anticipated being flooded with contributions of narrative essays that used the authors' lived experience and personal insights to reflect on the meaning of whiteness. Their expectations were not met, however, in part because a large number of the invited feminist philosophers did not want to contribute personal narratives. As one of them admitted, she was afraid that what she would write would be hurtful to members of her family.[4] Even though the invited feminists presumably considered the topic of whiteness to be philosophically valuable, the safest route for them was to avoid writing on it. Choosing to stick to philosophical topics that did not risk self-disclosure and the exposure of the lives of loved ones apparently was seen as the most prudent way to shape an academic career.

Part of what makes these editors' experience significant and somewhat surprising is that feminist philosophy regularly includes reflection on personal life. After all, the personal is the political, as the feminist cliché goes. This is not to claim that all feminist philosophy incorporates personal reflection. Indeed, the field arguably has become somewhat more impersonal as it has gained institutional credibility. Feminist philosophy nonetheless tends to include a commitment to connecting philosophical theory to lived experience, especially that of women. So it might seem odd that feminist philosophers would shy away from the risk of writing a narrative essay, on race or any other topic. But their reluctance to write on whiteness is not as surprising when one factors in the different relationship to domination that white feminists have in the case of gender versus that of race. The risk involved when writing as a (white) woman about sexist oppression is very different from that involved when writing as a white person (woman) about racist oppression. My point is not that white women, or women of color for that matter, can or should completely separate gender from race when thinking about either of these issues. Rather, my point is that the practice that white feminist philosophers have with self-disclosure in the case of gender does not necessarily or easily translate into a facility or willingness to self-disclose in the case of race. For a white woman to philosophically reflect on sexism generally is for her to be "in the right," a position that often is more psychologically comfortable for her (even though she is rightly wary of the danger that this position will be reduced to that of wronged victim) than a position that puts her "in the wrong," as reflection on racism tends to do. Simply put, to think of oneself as an oppressor involves greater confrontation with the uglier sides of oneself than thinking of oneself as oppressed. My guess is that for this reason, some white continental feminists tend to avoid philosophical reflection on issues of race. By avoiding the topic, they can steer clear of disturbing questions about their participation in systems of white domination.

Another reason that white continental philosophers probably neglect issues of race—one that, I suspect, is more commonplace and thus is more discouraging for the prospects of increased numbers of white philosophers writing on race—is that, like most white people in the United States, they are not convinced that severe problems of racism still exist. On a vaguely abstract level, of course, they might recognize that some slight biases against people of color persist, but in their view those biases appear to be fading with time and, in any case, do not seem (to them) like salient features of life in the Western world.

Add to this phenomenon the strange twist that France, and perhaps also other countries in western Europe, tends to think that racism is a quintessentially American problem, and one has an ideal recipe for the avoidance of race by white continental philosophy in the United States. Frantz Fanon exposed this tendency over fifty years ago. Mocking Dominique Mannoni's claim that "'France is unquestionably one of the least racialist-minded countries in the world,'" Fanon sarcastically counsels, "Be glad that you are French, my fine Negro friends, even if it is a little hard, for your counterparts in America are much worse off than you."[5] And critical race feminist Patricia Williams suggests that little has changed in France regarding this matter since the 1950s. She reports that when traveling recently to France following an extended stay in England, the French began to regard her as exotic and fantastical when they realized that she was American and not British. With curious fascination they began asking questions that clearly assumed that Jim Crow still existed, betraying a French image of contemporary life for black people in the United States as oppressive in ways that no western European country could match.[6] Together Williams and Fanon reveal a French tendency to believe that France is not and never has been as racist as America, which therefore (allegedly) entails that France is not really racist at all.

Given France's purported lack of racism, issues of race "naturally" would tend not to arise in the work of U.S. continental philosophers who focus on French thought. I am less familiar with German attitudes toward racism in the United States, so I am cautious about extending my point to Germany. Yet it is fairly common knowledge that Hitler greatly admired and even used America's eugenics programs as a model for "improving" Germany's racial-national health. Thus there is reason to believe that, for all its problems with anti-Semitism and increasing violence against the Roma, or "gypsies"—which has become one of the largest race-related problems in western and central Europe since 1989, especially with the creation and recent expansion of the European Union[7]—Germany too sees itself as relatively free of racism in comparison to the United States. In that case, race would not be perceived as a relevant or urgent topic for the two main, and virtually only, European countries focused on by U.S. continental philosophers. Located in the United States, which allegedly has conquered all its problems with racism, and writing and teaching about the philosophy of two European countries that supposedly never suffered from those problems in the first place, many white continental philosophers in the United States probably feel that issues of race have no proper place in their work.

Given this situation, the current philosophical focus on race (slight though it may be) can strike some white continental philosophers as opportunistic and faddish. Like feminist philosophy, critical philosophy of race sometimes is considered to be a hot trend that will cool once its "political correctness," professional cachet, and strategic utility for university administrators has faded. And that time is seen as coming soon. As one white person recently remarked in the company of other white people after an issue involving race was raised, "That's so nineties." For many white people in the United States, race is already passé. To bring it up is (allegedly) to introduce into a situation or gathering a contentious topic that otherwise would not have been and should not be in play. White people's boredom with race often turns to frustration in the academy when people of color are perceived as having no difficulty finding jobs merely because they are a hot commodity in limited supply. With their hire, philosophical rigor is seen as taking a backseat to political correctness, and supposedly highly qualified white philosophers sometimes experience themselves as victims of reverse discrimination.

The upshot of this grim picture is that many white continental philosophers do not think there is any enduring philosophical value in work that focuses on race. On this view, developing a continental philosophy of race would mean that philosophical rigor and profundity were being sacrificed for political and personal purposes, including crass career opportunism. In that case, the ignorance of race by continental philosophy cannot be seen as an accidental oversight, a gap in knowledge that the tradition eventually will get around to filling. It instead must be viewed as the result of a deliberate production of not knowing, carefully (if not necessarily or always consciously) maintained and encouraged. One should recall that the active verb "ignore" is at the root of the seemingly passive noun "ignorance."[8] Issues related to race and racism often are actively ignored by white continental philosophers because those issues are seen as second-rate fluff that no serious philosopher would waste his or her time on.

These issues also are actively (although, again, not necessarily consciously) ignored because ignorance of them helps maintain an academic status quo that economically and psychologically benefits white philosophers. This support is provided by a highly problematic philosophical position. In the charge that continental philosophy sacrifices intellectual rigor for politics when it takes up issues of race and racism lies an implicit claim that "real" philosophy is not and cannot be informed by political perspectives and concerns. (Ironically, this charge duplicates attacks made on continental and other pluralist philosophers by the analytic philosophical establishment in the United States.[9]) In this implicit claim can be found a covert denial of the situated, perspectival quality of human existence. For philosophy to be completely apolitical would be for philosophers to be able to lift themselves out of the various local, national, and international communities that sustain them. But human beings are not and cannot become neutral blank slates. They cannot remove themselves from their historical, economic, social, political, and other contexts to obtain an allegedly "God's eye" point of view. The world inhabits us as much as we inhabit it. Ironically, it is continental philosophy that has made this point most forcefully and done the most to discredit the liberal notion of the neutral individual. Yet when it comes to race, that notion tends insidiously to slip back in.

Political perspectives do not contaminate "serious" philosophy, and, further, they cannot be entirely avoided. An allegedly apolitical position that separates "real" philosophy from issues of race is itself a political stance that supports the status quo of white domination in U.S. philosophy. If philosophers are not supposed to talk about race, then they cannot use the sophisticated theoretical tools they have developed to uncover, decipher, and explain how race and racism function. Hidden and seemingly nonexistent, white domination can then hum along undisturbed and unchallenged. The psychological, economic, and other privileges that white philosophers enjoy because of the hegemony achieved through the exclusion of perspectives that would challenge them can then seem like the normal state of things and not privileges at all.

What then should white continental philosophers do if they want to disrupt the status quo by addressing issues of race, including the role that racism plays in contemporary academic life in the United States and Europe? The first step might seem to be confession: to acknowledge that one is guilty of ignoring race while reaping the benefits that it bestows. I am wary of this approach, however, because I do not think that white guilt does much to illuminate the construction and functioning of race and racism or challenge white domination and privilege. My claim is not that white people do not have good reason to feel guilty about their complicity in racial systems of exploitation and oppression; they generally do. It rather is that the act of confession is wholly compatible with continued engagement in the "sin" of which one is guilty. White confession too often tends to self-indulgently focus on white people's psychological distress over their realization that they are not as good and pure as they had thought. But this is news only to white people. People of color have long been aware of the malicious, sordid underbelly of white "civilization."[10] As Jean-Paul Sartre suggests in the epigraph above, white Western guilt tends to be a pitiful response to centuries of racist and colonialist exploitation; moreover, it is offensive if and when it is offered as a reason for white people to be pardoned or granted leniency for their wrongdoings. In the context of the white bourgeois colonialist's remark, Sartre adds: "All you have to do is look our aristocratic virtues straight in the face, for the first and last time. They are cracking up. . . . Formerly our continent [Europe] was buoyed up by other means: the Parthenon, Chartres, the Rights of Man, or the swastika. Now we know what these are worth; and the only chance of our being saved from shipwreck is the very Christian sentiment of guilt. You can see it's the end; Europe is springing leaks everywhere."[11] Europe's guilt, Christian or otherwise, is not so much an alternative to the white bourgeois "virtues" that support racist and colonialist violence as it is merely another last-ditch version of them. If those values are all that Europe and "that super-European monstrosity, North America,"[12] have to offer the people and countries they have exploited, then the white Western world is sunk. If its sinking merely means, as Sartre later suggests, that white colonialism and the racism that it generates and on which it depends can no longer stay afloat, then this is all for the good. But if it also means that white Westerners have no response to their nonangelic past and present except the expectation that it be partially or wholly offset by their remorse, then its sinking is extremely problematic. In the interests of justice, the white Western world must stay afloat so that it can make reparations for the damage that it has done. Its sinking is the easy way out, just another way for it to wriggle off the hook.

Fanon further develops this point in *The Wretched of the Earth*, on which Sartre is commenting as he condemns bourgeois colonialism. It can seem that the best thing to happen to a colonized land is for the colonial regime to completely withdraw, relinquishing all power to the ex-colonial country. But to do so historically has meant for the colonial power also to abandon any responsibility that it has for what happens to the newly independent land. As Fanon insists, "Colonialism and imperialism have not paid their score when they withdraw their flags and their police forces from our territories."[13] Particularly through the operation of capitalist "development," colonial imperialism tends to plunder the minerals, fuel, physical labor, and other resources of the country it occupies, increasing the power and wealth of the "first world" by creating the impoverished conditions that constitute the occupied country as "third world." The incredible imbalance of power and wealth produced by colonialism does not magically disappear with the formal withdrawal of a colonialist regime. The underdevelopment of the third world persists, only it is now regarded as evidence of the backwardness of the ex-colonial country rather than as the creation of imperialist exploitation. The independence of the former colony is transformed from a blessing to a curse as the colonial power effectively says to it as it leaves, "Since you wanted independence, take it and starve."[14] A fat and skeptical Europe then watches safely at a distance as the newly freed nation struggles unaided to eliminate the hunger, disease, and poverty that are colonialism's primary legacy.

Here one can see operating what Latin American philosopher Enrique Dussel calls the myth of modernity. According to this myth, conquest is for the benefit of the vanquished country, not for that of the vanquisher. "Backward" and "underdeveloped," the conquered people are said to experience themselves as needing and even desiring (!) the existence of their conquerors because of the latter's superiority. The conquered people thus allegedly bring on the violence of conquest themselves. As Dussel explains, "After the innocent Other's victimization, the myth of modernity declares the Other the culpable cause of that victimization and absolves the modern subject of any guilt for the victimizing act."[15] A conquered country that rejects the "help" of its conquerors thus is seen as doubly deserving its misery. It not only is backward, but is so backward that it willfully increases its own suffering.

Fanon insists that ex-colonial countries should not accept this situation. If "Europe is literally the creation of the Third World,"[16] then Europe and its offshoot, white America, owe the third world for the stolen wealth and labor that produced them. This is not an issue of guilt or charity on Europe or the United States's part, and certainly not one of gratitude on the part of Africa, Asia, or Latin America. It instead is an issue of justice. In this context, Europe's or the United States's withdrawal of all capital from newly risky investments in an ex-colony—an all-too-common pattern, since "the spectacular flight of capital is one of the most constant phenomena of decolonization"[17]—is more an evasion than a fulfillment of responsibility, an extension rather than a reversal of oppression. There is no way for Europe or the United States to be neutral, uninvolved spectators of the third world. Their distance is itself a type of irresponsible involvement. A better type of involvement would actively seek to repair the damage of colonialism. Europe and the United States must stick around to help clean up the imperialist mess they have made.

Likewise, white people must help clean up the racist mess they have made, and they can only do so if whiteness continues to exist. The disappearance of whiteness is too easy a "solution" to problems of racism. It merely lets white people off the hook. Admittedly, since whiteness historically has tended to mean only white supremacy, domination, and privilege, it can be tempting to think that combating racism requires the abolition of whiteness.[18] Given that there are no necessary and sufficient biological or genetic conditions for clearly dividing the human population into distinctly separate races, some philosophers have claimed that racial categories are a lie and that to believe in them is to act in Sartrean bad faith.[19] On this account, people who continue to think of themselves as white are choosing to participate in the hoax of race and thus to support the scandal of racism, all the while evading the fact that they could and should choose otherwise. But even if it were a good idea, abolishing whiteness is not as simple as choosing to think of oneself as race-free. To begin, in a liberal age when overt racial discrimination is illegal and largely socially disapproved of in most white Western countries, white domination increasingly functions covertly and unconsciously, often hand in hand with the currently popular rhetoric of multiculturalism and diversity.[20] Racialism and racism are constituted as much, if not more, by deep-seated bodily and psychical habits that are not easily accessed by consciousness. Given this state of affairs, racism and belief in racial categories can and often do continue to exist even when one is rationally convinced that there is no genetic or biological basis for them.

The situation is even more complicated than this, however, since one of the ruses of whiteness is to pass itself off as racially neutral, as the allegedly generic standard to which all racially marked people should aspire. If white is not a race, then "the problem of race" becomes a problem concerning everyone but white people. "What to do about black people?" was the way this "problem" often was expressed in the United States after the Civil War, as white Americans worried about how to keep newly freed African Americans "in their place" in such a way that did not produce racial unrest. With this focus, it was nearly impossible to see "the problem" as one of racial inequality caused by white domination. Problems in black communities, such as poverty, poor health, and crime, were (and often still are) viewed as inherent to those communities, rather than a product of complex factors involving the de facto continuation of slavery's white domination via Jim Crow. Through "the racial distribution of guilt," black culpability was created out of white people's unwillingness to take responsibility for the black problems they had created.[21] None of this can be adequately addressed unless the existence of whiteness is acknowledged. This does not mean believing that racial categories are biologically determined by one's genetic makeup. Race might indeed be fictitious from a scientific perspective,[22] but the biological sciences are not the sole or even primary determinant of reality. The social, political, economic, psychological, and other "fictions" produced by human history and practice are just as real as the so-called hard wiring of the body. Indeed, even the "hard-wired" components of the human body, including its DNA, cannot be sharply separated from environmental factors that are shaped by human activity and concerns.[23]

It is not bad faith to believe and act on the reality of racial categories. Sartre himself realized this even though his work on anti-Semitism aimed for the eventual elimination of distinctive ethnic, racial, and religious groups. He criticizes the "democrat" who claims to be a friend of the Jews but ultimately is not unlike the anti-Semite in his or her hostility to them. Sartre's democrat adopts the allegedly antiracist strategy of color blindness: "He recognizes neither Jew, nor Arab, nor Negro, nor bourgeois, nor worker, but only man."[24] But this "defense" of the Jew, which seeks to assimilate her into a universal humanism, paradoxically succeeds only by denying her Jewishness. As in the case of anti-Semitism, race and ethnicity (read: nonwhiteness) continue to be seen by the democrat as an obstacle to inclusion in the community of those who matter. In contrast, combating the racism of liberal humanism means positively recognizing people of color *as* people of color, just as it requires acknowledging that white people also are raced.

Sartre would agree with this claim as long as the positive recognition of race had a limited time span. He would disagree that such recognition should be a long-term goal of antiracist struggle. His call for a socialist revolution that would eliminate racial, class, and other forms of pluralism springs from a distrust of social groups that (ironically, given his criticism of the democrat) is grounded in an individualist, liberal ontology. For the Sartre of the 1940s, group identity can only lead to conflict, hatred, and domination. This chapter is not the place for a defense of the ontological and epistemological status of group identities, including the political practices that they make possible.[25] I instead want to emphasize that Sartre is wrong that all Jewish people long for assimilation and that, likewise, all black people seek the end of race. As Fanon points out, Sartre's philosophical support of black people in *Black Orpheus* turns out to be a betrayal in disguise, just as it was for the Jews.[26] Transforming negritude into a mere minor term in the dialectical progression toward racelessness, Sartre robbed Fanon's blackness of any enduring value, just as he drained Jewishness of any meaningful content by reducing it to "a *quasi-historical* community."[27] For Sartre, both Jewishness and blackness are transitional stages to be passed through, which means that compared with the final stage of racelessness, they are immature and incomplete.

Sartre's application of a Hegelian dialectic to issues of race produces results that are eerily similar to those of recapitulation theory. Popular in the United States in the late nineteenth and early twentieth centuries, recapitulation theory claims that the development of individual human beings from immaturity to maturity recapitulates the development of the human race as a whole. The human race supposedly progressed from its most "savage" and primitive state to full maturity when it became "civilized." Very young children are not merely similar to "primitive savages," for, on this view, the relationship of individual and racial development is not one of analogy. Rather, the allegedly earlier races of humankind are thought to be lived through literally; much as the human fetus is said to pass through a stage that includes gills, a savage child and then adolescent becomes a civilized adult. The progression to maturity is not, however, available to people of all races. The adults of races such as Native Americans and Africans, who were seen as representing primitive savagery, were considered incapable of becoming civilized. Recapitulation theory, in other words, is a developmental theory about white people only (and only white males at that), who are supposed to indulge the rough savagery of their male children knowing that this is a necessary stage for their growth into full, civilized manhood.[28]

Although not the intention of its creators, recapitulation theory exposes the affirmation of violence that is at the heart of the Western ideal of white masculinity. It also explains the perverse "logic" behind the only recently eliminated U.S. custom of white people's calling a grown black man "boy." Recapitulation theory posits people of color as frozen in a stage of immature underdevelopment. Seen as eternally childlike, they are allegedly irrational and incapable of self-government, but they also are considered somewhat innocent because ignorant of and unspoiled by the complexities of civilization. Recapitulation theory thus allows white people to either demonize or romanticize people of color—or both—depending on their particular desires and needs. In neither case, however, are the needs and perspectives of people of color taken into consideration, nor are people of color ever seen as the equals of white people.

When Sartre characterizes negritude as a minor term to be surpassed in dialectical progression, he might as well have called Fanon's blackness immature savagery. Civilization is that stage that lies beyond both blackness and even (allegedly) racial categories altogether. The affirmation of blackness and all racial categories more generally is a necessary stage for humanity to pass through, but pass through it will. As Fanon says while speaking as the "rational" white man who counters the purported importance of negritude, "Now and then when we are worn out by our lives in big buildings, we will turn to you as we do to our children—to the innocent, the ingenious, the spontaneous. We will turn to you as to the childhood of the world. . . . Let us run away for a little while from our ritualized, polite civilization and let us relax, bend to those heads, those adorably expressive faces. In a way, you reconcile us with ourselves."[29] The innocent savagery of blackness, or nonwhiteness more generally, enables a return of white people to themselves, but it is a return that does not leave them in the same place as before. The dialectical progression at work here is like a spiral rather than a circle. For Sartre, the antithetical value of blackness enables a reconciliation with whiteness that is not a mere repetition of the thesis of white supremacy, but instead a "higher," synthesized form of it, otherwise known as racelessness.[30]

Julia Kristeva's work on foreignness presents another Hegelian-influenced attempt to deal with racial and ethnic difference that is in fact a wolf in sheep's clothing. Writing in the context of immigration from North Africa and eastern Europe to France (and herself an immigrant from Bulgaria), Kristeva argues that the remedy for the aversion felt toward strangers is the recognition that we are all strangers to ourselves. The strange, the frightening, and the repulsive are not just that which is outside me, according to Kristeva; they are also a part of me. I am other to myself, which means that the world cannot be cleanly divided into those who are familiar and the same and those who are foreign and different. Kristeva suggests that acknowledging that the cause of my "choked up rage deep down in my throat" is part of myself will eliminate violence and discrimination against immigrants and other foreigners.[31] As she argues, "The foreigner is within me, hence we are all foreigners. If I am a foreigner, there are no foreigners."[32]

One significant feature of Kristeva's account is that it does not so much eliminate repulsion toward and hatred for the perceived foreign as it increases those attitudes by universalizing them. Foreignness is still disgusting and detestable on her view; it just cannot be localized in any one person or group of people. Its ubiquity is what ultimately will defang it. Or, more precisely (since it can never be completely defanged, on Kristeva's view), its ubiquity will ensure that it does not lead to violence toward other people, for the violence it inspired now can be turned inward. Much like Nietzsche's newly tamed man in possession of a conscience, Kristeva's stranger-to-herself is just as violent before as after her turn inward; the only difference is that her violence has a new direction and target.

I disagree with Kristeva that strangeness necessarily produces revulsion and hatred. Setting that issue aside, however, my main concern with her account of *étrangeté* is that it does little to counter a white Western view of nonwhite immigrants as disgustingly and infuriatingly strange. It tends to occupy the perspective of a white Westerner who is unreflective about the particularities of his or her point of view, assuming that all people find the strange to be horrific, and implicitly racially coding the foreigner as nonwhite. How different is W. E. B. Du Bois's account of whiteness as simultaneously horrific and all too familiar. Speaking of the "souls of white folk," Du Bois claims, "I see in and through them.... Not as a foreigner do I come, for I am native, not foreign, bone of their thought and flesh of their language.... I see these souls undressed and from the back and side. I see the working of their entrails. I know their thoughts and they know that I know. This knowledge makes them now embarrassed, now furious.... I see them ever stripped—ugly, human."[33] How different also is Fanon's reference to the foreigner not as an immigrant, but as a colonialist settler who forces himself on another country by means of guns and machines.[34] Contra Kristeva, the foreigner often is the "civilized" person who initiates violence by leaving his home to forcibly rule a non-Western country, not the one who emigrates from it. Kristeva's advice to find the stranger within oneself also fails to acknowledge that often it is intimacy and familiarity, not foreignness, that tends to produce anger and hostility toward others. For these reasons, Kristeva's account will do little, I fear, to help white Westerners challenge their complicity with racist and colonialist oppression.

I have outlined more strategies for white continental philosophers to avoid than to pursue if they wish to take up issues of race in antiracist ways, but in either case, it is important that a continental philosophy of race address how continental philosophy today is implicated in structures of white privilege and domination. I do not mean that a continental philosophy of race should not use or address historical figures in the tradition, only that the history of philosophy should not function as a way for contemporary philosophers to make race and racism abstract topics far removed from the twenty-first century. Such historical distance and abstraction would allow white philosophers to evade hard issues of race and racism all in the name of supposedly addressing them. Like the abolition of whiteness, this approach lets white continental philosophers off the hook too easily. A truly effective continental philosophy of race must include a contemporary focus.

One thing entailed by this focus is the need for white continental philosophers to reflect on their reasons for engaging issues of race. In my case, a key motivation for my initial work in critical philosophy of race concerns my work as a feminist.[35] I have always thought that feminism must involve men as well as women. Gender and sexist oppression do not just affect the lives of women; thus for feminist struggle to be successful it needs to be a project for all people (and not just "women's work"). Especially when teaching feminist philosophy, I have been curious about men's relationships to feminist theory and practice. To imagine that relationship, I have tried to understand what it is like to be the one with relative privilege, addressed (sometimes angrily, often critically) by those who suffer because of that privilege. Although not the only available route, the easiest way for me to do that has been to think about my own position of privilege as a white person. While not assuming that race and gender operate in identical ways, I was initially motivated to think about white privilege by feminist concerns to better understand men's relationship to feminism.

Although it might seem counterintuitive given my earlier account of some white feminists' relationships to issues of race, I found (and often still find) it easier to confront other people with the importance of struggling against oppression when talking about race rather than about sex and gender. This is not because, for example, my undergraduate students are more receptive to discussions of race than sex and gender. In fact, at the white-dominated university at which I teach, the opposite is generally the case. Instead, it is because I find such confrontation easier precisely when it involves sites of oppression in which I am in a privileged position. In that case, I do not appear to be struggling on my own behalf; I am struggling on the behalf of other people, and any criticisms that I make are, at least implicitly, made of myself as much as anyone else.

Sex, gender, and race transact in complex ways in my work in feminist philosophy and critical philosophy of race. My being a woman and a feminist led me to focus on and hopefully better understand race and white privilege. Another way of explaining this shift in focus, however, is to say that I began to concentrate on race and white privilege because of sexism. I did not want to be perceived as "complaining" about oppression, a perception that feminist but not antiracist struggle risked in my case. The effects of male privilege on my gendered habits are clear. More comfortable being in the background with the focus on someone else, I am in this regard stereotypically feminine, and this femininity finds its expression, in part, in my turn to critical philosophy of race.

And the situation is even more complex because my gendered habits are middle-class through and through. Struggling for others because "proper" women are not "supposed" to speak out on their own behalf is not just the result of sexism and male privilege; it also is a classed—and classic—means by which privileged white women have contributed to the oppression of people of color and the domination of colonized lands. With her self-sacrificing moral purity, the white, middle-to-upper-class woman savior is able to speak out on the behalf of the helpless underclass wretches who are too underdeveloped to understand or articulate their needs for themselves—or so the story goes. A product of male and class privilege, middle-class white women's self-abnegation is often an ideal tool for the furthering of white privilege, and she often takes pleasure in using it even if she cannot consciously admit that to herself. To the extent that my foray into critical philosophy of race is fueled by such self-denial, it contributes to white privilege (with all its connections to class and first world privilege) even though I do not intend that result.

The point of this bit of self-reflection is not to confess my guilt. It concerns instead the importance of recognizing complex relationships among race, gender, class, nationality, and other salient features of contemporary human existence. Even more crucial, it also concerns the need for white people to give up the dream of perfection, purity, and mastery. Not only is that dream yet another manifestation of white privilege, it also interferes with white people's ability to act against racism. If a person has to be in a perfectly pure state of total control, with no possible danger that what she does will be interpreted as, or in fact be an enactment of, racism, then she will never have to try to work for change. This produces for white people a very comfortable position that maintains the racial status quo, and all in the name of wanting to challenge white privilege. Yet another way of wriggling off the hook, white people's quest for perfection when engaging in antiracist struggle must be resisted.

White continental philosophers also should not wait for an influx of philosophers of color in the continental tradition before doing something about its perpetuation of white domination. This is not to say that more people of color are not needed in philosophy in the United States, continental or otherwise. Efforts by influential white philosophers, such as Robert

Bernasconi, to recruit black graduate students to the discipline of philosophy are extremely important. But continental philosophers should avoid the trap of thinking that problems of racism can only be dealt with by people of color, or by white people if and when a sufficient number of people of color (and what number would that be?) have entered the field. White continental philosophers can and should act now by taking up issues of race in their writing, teaching, and everyday life. The situation is as simple as that. And it is as terribly complicated as that: I am not Pollyannaish about the likelihood that a large number of white continental philosophers are going to flock to critical philosophy of race any time soon. Delay tactics nonetheless need to be recognized as the subtle operation of white domination that they usually are. Fanon is probably right that "philosophy has never saved anyone,"[36] but in the United States, Europe, and elsewhere, it can and does affect which issues are seen as worthy of engagement, at least in intellectual and educational circles. Race and racism surely are among the most important of those issues, and this should be reflected in continental philosophy today.

NOTES

1. Robert Bernasconi, "Who Invented the Concept of Race? Kant's Role in the Enlightenment Construction of Race," in *Race*, ed. Robert Bernasconi (Malden, Mass.: Blackwell, 2001), 11–36. See also Robert Bernasconi, ed., *Race and Racism in Continental Philosophy* (Bloomington: Indiana University Press, 2003); Robert Bernasconi and Tommy Lott, eds., *The Idea of Race* (Indianapolis: Hackett, 2000).

2. See, for example, Linda Martín-Alcoff, "Towards a Phenomenology of Racial Embodiment," *Radical Philosophy* 95 (1999): 15–26; Judith Butler, *Bodies That Matter: On the Discursive Limits of "Sex"* (New York: Routledge, 1993), chap. 6; Tina Chanter, "Abjection and the Constitutive Nature of Difference: Class Mourning in *Margaret's Museum* and Legitimating Myths of Innocence in *Casablanca*," *Hypatia* 21, no. 1 (2006): 86–106; Ladelle McWhorter, "Where Do White People Come From? A Foucaultian Critique of Whiteness Studies," *Philosophy and Social Criticism* 31 (2005): 533–56; Kelly Oliver, *Witnessing: Beyond Recognition* (Minneapolis: University of Minnesota Press, 2001), chap. 7; Ofelia Schutte, "Continental Philosophy and Postcolonial Subjects," in *Latin American Philosophy: Currents, Issues, Debates*, ed. Eduardo Mendieta (Bloomington: Indiana University Press, 2003), 150–64; Jacqueline Scott and A. Todd Franklin, eds., *Critical Affinities: Nietzsche and African American Thought* (Albany: State University of New York Press, 2006); Cynthia Willett, *The Soul of Justice: Social Bonds and Racial Hubris* (Ithaca: Cornell University Press, 2001). See also Shannon Sullivan, *Revealing Whiteness: The Unconscious Habits of Racial Privilege* (Bloomington: Indiana University Press, 2006).

3. Chris J. Cuomo and Kim Q. Hall, eds., *Whiteness: Feminist Philosophical Reflections* (Lanham, Md.: Rowman and Littlefield, 1999).

4. Chris J. Cuomo and Kim Q. Hall, "Introduction: Reflections on Whiteness," in Cuomo and Hall, *Whiteness*, 7.

5. Frantz Fanon, *Black Skin, White Masks*, trans. Charles Lam Markmann (New York: Grove Press, 1967), 92.

6. Patricia Williams, "Racism Explained to My Son," in Tahar Ben Jelloun, *Racism Explained to My Daughter* (New York: New Press, 1999), 83–84.

7. For more on the Roma in central Europe, see Shannon Sullivan, "Racialized Habits: Dewey on Race and the Roma," in *Pragmatism and Values: The Central European Pragmatist Forum*, vol. 1, ed. John Ryder and Emil Višňovský (Amsterdam: Rodopi Press, 2004), 139–48.

8. Marilyn Frye, *The Politics of Reality: Essays in Feminist Theory* (Freedom, Calif.: Crossing Press, 1983), 118–19.

9. A. J. Mandt, "The Inevitability of Pluralism: Philosophical Practice and Philosophical Excellence," in *The Institution of Philosophy: A Discipline in Crisis?* ed. Avner Cohen and Marcelo Dascal (La Salle, Ill.: Open Court, 1999), 77–101.

10. David R. Roediger, ed., *Black on White: Black Writers on What It Means to Be White* (New York: Schocken Books, 1998).

11. Jean-Paul Sartre, preface to Franz Fanon, *The Wretched of the Earth*, trans. Constance Farrington (New York: Grove Press, 1963), 27.

12. Ibid., 26.

13. Fanon, *Wretched of the Earth*, 101.

14. Ibid., 97.

15. Enrique Dussel, *The Invention of the Americas: Eclipse of "the Other" and the Myth of Modernity*, trans. Michael D. Barber (New York: Continuum Publishing, 1995), 64.

16. Fanon, *Wretched of the Earth*, 102.

17. Ibid., 103.

18. For arguments in support of contemporary abolitionism, see the journal *Race Traitor*, and esp. Noel Ignatiev, "Abolitionism and the White Studies Racket," *Race Traitor* 10, no. 3 (1999): 3–7.

19. Naomi Zack, "Race, Life, Death, Identity, Tragedy, and Good Faith," in *Existence in Black: An Anthology of Black Existential Philosophy*, ed. Lewis R. Gordon (New York: Routledge, 1997), 99–110.

20. Sullivan, *Revealing Whiteness*, 192–96.

21. Fanon, *Black Skin, White Masks*, 103.

22. Although, in fact, it is not. While critical philosophers of race often like to claim that the concept of race has been completely scientifically discredited, this claim is a misleading simplification of the current state of biomedical research and human population genetics. See Stephanie Malia Fullerton, "On the Absence of Biology in Philosophical Considerations of Race," in *Race and the Epistemology of Ignorance*, ed. Shannon Sullivan and Nancy Tuana (Albany: SUNY Press, 2007), 241–58.

23. For example, somewhere between 23 and 40 percent of the human genome currently is retroviral detritus, and this percentage has been increasing over humans' evolutionary history. Thanks to Blake Whitaker, epidemiologist at the University of Southern Maine, for providing this information.

24. Jean-Paul Sartre, *Anti-Semite and Jew: An Exploration of the Etiology of Hate*, trans. George J. Becker (New York: Schocken Books, 1976), 55.

25. Linda Martín-Alcoff defends group identity in "On Judging Epistemic Credibility: Is Social Identity Relevant?" in *Engendering Rationalities*, ed. Nancy Tuana and Sandra Morgen (Albany: SUNY Press, 2001), 53–80; and *Visible Identities: Race, Gender, and the Self* (New York: Oxford University Press, 2006).

26. Fanon, *Black Skin, White Masks*, 132–33.

27. Sartre, *Anti-Semite and Jew*, 145; italics in the original.

28. Gail Bederman, *Manliness and Civilization: A Cultural History of Gender and Race in the United States, 1990–1917* (Chicago: University of Chicago Press, 1995), 77–120.

29. Fanon, *Black Skin, White Masks*, 132.

30. For more on Sartre's reading of Fanon and Fanon's subsequent criticism of Sartre, see Robert Bernasconi, "On Needing Not to Know and Forgetting What One Never Knew: The Epistemology of Ignorance in Fanon's Critique of Sartre," in Sullivan and Tuana, *Race and the Epistemology of Ignorance*, 231–40.

31. Julia Kristeva, *Strangers to Ourselves*, trans. Leon S. Roudiez (New York: Columbia University Press, 1991), 1.

32. Ibid., 192.

33. W. E. B. Du Bois, *Darkwater: Voices from Within the Veil* (1920; repr., Mineola, N.Y.: Dover Publications, 1999), 17.

34. Fanon, *Wretched of the Earth*, 40.

35. The following four paragraphs have been adapted from pages 11–12 of Sullivan, *Revealing Whiteness*.

36. Fanon, *Black Skin, White Masks*, 29.

4

RACISM AND BIOPOWER

Ladelle McWhorter

Introduction: Confusion and Silence

While ignorance, or at least a lack of clear and distinct experience, does not seem to have stopped our predecessors from philosophizing about all manner of things from matter to immortal souls, in the latter half of the twentieth century North American philosophers became increasingly timid about advancing propositions based primarily not on logic informed by material evidence but on intuition, creative imagination, and passionate desire. By the 1960s our generation's teachers and mentors, perhaps battered by the McCarthy years or humbled by the dazzling successes of their colleagues in the "hard" sciences, had redrawn the disciplinary boundaries tightly enough to make almost any speculative work fall outside the realm of legitimate philosophy and into the realm of liberal politics or sociology (read: soft-headed nonsense) or that of literature (read: girl stuff). In this way they sought to purify and legitimate the discipline. Even still, at the beginning of the twenty-first century, North American continentalists labor under and around these intellectual and institutional (and highly gender-coded) dividing practices and defensive barriers; much of our work is still considered by about 90 percent of our Anglo-American philosophical contemporaries to be irrational poeticizing or manipulative politicizing. And of course in most circles our masculinity is still in serious doubt.

    Nevertheless, we carry on. We write about cultural and political issues; we take history seriously; we critique logic as well as social structures; and we often do so with unabashed passion. Some of us are avowed feminists, and a few are flagrantly female. Clearly we are willing to take some pretty big risks. So why is it that, until very recently, we have had so little to say about racism? Surely we have noticed it. We may have even suffered from it. Most likely we have abhorred it and denounced it on our campuses and in our communities. But with a few exceptions we have not written about it. Why not?

I can't answer for anybody but myself—and really I don't think I can explain myself terribly well either—but one reason, I think, is that I am deeply confused about racism and have been so virtually all my life, even while encountering and experiencing it daily. Michael Omi and Howard Winant suggest that most North Americans are similarly confused. "Since the ambiguous triumph of the civil rights movement in the mid-1960s," they write, "clarity about what racism means has been eroding."[1] Given their periodization, this process of conceptual erosion has been going on just about ever since I became aware of the world. I have never lived in a time when there was widespread agreement about what racism is.

Prior to the mid-1960s, Omi and Winant continue, "the problem of racial injustice and inequality was generally understood . . . as a matter of prejudiced attitudes or bigotry on the one hand, and discriminatory practices on the other" (69). But by the late 1960s, a significant and widely observed theoretical shift had taken place. A large number of social critics, especially many within social justice movements, had begun to locate racism less in the individual psyche than in institutional structures: "Discrimination, far from manifesting itself only (or even principally) through individual actions or conscious policies, was a structural feature of U.S. society, the product of centuries of systematic exclusion, exploitation, and disregard of racially defined minorities" (69). While a structural conception perhaps better reflected some of the realities of the late twentieth century, the 1970s saw a neoconservative appropriation of the rhetoric of civil rights, and a concomitant return to the ideal of a color-blind society and to a conception of racism as injuries done to individuals by individuals. Given these twists and turns, by the 1990s, after thirty years of epistemological contestation, the concept of racism had entered what Omi and Winant term "an overall crisis of meaning. . . . Today, the absence of a clear 'common sense' understanding of what racism means has become a significant obstacle to efforts aimed at challenging it" (70).

In fact, that absence is a significant obstacle to thinking systematically about race and racism at all. It is difficult to philosophize about something if you don't know what it is. Not that such ignorance gives us permission not to try, but it does make the job a lot more difficult and daunting than it might otherwise be. Couple the enormity of the undertaking itself with the professional risks of venturing into a relatively uncharted philosophical terrain and the emotional risks of closely examining phenomena that have shaped and scarred us all since early life, and you may have a partial answer to why so few of us have made much of an attempt. The prospect is just plain scary.

There is a further reason as well, I think, which is that by definition continental philosophers focus on European philosophy, mostly European philosophy produced in the twentieth century. We rarely philosophize about anything without a text to depart from (or, more often, to stay right with, reading *closely*), a text authored by someone with either a French or a German last name. So we end up more or less stuck discussing the topics those people thought were important. Not very many of them had anything at all to say about racism in North America. As long as we let our texts set the agenda, we probably won't have a whole lot to say about it either.

In the next section of this chapter, I will briefly examine some of the very few "canonical" twentieth-century continental texts that do deal with racism, namely, some works by Sartre, Horkheimer, and Adorno. I will argue that these analyses are inadequate for thinking through North American racism and the concept of race operative here. Then I will turn my attention to some texts—especially two late works by Michel Foucault—that do not directly address North American racism but, I believe, hold a great deal of promise for such a project. I will examine part V of *The History of Sexuality*, vol. 1, *An Introduction* and several chapters of *"Society Must Be Defended"*[2] in conjunction with works by U.S. historians to give a sketch of a genealogy of Anglo-American racism. I will contend that cultivating a genealogical awareness of the racism that shapes our society and our selves is a powerful beginning on the way toward diminishing our confusion about race and racism, and, even more important, toward overcoming our racist culture and our racist selves.

Continental Resources: Some Philosophers with French and German Last Names Who *Did* Write About Racism in North America

Jean-Paul Sartre is an apparent exception to the resounding European silence on the issue of racism. His most systematic philosophical exploration of bigotry is his *Anti-Semite and Jew* (first published in France in 1946 under the title *Reflexions sur la question juive*). This very readable volume offers a provocative analysis of the existential psychology of anti-Semitism as a personal choice rooted in a bad faith disavowal of the human condition of radical freedom. Unfortunately, in the end it does not tell us much about racism. Sartre writes, "For the anti-Semite, what makes the Jew is the presence in him of 'Jewishness,' a Jewish principle analogous to phlogiston or the soporific virtue of opium. We must not be deceived: explanations on the basis of heredity and race came later; they are the slender scientific coating of this primitive conviction."³ Anti-Semitism is a reifying strategy; it is a way of making the world be still, of keeping everyone in his or her carefully delineated place so that new circumstances will not arise in which new choices will have to be made. Sartre writes: "The existence of the Jew merely permits the anti-Semite to stifle his anxieties at their inception by persuading himself that his place in the world has been marked out in advance, that it awaits him, and that tradition gives him the right to occupy it. Anti-Semitism, in short, is fear of the human condition. The anti-Semite is a man who wishes to be pitiless stone, a furious torrent, a devastating thunderbolt—anything except a man" (54). The underlying issue is not anti-Semitism, then, or even racism in general; it is bad faith.

Sartre did produce some work on antiblack racism in the United States, which one might think would be of more help to U.S. continental philosophers. Since he claims that antiblack racism, too, is a but another line of flight from freedom, one of the many apparently interchangeable guises of bad faith rather than a phenomenon to be studied in itself, however, his descriptions of the U.S. situation offer no more insight than what we can glean from *Anti-Semite and Jew*. As Julien Murphy has pointed out in her essay "Sartre on American Racism," Sartre fails to develop any analysis that gets at what is particular about racism in the United States.⁴ Even when writing on horrific housing conditions in Chicago's black ghettos, Sartre does not distinguish racism from any other form of oppression; instead, he subsumes African Americans into the international proletariat and insists that the interests of African Americans are identical with the interests of workers in a socialist revolution;⁵ racism is just an outgrowth of capitalism.⁶ Thus, strangely enough, using Sartre's work to understand racism very quickly leads us away from any analysis of racism. Racism as a primary object of inquiry dissolves in a critique of capitalism and of individual subjectivity in bad faith.⁷

A similar limitation characterizes another apparent exception to European philosophers' silence on the issue of race, namely, Horkheimer and Adorno's *Dialectic of Enlightenment*, together with the Frankfurt School's massive empirical study *The Authoritarian Personality* (authored by Adorno and others). Whereas Sartre maintains that the motive for anti-Semitism and racism is the fear of radical freedom and the responsibility it entails (it is a kind of metaphysical cowardice), the Frankfurt School authors take a less moralistic tack, holding that the motive is merely the satisfaction of certain psychological needs.⁸ These two accounts could be reconciled, though, if we construe "need" to include the desire to conceal from oneself one's feelings of fear and inadequacy in the face of what Sartre calls "the human condition." That done, the two descriptions are remarkably similar. Both accounts take anti-Semitism to be the most prevalent and virulent form of bigotry in the modern West, but both construe anti-Semitism as just a particular version of a more general phenomenon that is, or includes, all forms of racism. Thus, according to the Frankfurt theorists, an analysis based on anti-Semitism should be adequate to account for antiblack racism as well. Say the authors of *The Authoritarian Personality*, "Evidence from the present study confirms what has often been indicated: that a man who is hostile toward one minority group is very likely to be hostile against a wide variety of others" (Adorno et al., 9). And as Horkheimer and Adorno assert in *Dialectic of Enlightenment*, "It is not so much that such people react originally against the Jews as that their drive-structure has developed a tendency toward persecution which the ticket [meaning the party in power] then furnishes with an adequate object."[9] In other words, anti-Semitism is an expression of a kind of personality under certain social conditions; under other social conditions that same kind of personality would express itself in antiblack racism, hatred of Mexicans or Arabs, or even hatred of homosexuals or Catholics (Adorno et al., 142–45).

Hence, like Sartre's analysis, that of the Frankfurt School turns out on close inspection not to be an analysis of *racism per se*. In fact, chapter 4 of *The Authoritarian Personality* critiques the very concept of "race," asserting that it is inadequate for any classification of human beings (Adorno et al., 103); instead of "racism," therefore, this critical study addresses itself to "ethnocentrism." To be ethnocentric means "to be rigid in [one's] acceptance of the culturally 'alike' and in [one's] rejection of the 'unlike'" (Adorno et al., 102). The concept of ethnocentrism represents an improvement over the concept of racism, we are told, in that it enables study not only of race hatreds but also of hatred directed toward groups not classifiable as races under any schema; the text mentions zoot-suiters and Okies in particular. Once again, the framework offered does not purport to be a framework for analyzing racism, except insofar as racism is a symptom of or a disguise for something else.

These analyses share many assumptions with what Omi and Winant term the pre–civil rights era view of racism, wherein racism was understood as a function of individual action and belief—individual prejudice against and deliberate mistreatment of other individuals. Both analyses focus on subjectivity as the locus of racism and the appropriate focus of opposition to it. This attention to subjectivity is typical, of course, not only of understandings of racism in the first half of the twentieth century but also of European philosophy in general. Phenomenology—out of which

Sartrean existentialism comes—is all about subjectivity as the ground on which sense is to be made of the world. It is a legitimate heir to Hegel, Kant, and Descartes. So it should come as no surprise to us that this strain of continental philosophy would founder in the face of the kinds of structural analyses of racism that began to come out of the Black Power movement, for example, by the late 1960s. Nor is it any surprise that philosophical Marxism, which one might think could help generate structural analyses, also failed to produce an analysis of racism that did not dissolve it in a more generic global struggle for economic ascendancy.

This leaves continental philosophers in the United States facing an enormous issue without clearly applicable philosophical models. We who are so unremittingly textual in our orientation—who can barely utter a sentence without a European author's name attached—find ourselves on a distinctly American frontier without a legible map. Nevertheless, I don't think we are completely without continental resources—just not models or theoretical frameworks premade for use in our geopolitical context. I want to use the rest of the space allotted to me here to make a case for the importance of Foucault's thought for the work we have to do.

Race and History

History shows no shortage of group-based animosity. People have hated other people and have gone so far as to torture and massacre them in droves for all sorts of reasons—their religion, their morals, the language they spoke, because they were Saracens or Croats or Romans or damn Yankees or vagabonds or infidels. The point was they just weren't *us*, and they had something we wanted or posed a threat to us either materially or psychologically. To call all these phenomena instances of racism, it seems to me, would be to dilute the meaning of the term wantonly, without any conceptual gain. Whatever racism is, it has something to do with whatever it is that we call *race*. Where there is no concept of race, where differences between people are not identified as racial differences, animosity, hatred, oppression, and genocide might be very bad things, but they are not racist.

The first known use of the term *race* in English occurred in 1508; it, like its French and German equivalents, derives from the Italian *razza*, which is not much older.[10] Thus, given my stipulation that group animosities not rooted in racial divisions are not racisms—even if their adherents point to morphological traits as indicative of group membership—whatever racism is, it did not exist among English-speaking peoples any earlier than the sixteenth century.

Nevertheless, racism did not necessarily come into existence when the concept of race did. The concept of race is no more essentially racist than the concept of sex is essentially sexist. On the contrary, early uses of the term *race* are so different from familiar racist uses of the word that it is very unlikely that the concept was first used as a tool for making broad and unjust political, economic, or moral distinctions among human beings. In the sixteenth century, the term *race* occurs most often in reference to groups of animals and plants—what we might call subspecies, breeds, strains, or varieties. There is no clear scientific definition until the late eighteenth century. This very early use of the term persists in present-day bird-watching manuals. Robert Burton, writing for the National Audubon Society in 1999, elaborates on his description of the Northern Flicker: "There are three races, showing variations in color under the wings and tail. The red-shafted, west of the Rockies, has red, and the gilded flicker, of the southwest, is golden. The yellow-shafted, east of the Rockies, has yellow, with red on the back of the head, and a black mustache."[11] I have no reason to think that Mr. Burton holds one or another of these races of birds to be inferior or superior, insofar as they are red-shafted, yellow, or golden, mustachioed or clean-shaven. Nor is there reason to believe that the birds have established some sort of racist hierarchy among themselves or hold one another in racist contempt. As this example shows, classification of beings into races is not necessarily a racist practice. Presumably that could be true even if the beings so classified were human, as they were in the English-speaking world by 1580.[12] Only after 1580 did the concept of race somehow enable or begin to play a role in practices that most people would call racist. Clearly racism, whatever it is, is not a natural phenomenon, an ahistorical given; racism emerges in history.

European philosophers of the twentieth century may have neglected to say much about racism, but they have had a lot to say about history and the historicity of things often taken to be ahistorical. Accordingly, insofar as we take racism to be a historical phenomenon, we continentalists may be in a very good position to develop some understanding of it. Foucault's thought stands out in this regard, both because he produced so much work that investigates the concrete genealogies of cultural realities—like mental illness, criminality, sexuality, and so forth—thus giving us a set of tools for undertaking such investigations ourselves, and because he actually did some work on the history of European racisms himself, most notably in part V of *The*

History of Sexuality, vol. 1, *An Introduction* (1978) and in his 1976 lecture series at the Collège de France, *"Society Must Be Defended"* (2003). I will spend the rest of this chapter exploring the use of these works as a basis for developing a genealogical account of modern racism in the United States.

Raciality as a *Dispositif*

Foucault tells a genealogical story about racial discourse that begins in England around 1630, fifty years after the concept of race began to be used to classify groups of human beings. Foucault's is a story not of racism but rather, as he terms it, of race war. The story goes like this: Various factions in English society, principally those more or less disempowered and humiliated by what they called the Norman government of James I, claimed that the Stuart monarchy was illegitimate. Oppressed by a king and court that had blood and religious ties to a foreign country and that conducted state affairs in a foreign language, a self-proclaimed Saxon underclass began to speak of themselves as an indigenous race aligned against a race of conquering aliens.[13] The laws these aliens brought with them and imposed were not a means to peace (as laws are allegedly supposed to be) but a weapon of continued subjugation of the general populace, the rightful inhabitants of the land. What underlay and pervaded all of seventeenth-century English society, according to these thinkers and rebels, was war—"basically, a race war" (Foucault, 2003, 60), one that had been ongoing since 1066.[14]

Thus the concept of race as race war emerges in the English-speaking world, Foucault maintains, first as a means of locating and underlining the existence of ongoing and egregious injustice. It surfaces among the Puritans, circulates in modified form among the Parliamentarians, and erupts in the demands of the Diggers and Levellers. In each case, different though they may be, it operates as a wedge for separating the people from the sovereign, the better to lay hold of an alternative conception of the nation, not as the sovereign's property but as a kind of popular hereditary home. The concept of race thus makes its first explicitly political appearance not on the side of a powerful oppressor group but on the side of the oppressed. It enables a counterhistory. It rallies a people for revolutionary action.

This is decidedly not the same discursive formation that supported the biologistic conceptions of race that circulated in the twentieth century: "Although this discourse speaks of races, and although the term 'race' appears at a very early stage, it is quite obvious that the word 'race' itself is not joined to a stable biological meaning" (Foucault, 2003, 77). Instead of groups of different types of bodies with different capacities for development, race at this time typically named groups that differed in language and religion; it was therefore allied with lineage, ritual, and custom, but was not essentially determined by heredity or necessarily marked by morphological traits. Race did not mean in 1630 what it came to mean in the nineteenth century and what it often still means now. Nor was racial animosity and hatred the same phenomenon as our post-Darwinian racism. That is not to say, however, that the discourse of race war was solely the property of the downtrodden: "It should in fact be immediately obvious that it is a discourse that has a great ability to circulate, a great aptitude for metamorphosis, or a sort of strategic polyvalence" (Foucault, 2003, 76). The discourse of race war was a wonderful way, in all kinds of political contexts, for distinguishing between "us" and "them." Once invented, it was available as a means for rallying forces for reactionary as well as revolutionary acts of expulsion or extermination of those deemed alien ("them"). It was used by just about everybody. Foucault goes on to trace the career of race war discourse in transmuted form in late seventeenth-century France among an aristocracy battling both a tyrannical monarch and a rising underclass. But we need not examine that history here, since our concern is with the genealogy of racism in Anglo-America.

It should be an easy matter for historians to trace the migration of race war discourse from England to the Anglo-American colonies. Although the Plymouth Puritans arrived in New England before 1630, plenty of English dissenters found themselves in the "New World" after the discourse became current in England; they would have heard the racial rallying cries before they got on the boat. During Cromwell's rule in the 1650s, Puritan factions held power in a number of American colonial governments, including Virginia and Maryland.[15] After the Restoration of the Stuart monarchy in 1660, Charles II sent a number of Cromwellians into bond-servitude in the Virginia colony.[16] Since Anglo-America was a handy repository for royal enemies, it is quite likely that a great many of the "settlers" (most of them chattel bond-laborers) in Virginia and elsewhere were well acquainted with the dissenter rhetoric of race war between the Saxons and the Norman usurpers.[17]

Beyond giving a voice to seething resentment toward the Stuart king who bound and exiled his enemies to the malarial marshlands of the Chesapeake, however, such a discourse might have had little application in colonial territories like Maryland, Virginia, and Carolina. Who, after all, was being conquered there? Clearly not the Saxons. There it was native peoples who were placed under laws that operated more like weapons against them or were killed or sold by the thousands into slavery in the colonies of the Caribbean. The Puritan discourse of race war does not seem especially applicable, except possibly in reverse. Therefore it does not seem to have given rise in any direct way to the racial discourses that eventually came to characterize the incipient United States of America. Benjamin Franklin's and Thomas Jefferson's racial discourses are not reminiscent that of seventeenth-century dissenter race war; the concept of race itself had undergone significant change by their time, and they write from out of a very different political milieu.[18] What happened, and what differences did it make?

According to Foucault, there are two major points of historical transformation in racial discourse on the European continent after the seventeenth century. The first is what he calls "an openly biological transition," when race becomes a biological concept. This occurs in the latter half of the eighteenth century and reaches full articulation very early in the nineteenth. Foucault correlates this move—which he sees as politically highly ambiguous—with "nationalist movements in Europe and with nationalities' struggles against the great State apparatuses (essentially the Russian and the Austrian)," and with eighteenth-century policies of colonization (2003, 60). I would venture to say that it is highly likely that Anglo-Americans participated fully in this development, possibly influencing Europeans' thinking as much as European thinking influenced theirs, and certainly helping to create the concepts and theories from which later Americans would draw. Anglo-Americans had a lot to gain from reworking the concept of race and using it to divide an often-rowdy population into distinct groups according to both custom and law. I doubt they waited to *follow* European trends, even if they did eventually incorporate a great deal of European racial thinking into their own.

Historian Theodore Allen's 1997 work *The Invention of the White Race* is very suggestive along these lines. He argues that the "white race" was a North American invention of the eighteenth century, to a great extent deliberately produced by a capitalist elite as a means of controlling a rebellious labor force made up of bond-laborers from all over the world. Allen marshals pages and pages of evidence to show that the colonial labor force was in fact extremely rebellious and prone to act with solidarity across what we now perceive as racial lines.[19] He documents numerous examples of European and African bond-laborers escaping their masters together, many of them running for asylum to neighboring native communities that sheltered and eventually incorporated them. Many planters found it necessary to separate European and African bond-laborers from native slaves (and many objected to having native laborers at all, preferring to sell them to dealers for shipment out of the colony), because the natives, with their knowledge of the local geography and environment, were apt to be successful at escaping into the hinterland and frequently took their European and African comrades along.[20] There are also many examples of seventeenth-century resistance to individual masters, and to bond-servitude in general, where European and African laborers cooperated with one another without any apparent racist discord. Allen's central example of this is Bacon's Rebellion in the Virginia Colony in 1676, wherein hundreds of bond-laborers of both European and African descent united, took up arms, and fought to destroy the institution of chattel slavery in the Virginia Colony.[21]

Unlike production of sugar in the colonies of the Caribbean, which required a lot of capital for equipment and a highly skilled labor force, production of tobacco required little more than land and hands. Anyone who could get land and force enough people to work for him could, theoretically, get rich. But if the hands came as indentured servants to whom land was owed after a certain number of years of servitude (and if those indentured servants actually lived longer than their term of service, which rarely happened in the first decades of the Virginia Colony), the number of landowners among whom tobacco profits had to be shared would grow (because the price would drop as production increased), and the number of people available to use as laborers would decrease. Lifelong bond-servitude looked like a good solution from the perspective of propertied profit seekers; if bond-laborers were never set free, no freedom dues (land and tools) would be owed and the cost of labor would stay at a minimum (corn mash and an occasional suit of clothes). Allen shows that there were many attempts on the part of Virginia landowners to reduce their European labor force to the status of chattel slaves, and in many instances they succeeded. But these efforts were clearly out of keeping with British law and difficult to reconcile with emerging classical liberal political principles. Once the British chartered the Royal Africa Company in 1667 to exploit their newly acquired direct access to African coasts following the Second Anglo-Dutch War, it was much easier to enforce lifelong servitude on laborers with no indenture papers and no ties to European governments that might protect their rights or interests. Why fight with the authorities over the status of European laborers when the same work could be wrung out of people with no government to protect their interests?

Still, if European bond-laborers or small-claims freedmen identified with the plight of the African life-term bond-laborer or understood their economic interests to be compromised by the rise of this source of cheap labor,[22] elite capitalist control of the population would remain very difficult. Hence, Allen argues, the colonial government in the tobacco colonies, and later the U.S. government as an extension of those colonial governments, deliberately sought to drive an ideological wedge between African American laborers and those whose ancestors came from European lands. They did this by more or less systematically degrading not chattel slaves but *free* Africans and African Americans through legal and economic means, while setting up a contrasting and higher legal status for European Americans. The legal code of Virginia was revised in 1705, at which time the General Assembly created a number of new laws to lower the status of free African Americans and simultaneously raise the status of European American bond-servants. More such laws were enacted over the next two decades, and Allen notes that not only did these laws change the status of free African Americans from its previous level of civil equality with free European Americans, but, further, "the ruling class took special pains to be sure that the people they ruled were propagandized in the moral and legal ethos of white-supremacism." Allen continues:

> For consciousness-raising purposes (to prevent "pretense of ignorance"), the laws mandated that parish clerks or churchwardens, once each spring and fall at the close of Sunday service, should read ("publish") these laws in full to the congregants. Sheriffs were ordered to have the same done at the courthouse door at the June or July term of court. If we presume, in the absence of any contrary record, that this mandate was followed, we must conclude that the general public was regularly and systematically subjected to official white-supremacist agitation. It was to be drummed into the minds of the people that, for the first time, no free African-American was to dare to lift his or her hand against a "Christian, not being a negro, mulatto, or Indian" (3:459); that African-American freeholders were no longer to be allowed to vote (4:133–34); that the provision of a previous enactment (3:87 [1691]) was being reinforced against the mating of English and Negroes as producing "abominable mixture" and "spurious issue" (3:453–54); that, as provided in the 1723 law for preventing freedom plots by African-American bond-laborers, "any white person... found in company with any [illegally congregated] slaves" was to be fined (along with free African-Americans or Indians so offending)

with a fine of fifteen shillings, or to "receive, on his, her, or their bare backs, for every such offense, twenty lashes well laid on" (4:129).²³

If European Americans *already* considered African Americans their inferiors, *already* discriminated against them by custom socially and economically, and *already* disdained their company and ignored their interests and needs, why would such laws have been enacted and why would such care have been taken to make sure European Americans were reminded of their existence three times per year? Why were these actions taken if not to divide an as-yet *undivided* working class in such a way as to cripple or preclude at the outset any movement that might challenge the rich planters' control? For the colonial capitalists' purposes it was necessary, Allen argues, not just to enslave African Americans for their entire lives and bind their children into life-term servitude as well, but also to convince European Americans to tolerate a system that ran counter to their English traditions, their emotional ties, and their economic interests, and even to help uphold it by keeping surveillance over slave populations and taking up arms to defend the planters against African American rebellions. "Thus," Allen concludes:

> was the "white race" invented as the social control formation whose distinguishing characteristic was not the participation of the slaveholding class, nor even of other elements of the propertied classes; that alone would have been merely a form of the "beautiful gradation" of class differentiation prescribed by Edmund Burke. What distinguished this system of social control, what made it "the white race," was the participation of the laboring classes: non-slave-holders, self-employed small-holders, tenants, and laborers. In time this "white race" social control system begun in Virginia and Maryland would serve as the model of social order to each succeeding plantation region of settlement.²⁴

The white race was thus an element in what Foucault could call a *dispositif*, a vast institutionalized apparatus of power. Its creation was not masterminded by one small group of people or brought into existence by one official act, but rather was a historical creation that served a great many confluent interests.

Racial whiteness, a form of embodiment, became a form of subjectivity—a form of citizenship, a form of social status, and a form of personal identity in North America over the course of the eighteenth century. Whereas earlier racial discourse tended to emphasize lineage and language above physical appearance, now physical appearance was paramount. And whereas before racism might consist in animosity or violence among races, now it tended to consist in universalized hierarchical rankings and the oppression that such rankings were deemed to justify. By the late eighteenth century, race had become something much more like a biological concept.

Still, as Foucault points out and as many other writers have as well, until the nineteenth century race was not a salient *scientific* concept. While race had a kind of quasi-biological existence outside the science of biology, it did not become a significant category for biologists, and for political discourses ostensibly predicated on biology, until a bit later. And, according to Foucault, this development, when it occurred, enabled the creation of what he calls "state racism," the most extreme form of which is exemplified in the Third Reich.

Foucault maintains that this second transformation in the concept of race emerges in nineteenth-century Europe just as popular discourse of class struggle begins to supplant race discourse altogether. I think this part of his European story diverges somewhat from the account we would have to give of the career of race in North America, but before addressing that issue, I will simply recount Foucault's narrative.

Foucault asserts, "At the time when the notion of race struggle was about to be replaced by that of class struggle . . . it was in fact only natural that attempts should be made by one side to recode the old counterhistory not in terms of class, but in terms of races—races in the biological and medical sense of that term" (Foucault, 2003, 80). To retain control over their labor forces and to reassert their power and moral authority, the ruling classes developed their own racial counterdiscourse (in opposition to the discourse of race war and to the emerging discourse of class struggle), but their reactionary version stripped racial discourse of its historical dimension and its emphasis on battles and conquests, substituting a "postrevolutionist theme of struggle for existence . . . the differentiation of species, natural selection, and the survival of the fittest species" (80). From that time on, as Foucault points out, European nations were not conceived as divided into two (or more) conflicting groups with different lineages, languages, and laws, but rather as one biological entity, one body, threatened in its biological continuity by heterogeneous elements that must be purged to maintain its health and insure its survival: "Hence the idea that foreigners have infiltrated this society, the theme of the deviants who are this society's by-products" (81). These people, both alien "germs" and indigenous "cancers," had to be identified and eliminated before the contamination they constituted could weaken and destroy "our" society.

In the earlier European discourses of race war, the state was seen as the enemy of justice, the weapon in the ongoing war of the alien conquerors over the native race. In this new European discourse of race as biological contamination, "the State is no longer an instrument that one race uses against another: the State is, and must be, the protector of the integrity, the superiority, and the purity of the race" (81). This is a ruling class discourse, then, one that could only be perpetrated by a group already in control of the state apparatus and ready to use it to contain and neutralize their enemies.

This is where Foucault locates the origin of modern racism: "I think that racism is born at the point when the theme of racial purity replaces that of race struggle. . . . At the moment when the discourse of race struggle was being transformed into revolutionary discourse [meaning, here, something like a Marxist discourse of class struggle], the revolutionary project and revolutionary propheticism now began to take a very different direction. Racism is, quite literally, revolutionary discourse in an inverted form" (81). It is this racial discourse—that of the state's imperative to purify the race of the contaminants that threaten its biological existence and continued viability in a post-Darwinian world—that leads to fascism, elements of which persist in every modern nation-state throughout the twentieth century.

This is Foucault's genealogy of race and racism. The story begins in England in 1630, where race is conceived nonbiologically in terms of language, lineage, law, and conquest. The discourse undergoes a transformation as it becomes part of a biological discourse in the late eighteenth century, and then a further transformation when that biological discourse becomes a tool in the hands of capitalists and state officials in the nineteenth century who seek control over national populations, especially laborers. I will leave it to students of European history to examine the details of this account. My concern is with North America, where history unfolds somewhat differently.

Speculations on the Genealogy of Race in North America

Foucault, as was said above, sees two shifts in European racial discourse after its inception as race war. First there is the shift in the meaning of the term *race* from a loose designation of cultural affiliation to a description of heritable morphology. This occurs in the late eighteenth century, according to Foucault, and subsequent scholarship has suggested that it may achieve its most systematic expression in the work of Immanuel Kant between 1775 and 1788.[25] Second is the incorporation of race into biological science, eugenic policy, and technology beginning in the mid-nineteenth century. In this latter move the idea of race as heritable morphology is incorporated into a biological science that emphasizes function and development over anatomy and structure. In this new context, heritable race encompasses not only physical appearance (and not even necessarily that) but also characteristic physiological processes and functions, including sexuality, cognitive development, and vulnerability to degenerative disease.

In work that predates his study of race by at least a decade, Foucault described the advent of biological science at the very beginning of the nineteenth century. Biology, he maintains, eclipses its older rival natural history when scientists first isolate and define the concept "life" as an object of study. Natural historians gave accounts of plants and animals that focused on the visible body, the appearance and architecture of entities. Some, like Linnaeus, were interested in classifying beings as like or unlike other beings in form. Others, like Kant (who was primarily a geographer rather than a natural historian), insisted on taking history seriously as the medium in which form arises, but still the accounts produced concentrated on visual appearances or structural forms. As Foucault put it, "The naturalist is the man concerned with the structure of the visible world and its denomination according to characters. Not with life."[26] Life, as biologists began to understand it, was in effect process; it was the process of material assimilation and growth, the process of reproduction, the process of aging and deterioration, even the process of death. Living beings were organisms made up of functional systems whose processes were both cyclic (like respiration and digestion) and longitudinal (like sexual maturation). Organisms do not simply exist; they develop, and eventually decay.

These processes that, taken together, make up *life* can be normed—that is, their speed and trajectories can be measured and data compiled so that it becomes possible to say what rate and type of development is normal in a given type of organism. For example, on average female human beings become fertile between (say) ten and fifteen years of age. A girl who reaches menarche at seven or at twenty is unusual; her development deviates from the norm, and she can be classified as abnormal in a certain specifiable degree. The nineteenth century ushered in an age of statistics wherein virtually every phenomenon is normalized, every event rendered knowable by means of its degree of deviation from some norm.

As this new scientific life began to operate as an organizing principle in an ever-widening circle of theoretical undertakings, European racial theories underwent alteration. No longer was race simply an observable morphological phenomenon that might (or might not) signify a metaphysical difference; race became a mark of deviance explicable in terms of the process of human development, the development of civilization.[27] There was only one normal developmental path from savagery to civilization. Some human groups were either dallying along that path—retarded in their development—or had deviated from it and were either permanently arrested at a primitive stage or retrogressing toward savagery. Everyone who was not a _____ (depending on the theorist, in this blank would be written English, Saxon, Caucasian, Aryan, etc.) was either a racial retard or a racial degenerate. Either way, race had become, inherently, a matter of both hierarchy and health.

We see the same two major trends in racial discourse in Anglo-America. The first shift may have occurred somewhat more rapidly in the tobacco colonies, predating Kant's work certainly and even influencing it—particularly his changing conception of the racial status of native North Americans between 1775 and 1785. (Kant insists in his earlier work that Americans do not constitute a fully formed race but are the imperfectly adapted progeny of "Hunnish"—he also calls them Mongol or Kalmuck—peoples once living in northeastern Asia. In his later work, he holds the Americans to be a separate "red" race, distinct from the "yellow" races of the East. This change may have come as a result of reading Anglo-American sources, since the idea that Native Americans are red apparently originated with Native Americans themselves or within verbal encounters between them and Anglo-Americans; in fact, Native Americans do not have red skin, and no Anglo-American spoke of natives as red before the 1720s.[28]) Whatever the conceptual status of the morphological concept of race in North America relative to Europe, it is clear that Anglo-Americans were far more willing much earlier to use morphological race as the basis of political dividing practices. In 1723 the Virginia General Assembly passed "an Act directing the trial of Slaves, committing capital crimes; and for the more effectual punishing conspiracies and insurrections of them; and for the better government of Negroes, Mulattos, and Indians, bond or free." Shortly thereafter, British attorney general Richard West made inquiry as to why free Negroes, mulattoes, and Native Americans were to have no right to vote in any election in the colony, a clear departure from English law and from previous colonial statutes. West wrote, "I cannot see why one freeman should be used worse than another, merely upon account of his complexion."[29] Colonial governor William Gooch explained that free Negroes and mulattoes would undoubtedly remain sympathetic to slaves—as they apparently had in a recent slave uprising—and thus must have affixed to them "a perpetual Brand . . . by excluding them from that great Privilege of a Freeman."[30] It should be noted that Gooch evinces no small amount of class consciousness when he points out that mulattoes in particular were troublesome, "as most of them are the Bastards of some of the worst of our imported Servants and Convicts." Race (or a sort of ingrained or habitual racism) was obviously *not* the fundamental reason for racial distinction in law, according to Gooch; the fundamental reason was political and strategic. Because of their personal histories and affiliations, such people simply could not be trusted to act as loyal subjects of the Crown. The easiest way to contain them was to create law that marked their race as an underclass. Thus was the morphological concept of race shaped and extended more or less deliberately through the mechanism of colonial law.[31]

Pigmentation was the premiere morphological mark of race, replacing the older conception of race as cultural or linguistic affiliation and lineage, although obviously pigmentation was believed to be heritable and thus a concomitant of lineage. There were certainly other morphological considerations, such as head shape, hair color and texture, and facial features. But pigmentation was the easiest to see at a distance, which was important in tracking fugitive servants and slaves and spotting hostile natives. For the most part, then, in Anglo-America pigmentation was paramount; it was the difference that could most readily be used to make a difference. Studies of the other aspects of racial morphology were generally only needed to bolster later claims that racial hierarchy was somehow natural rather than simply politically expedient.

The prevailing theoretical view of race in eighteenth-century Anglo-America seems to have been something like what Samuel Stanhope Smith offered in his 1785 address to the American Philosophical Society (which was later published as *An Essay on the Causes of the Variety of Complexion and Figure in the Human Species* in 1787). Rev. Smith claimed that there was but one original human pair from which all living persons are descended, and that pair was white.[32] Some of their progeny, however, migrated to lands where the environmental conditions changed their skin, giving rise to peoples of black, tawny, and yellow complexions that were inherited by successive generations. Smith was very familiar with European racial theories of his time and drew on them freely in his essay. His view differed from that of his contemporary Immanuel Kant in that Smith believed as races migrated into new lands, their pigmentation and other features would gradually alter further, according to climate; Kant, of course, believed that once the original "germs" had matured into racial types, people of each type lost the ability to produce children with features carried by the other germs, so races were now fixed regardless of the climate inhabited.

Smith's monogenetic view of the etiology of race prevailed in North America for about fifty years. By that point it was clear that dark-skinned people were not lightening, light-skinned people were not darkening, and neither Europeans nor Africans were turning tawny, olive, yellow, or red like the native groups (depending on which observer one consults). By the 1830s, with the work of Charles Caldwell (*Thoughts on the Original Unity of the Human Race*, 1830) and Samuel George Morton (*Crania Americana*, 1839), Anglo-American thinking began to change dramatically; by 1851 Morton was openly declaring what he had only implied twelve years earlier, namely, that each of the five races (he held there were five, as did Blumenbach, but this was subject to debate; Kant had said there were four) were separate species with separate origins.[33] Although Morton's work was controversial—in part because it contradicted the idea that species could be distinguished on the basis of whether cross-progeny were fertile, which clearly mulattoes and mustees were[34]—from midcentury on, polygenist views held sway in the United States, finding voice and reinforcement in the work of George Gliddon, Josiah Nott, and Louis Agassiz.[35]

Samuel Stanhope Smith's work coincides with the beginning of the national debate about whether to abolish slavery. At that point, according to Michael Banton, "Only a handful of pro-slavery writers asserted that blacks were inferior; most pointedly rejected such views except in so far as they contended that only Negroes could work in extreme heat."[36] (It is not self-evident that heat tolerance is a sign of inferiority; in this age of perforated ozone, heat and sun tolerance may be the trait that marks those fittest for survival. But Thomas Jefferson among others suggested that this trait in the Negro indicated fitness for manual as opposed to mental labor.[37]) Slave traders' testimony in parliamentary inquiries on the subject amounted to "detailed information which revealed mistrust and ethnocentric contempt but no assumptions about permanent superiority and inferiority."[38] The debate was not primarily over whether Africans were inferior to whites but over whether enslavement of human beings was morally permissible. Smith's essay was often used by abolitionists as a foundation for arguments against slavery. In 1810, two years after abolition of the slave trade, Smith's essay was reprinted, so it was still enjoying wide popularity, but the days of monogeny's ascendancy in the United States were numbered. The subsequent rise of polygeny theory coincided with a period in which the only legal way to increase the slave population was to impregnate African American women. Black men could be used for that purpose, but very often slave owners took the duty on themselves or delegated it to their sons—which of course meant that large numbers of enslaved individuals in the years following 1808 were of European as well as African descent. As the actual hereditary lines between Americans of varying pigmentation became indistinct, the theoretical biological lines between American races were sharpened.

Following the abolition of racial slavery in 1863 and the conclusion of the Civil War in 1865, a new era began in the United States, especially in the once politically dominant South. While the imperialistic nations of Europe were honing their management skills in the creation of technological bureaucracies, the United States was trying to build an economy virtually from the ground up. Except for a few cities like Richmond where negotiation prevented outright razing, the South's urban infrastructure and transportation system was utterly destroyed by fire, looting, and four years of violence and neglect. Much of the labor force was displaced. Thousands of former slaves simply marched along behind the liberating armies for lack of any idea where to go or what to do; military leaders managed to feed and resettle some of them, but many were left without any provision at all. One out of every four white Southern males above the age of twelve had died in battle or of starvation, exposure, or disease between 1861 and 1865. In fields outside Petersburg, Virginia, alone, thirty thousand bodies lay scattered; most would never be identified.

There is no economy without a labor force. But within the defeated Confederacy most of the laborers in 1865 were either displaced or dead, and those who remained or could be rounded up were destitute, unruly, largely unskilled, and filled with high expectations and intense fears and suspicions. This posed a huge administrative problem, but it also presented a variety of interesting opportunities. In any case, the South constituted an enormous laboratory for experimentation in the management of populations, which set the North American stage for the widespread development of what Foucault calls "biopower."

Biopower

The science of life aided two parallel governmental developments, which Foucault describes in both part V of *The History of Sexuality*, vol. 1, and *"Society Must Be Defended."* The first is that of normalizing disciplinary control of individuated bodies, familiar to readers of Foucault's *Discipline and Punish*. Normalizing discipline takes shape in the late eighteenth century in response both to increasing numbers of individuals requiring management in institutions like the military, schools, hospitals, and factories and to the requirements of technological innovations in mechanized production and weaponry. This Foucault calls "an *anatomo-politics of the human body*" (Foucault, 1980, 139). The second governmental development, which began to take shape in the nineteenth century, "focused on the species body, the body imbued with the mechanisms of life and serving as the basis of the biological processes: propagation, births, and longevity, with all the conditions that can cause them to vary" (139). This involved a series of interventions and regulatory controls, as opposed to normalizing disciplines. Foucault terms this "*a biopolitics of the population*" (139). These two poles of development in governmental practice and institutional power structures constituted "an explosion of numerous and diverse techniques for achieving the subjugation of bodies and the control of populations, marking the beginning of an era of 'bio-power'" (140). As European nation-states become modern technological bureaucracies, biopower emerges and extends its reach through groups now defined as *populations*. It justifies itself and broadens its purview on the basis of its claim to manage life processes (health) at the level of the social body. Its institutions and practices purport to work for the good of the people, its subjects, as a collective mass. Government's job becomes not simply defending and perhaps enlarging the sovereign's territory and wealth but, and much more important, protecting and strengthening the nation, conceived as a people or race.

Biopower is Foucault's word for the mechanisms and institutions, policies and procedures, that officials created in pursuit of that goal. These have included such things as programs for public hygiene, mandatory inoculation or quarantine, "managed" health care, insurance regulation, campaigns to promote marriage and fertility or to achieve zero population growth or put an end to the consumption of dangerous substances (from alcohol to marijuana to tobacco), state regulation of reproductive technology, institutional efforts to improve the public morals, public surveillance to reduce crime or prevent masturbation or identify bioterrorists, and on and on. The main, or at least the ostensible, point of such efforts is to strengthen the nation considered as a living population rather than as individuals, so that restrictions on liberty for individuals are considered to be largely justified. But the issue is not so much what people decide to do and how to entice them to do what meshes with the aims of power structures; the issue is, at least very often, who people are, what deviant groups they belong to or identify with. Deviance may weaken the nation; pathology, perversion, and all forms of degeneracy contaminate it and threaten its life. The state has become the great administrator of the national *bios*, which means that it must act as the great divider, the mechanism for purifying the public body of contaminants by excluding or eliminating those "elements" that the body cannot healthfully assimilate.

What—or who—count as internal contaminants? In European nations answers could vary—in fact, answers have varied a great deal across national boundaries and over time. But it is no surprise that the usual suspects include the "idle," the poor, the sick, the criminal, and the stupid, as well as anyone else who refuses to adhere to the standards of productivity, hygiene, lifestyle, and reproduction set by the state.

Morphological racism was already entrenched in most European societies in one form or another by the nineteenth century, so persons of races other than whatever was allegedly best (be it white, Caucasian, Saxon, Nordic, Aryan, etc.) were already members of an underclass, usually economically deprived and evincing the effects of that deprivation (illness, the filth of poverty, thievery and violence, illiteracy and ignorance, and so on). Entire morphologically defined races were easily subsumed into this new category of biological degenerates held responsible for the disease and corruption of an otherwise-healthy social body. As a thoroughly biologized concept, as a category of normalization, race came to operate as one way—but a major way—of identifying degenerates. Late nineteenth- and early twentieth-century studies of racial physiology dovetailed nicely with similar studies of the physiology of criminals, alcoholics, morons, and sexual perverts. And all these social contaminants—physiologically defined and morphologically identified—could be held to be pathogens in the public body, and therefore enemies of the state.

This was an especially valuable tool for European colonial administrators who could, under the auspices of the authority of a state committed to enhancing life, kill thousands upon thousands of the people under their control. Without the new scientific theories of race as arrested development or deviance, a glaring contradiction would have threatened the authority and legitimacy of imperialistic national governments. If government's job is to maintain the health of populations, should it not treat its colonial populations as groups in need of purification in relation to the motherland? If race had simply meant morphological difference, European administrators should have taken the same approach to rooting out impurities—criminals, imbeciles, madmen, perverts—in the colonial territories as their counterparts did in Europe. Instead, the entirety of colonial populations were treated as biological threats to European peoples. Thus, Foucault asserts, the kind of racism that operates in the twentieth century, the kind we all grew up with and know from intimate experience, "first develops with colonization, or in other words, with colonizing genocide. If you are functioning in the biopower mode, how can you justify the need to kill people, to kill populations, and to kill civilizations?" (2003, 257). Modern, scientific theories of race created a set of developmental distinctions that allowed colonial governments to exterminate their own colonial populations or deprive imported colonial workers of basic necessities, not to mention basic rights. Racism, Foucault writes, "is primarily a way of introducing a break into the domain of life that is under power's control: the break between what must live and what must die" (258). It is a way of marking out, in biological terms, those individuals who pose an alleged threat to the corporate *bios*—that is, the life, health, strength, and longevity—of the nation (255). Hence state racism—which interlocks with scientific racism—is a virtual inevitability, Foucault insists, in a nation that constitutes itself by means of the techniques of biopower; to function and extend itself, biopower requires biologically based dividing practices that justify—in fact dictate—that some people will be sacrificed either by direct elimination from the population or by deprivation of vital resources. To protect its life, it will be argued, the population must be made secure against various internal (or annexed and internali*zed*) contaminants.

As we have seen in the previous section of this chapter, the United States (perhaps unlike European nations) practiced state racism from its inception. Racism—and not just racial slavery—was enshrined in its laws from the very beginning.[39] Our laws and governmental institutions have never been "color-blind," have never operated in the absence of racial dividing practices. If Anglo-America was perhaps a step ahead of Europe in producing a concept of race as heritable morphology, it may also have been at the forefront of the development of racist population management.

In a U.S. context, we must make a distinction that Foucault does not make: we must distinguish between state racism and scientific racism (which came later and was used extensively by the state once it was articulated). But the basic distinction that Foucault draws still holds: there is a crucial difference between race conceived as heritable morphology and race conceived as heritable physiological functioning. The development of the latter concept—which enabled the kind of administration of populations that now characterizes the industrialized West—required a major shift in scientific thinking, which Foucault locates at the turn of the nineteenth century with the demise of natural history (the rubric under which Kant's work on race clearly fits, as he himself adamantly asserts) and the rise of biology (the rubric under which Darwin's work and the work of the eugenicists following Galton clearly fit). State racism requires nothing more than some kind of racial dividing practice that enables oppression of one or more racially defined groups. Scientific racism—which I would agree with Foucault is what we today understand and experience as modern racism—amounts to a major expansion of the tools of state racism in nineteenth- and twentieth-century America.

So Racism Is *What*?

It is hard for any philosopher to resist the Platonic imperative to define everything. I have argued here that, whatever else it might be said to be, racism is a *dispositif*, a vast apparatus of repeating, self-reinforcing power relations that emerges in the English-speaking world in the seventeenth century. It functions to divide people—first primarily laborer from laborer—and to apportion resources such as health care, insurance, police protection, education, and personal wealth unequally. While it is true that racism requires the concept of race, it did not require a very precise or stable concept; as racism has evolved in conjunction with global economic and technological change, it has produced racial sciences that have given the world concepts of race different from those that enabled its initial founding. Neither race nor racism is a historical constant, much less a natural constant.

I have argued, further, that the concept of race operative in modern racism is not primarily a morphological concept as it was in eighteenth-century racism, but is instead a physiological concept rooted in the nineteenth- and twentieth-century knowledges and practices that Foucault calls "normalization." It is an aspect or type of development—or the lack, arrest, or deviant trajectory thereof. Thus it is almost impossible to classify people racially in the twentieth century without importing into that practice some presumption of abnormality or pathology.

Racism persists regardless of whether the concept of race it employs is scientifically delineated, historically stable, or officially acceptable. It persists because it is the way that U.S. society was organized from its inception. But its persistence is not an indication that it is a permanent psychological (let alone biological) feature of human beings. Rather, its persistence is an indication that our society is deeply invested in maintaining economic inequality and extending the range and depth of mechanisms of social control. Racism has served these ambitions well for three hundred years. What all this means is that racism is not about to go away just because some geneticists have told us—and have been telling us since the 1940s—that our divisions of human beings into skin-color groups have no scientific basis. Racism can adapt to changes in the popular conception of what race is. If *race* comes to mean something like collections of statistical norms within larger gene pools that allegedly reproduce certain morphological and behavioral regularities in populations, racism can continue unabated. Recent moves to map many of society's so-called ills onto our genes—alcoholism, violent behavior, homosexuality, and so forth—testify to the commodious nature of the concepts of physiological racism. (I suspect that by the late 1940s U.S. racism was in fact already transforming and expanding, as genetic theory was gaining ground, to include these various kinds of deviant physiologies—which may be one reason why mid-century theorists like Sartre and Adorno saw racism as so multifaceted, as having so many target groups, and also as so stubborn.)

What, then, shall we do? As Foucault points out, there is no outside to power, and biopower is the name of the game in our age. But just as Foucault taketh away—our belief in social progress, our belief in the fundamental autonomy of the individual—he also giveth. And what he giveth is the idea that power is never monolithic. For a regime of power to persist, millions of what he calls "capillary" relationships must persist unchanged—that is, they must repeat themselves—from day to day. And there is always the chance that they won't.

We can enlarge that chance. We can disrupt capillary circuits of repetition. No, we can't hijack the whole system and make it fly at another altitude or crash it into the ground. There is no central control that we could commandeer. But each one of us can find points in the circulations of power that shape our lives where a refusal to act as we have in the past, an experimental move where before a habituated response would have been given, might begin to make a difference in our lives and the lives of those around us. Foucault refuses to give anybody a "right answer" to the question of what to do about any kind of injustice, but every word he ever wrote urges us to *try*. What emerges in history can disappear in history as well. Foucault was Nietzschean enough to believe that absolutely anything could—and would—one day be overcome. Progress is not inevitable, but change is. And what we do, consciously or not, creates that change.

What Philosophical Difference Any of This Makes or: Why This Is Philosophy and Not Just "Soft-Headed Girl Stuff"

What have I done in this chapter besides recount the work that some excellent U.S. historians have already done and relate it to some things a dead French guy once said about European history? Have I clarified a philosophical puzzle? Have I solved a philosophical problem? How can this enlargement on Foucault's work be construed as continental *philosophy*?

Foucault's friend and colleague at the Collège de France Pierre Hadot describes Hellenistic philosophy not as a body of knowledge or even a method for producing and verifying truth, but rather as a practice, a "way of life."[40] Philosophy, Hadot writes, was once something people did—and not just on occasion; it was something they did from dawn till dusk in everything that they undertook. It was a form of self-cultivation and self-governance. Foucault was very attracted by that idea, and so am I. I became a philosopher not because I wanted to solve puzzles but because I wanted to be better, in some indefinable way, than I was.

Twenty years later "better" remains underdefined, but my desire persists. Now it is a desire to explore possibilities rather than reach some imagined goal like Platonic Beauty or Truth. As Foucault has said, "In what does [philosophy] consist, if not in the endeavor to know how and to what extent it might be possible to think differently, instead of legitimating [or attempting to realize] what is already known?"[41] I want to think differently from how I have been taught to think, from how my racist, sexist society has constrained me to think. And this thinking differently is not a mere matter of changing my mind, restructuring or purifying my system of beliefs. This thinking is a practice; it lives in the actions that I take and the way that I live. When I say I want to think differently, I mean I want to live differently, and that means dismantling old habits and developing new ways of behaving and moving and interacting and perceiving. I very strongly believe that that concerted effort to think—to act, to be—differently *is* philosophy.

Genealogical exhumation of the ways our thinking was shaped, its predecessors, its differences from its own past that it often tries to pass off as inevitabilities rather than options, can help us think differently. It can "free thought from what it silently thinks";[42] it can break the intellectual, emotional, and behavioral bonds that hold us within a world shaped by the greed, the fears, and the desires of so many of our ancestors; it can estrange us from the habits and mores that heretofore seemed normal and therefore right. It can be a step toward becoming different people, people who can create a future different from our past. As Grace Hale puts it, "American history in its broadest sense—what has happened, how we have represented to ourselves what has happened, and how we will continue in this intersecting of making and telling—is vitally important here. If we understand the past as always having been only black and white, what will be the catalyst that makes the future different? the epiphany that erases the bloody divisions?"[43] Philosophy is about opening ourselves toward change, toward a future beyond what we are and know, a future that we do not dictate in advance. As such it is antithetical to the normalization and the management projects of our bioracist culture. Foucaultian genealogies, perhaps American-style, are tools we can use to effect some of those openings and, we may dare to hope, create a nonracist future. And this work of change (while neither hardheaded nor unambiguously masculine!) has absolutely everything to do with philosophy.

NOTES

1. Michael Omi and Howard Winant, *Racial Formation in the United States from the 1960s to the 1990s*, 2d ed. (New York: Routledge, 1994), 69.

2. Michel Foucault, *The History of Sexuality*, vol. 1, *An Introduction*, trans. Robert Hurley (New York: Random House, 1980); *"Society Must Be Defended": Lectures at the Collège de France, 1975–76*, trans. David Macey (New York: Picador, 2003).

3. Jean-Paul Sartre, *Anti-Semite and Jew*, trans. George Becker (New York: Schocken Books, 1948), 37–38.

4. Julien Murphy, "Sartre on American Racism," in *Philosophers on Race: Critical Essays*, ed. Julie K. Ward and Tommy L. Lott (Oxford: Blackwell, 2002), 222–40. Murphy lists four works by Sartre that focus on antiblack racism in the United States: his 1946 play *The Respectful Prostitute*; his unfinished essay on "Revolutionary Violence," published posthumously as an appendix to *Notebooks for an Ethics* (1992) and a piece of which was published in 1949 in *Combat*; as well as two untranslated reports he wrote in 1945 for *Le Figaro*.

5. Lewis Gordon, who has made the most use one could probably make of Sartre's work for an analysis of U.S. racism, has this to say about Sartre's equation of the proletariat with oppressed people of African descent: "It is not, as one might be inclined to think, that Sartre attempts to reduce blacks to the proletariat. It is instead that Sartre seeks to *elevate* blacks to such a level. Sartre appears to have been aware of the 'under-class' status of blacks." Gordon makes these comments in the context of a discussion of Sartre's *Black Orpheus*. See Lewis Gordon, "Bad Faith and Antiblack Racism," in Ward and Lott, *Philosophers on Race*, 251. See also Murphy, "Sartre on American Racism," 227.

6. It might seem that making racism a result of individual bad faith and, simultaneously, making it an effect of capitalism results in a logical quagmire, but these approaches are easily reconciled if we consider the final section of *Anti-Semite and Jew*. There Sartre says that the only way to end anti-Semitism as a social and political force (short of usurping the freedom of all those who choose it for themselves) is to restructure the situation in which people make personal choices. We need to construct a social and political field wherein the choice of anti-Semitism (or antiblack racism or any type of bigotry) is impossible. Sartre suggests that "anti-Semitism is a mythical, bourgeois representation of the class struggle, and that it could not exist in a classless

society" (149); further, it is founded on a certain conception of property that will "be cut at its roots" when the revolution comes (150). So, if we want to end bigotry, we should work for the revolution. Until the revolution comes, however, Sartre insists that we must work with the then newly forming Jewish League against anti-Semitism (151–52), or presumably with whatever twenty-first-century equivalents there might be. Not insignificantly, however, he does not say what it is that the Jewish League or its contemporary counterparts should actually do.

7. Of course I am aware that Lewis Gordon has worked hard to adapt Sartre's work as an analytic tool in a North American racial context. My contention is not that Sartre's work is impossible to use, only that it does not easily lend itself to the effort without a lot of alteration and critique, and it has serious limitations other than its lack of attention to racism per se, as I will detail below. For a lengthy sample of Gordon's extensive work, see his *Bad Faith and Antiblack Racism* (Atlantic Highlands, N.J.: Humanities Press, 1995).

8. Theodor W. Adorno, Else Frenkel-Brunswik, Daniel J. Levinson, and R. Nevitt Sanford, *The Authoritarian Personality* (New York: Harper, 1950), 9.

9. Max Horkheimer and Theodor W. Adorno, *Dialectic of Enlightenment: Philosophical Fragments*, ed. Gunzelin Schmid Noerr, trans. Edmund Jephcott (Stanford: Stanford University Press, 2002), 171.

10. This information is widely available, but see, for example, David Theo Goldberg, *Racist Culture: Philosophy and the Politics of Meaning* (Oxford: Blackwell, 1993), 62.

11. Robert Burton, *The Audubon Backyard Birdwatcher: Birdfeeders and Bird Gardens* (San Diego: Thunder Bay Press, 1999), 84.

12. Again, I am relying on Goldberg's etymology, *Racist Culture*, 63.

13. Actually they spoke of themselves as conquerors of longer standing. They were quite aware that the Saxons had not originated on the island, but had massacred and driven back the peoples there before them—notably the Celts, the ancestors of the Scots, the Welsh, and the Irish, who had retreated to the north and west. So their claim was not that conquest itself never constitutes a legitimate claim to land, but that the Norman laws were weapons aimed at them and should not be obeyed. Perhaps it was not that conquest was illegitimate but that the Norman Conquest was as yet incomplete and could still be turned back. The Normans may have agreed with at least part of this account. As Foucault points out, until the sixteenth-century rule of Henry VII, English political ritual stated that the king ruled by right of conquest. See Foucault, *"Society Must Be Defended,"* 99.

14. Footnote 22 of Foucault's February 4, 1976, lecture reads as follows: "The theory of the 'Norman yoke' (or 'Norman bondage') had been popularized in the sixteenth and seventeenth centuries by political writers (Blackwood, et cetera), by the 'Elizabethan Chroniclers' (Holinshed, Speed, Daniel, et cetera), by the Society of Antiquarians (Selden, Harrison, and Nowell), and by jurists (Coke, et cetera). Their goal was to 'glorify the pre-Norman past' that existed before the invasion and Conquest." See Foucault, *"Society Must Be Defended,"* 113.

15. See Winthrop D. Jordan, *White over Black: American Attitudes Toward the Negro, 1550–1812* (Chapel Hill: University of North Carolina Press, 1968), 87.

16. In 1663 a number of these men helped foment what historian Theodore Allen calls "the largest, most widespread insurrectionary plot of bond-laborers" in North American history. This occurred at Gloucester, Virginia, in September 1663 but was betrayed to authorities before it could get seriously underway. Most of the rebels escaped, however, and of those caught only four were hanged. See Theodore W. Allen, *The Invention of the White Race: The Origin of Racial Oppression in Anglo-America* (London: Verso, 1997), 152.

17. There is disagreement in historical texts about whether Europeans and Native Americans were colonial chattel slaves. This disagreement hangs, I suspect, on how one defines chattel slavery. If a person is purchased or somehow forced against his or her will to labor without remuneration for life, is that person a chattel slave? My intuition would tell me yes. If so, there were thousands of European and Native American chattel slaves in North America by the end of the seventeenth century. The first were perhaps the English women (loosely designated since many were but girls) brought to Jamestown in 1619 by the Virginia Company to be sold as wives to

planters there. They were purchased, forced to labor for another without remuneration, and bound for life (though most did not live more than a year). A similar situation obtained with regard to juvenile "apprentices." Many children as young as eight were more or less abducted from the streets of London and sold for a term of years to Virginia planters to work in the tobacco fields. Most of these children died before the end of their contracted servitude. Adult and adolescent indentured servants were brought—often forcibly—from England, Ireland, Scotland, and elsewhere and bound to labor without remuneration for a certain number of years, usually between four and seven. Most of them died before the end of their term of service, so in effect they served for life. Further, at the end of their term, if they could not produce their indenture papers and cajole their masters to go with them to court to have the term of indenture officially recognized as at an end, they could not cease their servitude. Finally, punishment for various sorts of infractions—from running away to fornicating with other indentured servants—often involved lengthening of term of service. In some cases servitude for life was the sentence pronounced. In effect, especially in the early years of the Virginia Colony, indentured servitude did not differ in any notable way from life-term slavery. English law forbade servants from being sold or bequeathed, which distinguished them from chattel property. But as Theodore Allen is at pains to show, this system broke down very quickly in the tobacco colonies, and bond-laborers became a circulating commodity. (Allen gives ample evidence of this; see Allen, *Invention of the White Race*, chap. 6.) So, was there slavery in Anglo-America before there was racial slavery? Were non-Africans in large numbers ever chattel? I think the answer is yes, and so do Allen and others, but many historians do not. It is certainly true that the chattel slavery system that developed in Anglo-America differed from anything that had come before it, and was thoroughly racialized by the early eighteenth century. But that does not mean that it was racialized from the beginning and that non-Africans were not treated, as Africans certainly were, as chattel. Hence my probably rather controversial use of the term. For a relatively brief history of slavery in Europe before the sixteenth century, see Robin Blackburn, "The Old World Background to European Colonial Slavery," *William and Mary Quarterly*, 3d ser., 54 (January 1997): 66–102.

18. It would be interesting to do a systematic comparison of the two men's writings on race. Jefferson devotes most of his attention to the kind of morphological race characteristic of discussions of racial slavery. Franklin seems to work with a morphological idea of race—identifying skin color as a mark of race—but he sees skin color differences where before Europeans would have simply have seen the old distinction of lineage, religion, and language. For example, he refers to the Pennsylvanian Germans, whose overwhelming numbers he deplored, as a tawny race. See Jordan, *White over Black*, 254.

19. In addition to his book, Allen develops his thesis in an article, "'. . . They Would Have Destroyed Me': Slavery and the Origins of Racism," *Radical America* 9 (May–June 1975): 41–63, esp. 44.

20. Most captured or purchased natives were sold to dealers and shipped out of the colonies, although in 1708 South Carolina held 1,400 native American bond-laborers (500 men, 600 women, and 300 children), amounting to about 25 percent of the total lifetime hereditary bond-labor force. See Allen, *Invention of the White Race*, 41.

21. Ibid., 214–15.

22. There is good evidence that many did at first understand that the institution of slavery compromised their economic interest as free laborers. Georgia was founded in 1732 with a principle of no slavery. South Carolina planters wanted the opportunity to develop the land with slave labor (as they had in their home state) and began agitating to repeal the rule. Allen quotes one Savannah citizen objecting with the claim that free laborers would be impoverished by such a move. See ibid., 252–53.

23. Ibid., 251.

24. Ibid. Winthrop Jordan also notes that the term *white* first begins to appear in place of the terms English or Christian in about 1680. See Jordan, *White over Black*, 95.

25. Robert Bernasconi has argued that Kant is the progenitor of our modern concept of race, although Kant's ideas developed within a context very different from our own. See Bernasconi,

"Who Invented the Concept of Race? Kant's Role in the Enlightenment Construction of Race," in *Race*, ed. Robert Bernasconi (Malden, Mass.: Blackwell, 2001), 11–36. For more discussion of Kant's role in the formation of this concept, see Emmanuel Chukwudi Eze, "The Color of Reason: The Idea of 'Race' in Kant's Anthropology," in *Postcolonial African Philosophy: A Critical Reader*, ed. Emmanuel Chukwudi Eze (Oxford: Blackwell, 1997), 103–40; Phillip R. Sloan, "Buffon, German Biology, and the Historical Interpretation of Biological Species," *British Journal for the History of Science* 12, no. 41 (1979): 109–53 ("The entry of Immanuel Kant into this discussion in the 1770s was crucial for the establishment, clarification, and amplification of the taxonomic concepts originally developed by Buffon" [125]); Mark Larrimore, "Sublime Waste: Kant on the Destiny of 'Races,'" in *Civilization and Oppression*, ed. Catherine Wilson (Calgary: University of Calgary Press, 1999), 99–125. For an account of how Kant's definition both informed and differed from what developed in nineteenth-century Europe, see Ladelle McWhorter, "Sex, Race, and Biopower: A Foucaultian Genealogy," *Hypatia* 19, no. 3 (2004): 38–62.

26. Michel Foucault, *The Order of Things: An Archaeology of the Human Science*, trans. Alan Sheridan (New York: Vintage Books, 1970), 161.

27. For more discussion of this, see Ladelle McWhorter, "Scientific Discipline and the Origins of Race: A Foucaultian Reading of the History of Biology," in *Continental and Postmodern Perspectives in the Philosophy of Science*, ed. Babette Babich, Debra Bergoffen, and Simon Glynn (Aldershot, UK: Avebury Press, 1995), 173–88.

28. Kant would have had two obvious sorts of sources for his view of Native Americans—travelers' reports of various kinds and the work of Linnaeus, who had mapped his delineation of race onto the doctrine of the four humors, which dictated that one must be red. Kant was, of course, criticizing Linnaeus's approach, since the latter merely described, so Kant says, rather than making any attempt to explain; therefore there is no reason for him to have accepted Linnaeus's idea that there is a red race. In fact, in his 1775 essay "On the Different Races of Man," Kant does not speak of a red race and holds Americans to be descendants of Asians. So it may well be that the change we see by 1785 has more to do with Kant's reading of Anglo-American sources than with the influence of Linnaeus. (Kant's 1775 essay is translated and published in Eze, *Postcolonial African Philosophy*, 38–48. A 1788 essay that holds there to be a red American race is translated and published as "On the Use of Teleological Principles in Philosophy," trans. Jon Mark Mikkelsen, in Bernasconi, *Race*, 37–56. For my own purposes I have had the generous use of Professor Mikkelsen's drafts of translations of three of Kant's essays—the above-mentioned two, plus "Defining the Concept of a Human Race" from 1785, all of which will be published in a forthcoming collection of German writings on race translated and edited by Jon Mark Mikkelsen.) We must remember, however, that Kant did not read English. He would have had to wait until the English writings were available in German before he could incorporate them into his view of Americans. Early encounters between English and native North Americans seem to have left most of the English with the impression that they were encountering people like themselves but pagan—not a distinct race, and certainly not a "red" people. Reports of the color of the natives usually employ words like "tawny," "yellow," or, frequently, "olive." Later on, as antagonisms developed and racial discourse became more systematic and organized, Anglo-Americans were much harsher in their appraisals of Native Americans and much more interested in setting them apart from themselves, with the help of racial categories. But why call them red? There is evidence that Cherokees—with whom tobacco colonists had many dealings and on whom they often depended for protection from more hostile tribes farther south and west—called themselves "red" people because they painted themselves red when they prepared for war. Gradually the Anglos began to refer to Cherokees as red people and slowly to all native tribes as "red." The first known uses of the term red to describe natives begin to surface around 1725. It would have taken a while before "red" was applied to all natives indiscriminately. It begins to appear in French diplomatic language and correspondence "as a generic label for Indians" in 1729, according to historian Nancy Shoemaker. In the southeastern colonies the English began to use the term broadly in the 1750s. See "How Indians Got to Be Red," *American Historical Review* 102 (June 1997):

625–44, esp. 628. It is quite possible that Kant did not encounter this usage, or was not persuaded of its descriptive accuracy, until the late 1770s. For a critique of Kant's rather unscholarly use of sources, see Eze, "The Color of Reason," 127–28. Bernasconi also remarks on Kant's unscholarly use of sources in his essay "Kant as an Unfamiliar Source of Racism," in Ward and Lott, *Philosophers on Race*, 148–49.

29. See Allen, *Invention of the White Race*, 241. The English were not only puzzled and skeptical but also positively outraged at the Anglo-Americans' use of castration as legally mandated punishment for slaves (and sometimes for free African Americans as well). Jordan writes, "In towering indignation, English officials called castration 'inhumane and contrary to all Christian laws,' 'a punishment never inflicted by any Law [in any of] H.M. Dominions,' and 'such as never was allowed by or known in any of the Laws of this Kingdom'" (*White over Black*, 156).

30. Quoted in Jordan, *White over Black*, 127.

31. Allen uses this letter of Gooch's to show that the process of legal racial marking was a conscious choice on the part of many colonial administrators and not an "unthinking decision," as Jordan would have it. Allen insists that morphologically based racism was a deliberate strategy on the part of colonial elites to divide and conquer their huge populations of impoverished and rebellious laborers of all races.

32. Jordan notes that there were Anglo-Americans who believed that the first race was tawny. See *White over Black*, 247–48.

33. See John S. Michael, "A New Look at Morton's Craniological Research," *Current Anthropology* 29 (April 1988): 349. According to George Stocking, polygeny (the view that there were numerous separate acts of creation and, thus, that humans beings are not all descended from one pair) was first advanced in a book called *Pre-Adamite* in 1655 by Isaac de la Peyrère. It was popularized by Lord Kames, a Scottish jurist, in a 1774 book titled *Sketches of the History of Man*. See Stocking, *Race, Culture, and Evolution: Essays in the History of Anthropology* (New York: The Free Press, 1968), 39.

34. The word *mustee* is similar in function to the word *mulatto*, indicating a child of parents of different races. In the case of a mustee one parent is Native American and the other either Negro or white. The word seems usually to have been applied to the child of a Native American and a Negro and has since dropped out of North American usage.

35. Wiegand, 1995, 34.

36. See Michael Banton, "The Classification of Races in Europe and North America: 1700–1850," *International Social Science Journal* 39 (February 1987): 50.

37. See Emmanuel Chukwudi Eze's introduction to excerpts from Jefferson's *Notes on the State of Virginia* in his edited volume *Race and the Enlightenment: A Reader* (Oxford: Blackwell, 1997), 95.

38. Banton, "Classification of Races," 50. Jordan's work reinforces Banton's assessment. See Jordan, *White over Black*, 231, 239, 259.

39. Most historians seem to mark the 1790 decision to restrict the right to acquire citizenship by naturalization to white people as the point at which racism per se became part of U.S. law.

40. See esp. Pierre Hadot, *Philosophy as a Way of Life*, trans. Michael Chase (Oxford: Blackwell, 1995).

41. Michel Foucault, *The History of Sexuality*, vol. 2, *The Use of Pleasure*, trans. Robert Hurley (New York: Pantheon, 1985), 9.

42. Ibid.

43. Grace Elizabeth Hale, *Making Whiteness: The Culture of Segregation in the South, 1890–1940* (New York: Pantheon, 1998), 10–11.

PART TWO

5

SOCIAL MINIMALISM IN A LIBERAL CULTURE
AND THE PROBLEM OF RACIAL HUBRIS

Cynthia Willett

Roy Martinez asks why the most influential white philosophers in the continental tradition in the United States have ignored the issue of race. The first response I would give is simple and straightforward. Philosophical thought begins in self-reflection, or at least in studying texts that develop our capacities for self-knowledge. Contemporary white philosophers typically do not think of ourselves as having significant racial or social identities, and so categories such as race do not tend to play a role in our philosophical reflection.

There are many reasons for the lack of reflection regarding the impact of race on our identities, but perhaps most prominent among these reasons is what also makes us suspicious of the nefarious uses of race, and that is liberal skepticism toward any social identity, including national identity, class elitism, and race. In fact, race as a social force constitutive of our individuality and even our style of thinking—in other words, as an essential topic for self-knowledge—challenges our liberalism, or at least the minimalist conception of sociality that undergirds liberalism and the professional culture of philosophy that it sustains. For liberals, it is not clear how race could be anything more than a shadow cast both on one's basic principles or core values and on the techniques or methods of philosophical reflection that a liberal culture sustains. Some of the most powerful books on race written by philosophers are read as having demonstrated why race matters not for philosophical principles but only for the application of those principles.[1] The implication is that race is important for social policy but not for philosophical reflection.

For cosmopolitan liberals, the thought that one belongs to a race, along with the idea that race could be a social unit akin to family or nation, is more than a little embarrassing. Groups insistent on such identities provoked twentieth-century mass slaughters, culminating in the genocide of World War II. The progressive rhetoric of the civil rights era urged us to move past race, and to view not just the country but the world as color-blind. The conception of equality that emerged out of the social movements of the 1950s and 1960s was, as Michael Walzer has observed, an abstract one: equality required that we think of ourselves in some fundamental way as the same, and that we construct progressive social policies to reflect this abstract sameness.[2] Just as the 1960s youth culture donned the uniform of jeans against artificial distinctions of status, so philosophers would think (or aim to think) as abstract persons defined by one's own actions and autonomous choices, and not by identities, communities, or cultures with histories. One might even expect to experience a tinge of guilt at the mere mention of race, as though by allowing one's thought to touch ever so lightly on the topic, one gives it greater credibility than it deserves.

To assert racial identities could then strike the liberal philosopher as a throwback to an era of segregation, when racial demarcations were prominent in our social codes and reinforced by laws. Against Jim Crow–era segregation we have tried to diminish racial categories from our perception as well as our thinking. Even liberal political programs important on college campuses may acknowledge the persistence of racial inequities, but they aim for a world in which merit wins out over race, not a world in which race matters. Many of us continue to take this goal of a color-blind and race-free society as a regulative ideal, and we understand this ideal as one that requires us to delete racial categories from our discourse as well as our philosophies, at least in the long run if not the short run. So to respond to Professor Martinez's question, of course we should not focus on race, at least not when pondering the ontological parameters of human existence or abstract and enduring domains of philosophical thought.

The ideal of a race-free society served as a progressive goal for a culture divided by legal segregation and social inequality. The civil rights movement established to some degree fair procedures rooted in equality for public institutions. The contributions of this notion of fairness, as well as the limitations of this notion, rest on the advance within liberalism of what Michael Sandel terms the procedural republic.[3] Fairness demands that procedures of our institutions either abstract from, or compensate for (via affirmative action), considerations of race to generate race-neutral political outcomes. The veil of ignorance that John Rawls employs to abstract from considerations such as race in proposing claims to justice exemplifies these liberal and left-liberal intuitions of what counts as fair. That is, many liberals or leftists insist that claims to justice should encourage procedures that abstract from race and focus on what really matters: either fair rules for decision making or the fair distribution of resources in the political economy. Our various policies of inclusion, such as affirmative action, are used to both counterbalance the artifact of race and clear space to tackle the deeper issues of justice, issues that are considered to be more substantial or real.

Beginning with the 1970s, and even more so after the end of the cold war, various groups pushed forth agendas based on asserting their social identities, as the older demands for abstract equality gave way to the recognition of racial, ethnic, or other differences. These groups have altered the language of racial equality to allow for the fact that we have not become raceless and colorless and show no signs of doing so anytime soon. Their aim is for a diverse society rather than a homogenous one. The danger is that a multicultural society may only superficially represent diversity, and may in fact fail to address deeper social and economic conflicts. In such a superficial society, individuals with diverse racial or other social backgrounds may gain positions of status and power as long as they exemplify the status quo values of the society and do not threaten any substantial social changes. For this reason, Patricia Hill Collins warns that multiculturalism leads to a new politics of containment.[4] Diversity amplifies our university curriculum and extends the philosophies that we teach, but it does not challenge the core principles of our thinking or the basic parameters of power.

It is this latter demand that renders the politics of recognition suspect.[5] Still, the politics of recognition, and specifically the Hegelian roots of this politics, does encourage greater attention to our social bonds and the identities that grow out of these bonds than typical of liberal thought and the culture of reflection that liberal institutions sustains. The politics of recognition has brought significant gains, and specifically because the quasi-Hegelian rhetoric of this politics gives us some way to understand how we depend on others for our identities. Our understanding of our social sources of identity can promote awareness of the role of race as a social force penetrating the core of thinking.

Yet even continental philosophers, those who trace their roots back to Hegel rather than simply to Kantian cosmopolitanism or Lockean liberalism, continue to treat race as a secondary concern. This is surprising because thinkers important for the continental tradition such as Merleau-Ponty, Nietzsche, and Freud have led us to reflect on the emotive, social, or cultural roots of thought, roots that predispose racial or related categories to persist not only in our lives but also on our most abstract level of reflection. The standard liberal position may defend abstract procedures of thinking, but even liberals, whether they are Lockean or Kantian or belong to yet another tradition, hardly abstain from attachments to their traditions and cultures of thought. These attachments betray identities that are far from neutral. The valorization of philosophical traditions and cultures of the Anglo-Saxons or the German Enlightenment functions as a social identity that shapes both reflection and our typical prejudices. And these limitations of thought carry substantial political consequences. The lack of interest in African philosophy in predominantly white universities is not unrelated to the abandonment of Africa to AIDS or wars of genocide or of urban populations in failing school systems.

One might think that U.S. philosophers in the continental tradition would be much more savvy about cultural, historical, and racial sources of identity, and more attentive to its implications. Any number of points of departure from continental philosophy should alert us to ways in which the primary focus on both neutral procedures of deliberation or abstract analyses of capital (neoliberal, liberal, or socialist) fail to reach the libidinal creatures that we are. Analyses of culture, history, and community play central roles in the philosophies of major thinkers of the continent who follow Hegel. Many of these systems of thought have emphasized the social and historical attachments that undermine the presumption of a reflective individual ontologically separable from the world, the core liberal ideal. Phenomenological studies inspired by Merleau-Ponty suggest that we cannot encounter ourselves, no matter how cerebral our experience, apart from the politics of what he calls flesh, and we might think as well in terms of the politics of skin. As Merleau-Ponty has demonstrated, philosophers following Descartes have attempted to understand space as an abstract set of positions. The Cartesian model empties space of intersubjective meaning and texture. Merleau-Ponty offers a poetics of space that gives us some way into understanding how space can be raced.[6] He developed his poetics of space from his study of depth and color in visual art. In this study he describes space as an interconnecting tissue of sensitivities and names this tissue "flesh." Space as an experience of depth and color, or an interconnecting "tissue" of sensitivities, offers a way of understanding the persistence of racial demarcations in institutions that are nominally racially neutral. Even though Merleau-Ponty did not think about ways in which the flesh is racially marked, his rich phenomenology of corporeality invites us to reflect on the politics of space that subtends both institutional procedures and individuals within those institutions who aim to make decisions that are autonomous or otherwise based on self-reflection.

Continental philosophers from the psychoanalytic traditions have tracked mythical fantasies and irrational impulses that constitute libidinal or destructive dimensions of our social world. Those fantasies and sublimated impulses do not allow us to encounter others or ourselves except through images or drives beyond our rational awareness. Some of these thinkers argue for an original sexual difference at the foundation of our identities. They may argue that this sexual difference cannot be deciphered through some single myth—such as the Oedipal dynamic of the heterosexual, Victorian family proposed by Freud—but that nonetheless this difference is ontological. Žižek argues that the ontological difference that determines how we become subjects is necessarily open to historical reinterpretation, and that different articulations of the sexual difference ground the possibility of history itself.[7] If ontological difference, however, is not a term meant to blind us to the contingencies of history, then why is it fixed rather single-mindedly around the category of sexuality? If historical narratives or ontological mythologies are crisscrossed by multiple forces irreducible to agents and their intentions, then why reduce this complex weave to sex? Do we not fantasize about sex through racial images, and about race through sex? Do not whites often cultivate emblems of black style to enhance their erotic capacities, putting on the black style to be cool? Why would sex but not race emerge as an ontological difference for the massively entangled social creatures that we are?

While Freud's legacy left some philosophers theorizing about what allegedly "perverse" desires occur in the privacy of the home and the hidden recesses of the mind, the public lynching of African Americans at white family picnics in twentieth-century America alters the paradigm of inside/outside, conscious/unconscious, and private/public considerably. To put the point provocatively, one would think that the psychoanalytic paradigms in the United States might turn not on the fantasies of Vienna's couches but on those of the American public barbecue. Race, perhaps even more but certainly as much as sex, lies at the emotive core of the discontents of so-called civilization in the twentieth century. For does not race emerge as a singular psychic force behind the concentration camps, the Holocaust, Hiroshima and Nagasaki, Vietnam, Rwanda, and, even more recently, the war on terror?

To be sure, the erotic fantasies behind the metaphorical and associative links for conscious thought do not consist only of sexuality. For Nietzsche our stronger drive is the will to power. Hegelians understand this drive in terms of agons for recognition. Along these lines, Bourdieu establishes that the autonomous individual prized by modern liberalism is not in fact free from the games of status and prestige that more evidently compose the social dynamic of premodern, honor-based social systems.[8] His point is that we judge the merits of others not through their actions alone but through their status and position in society. But then it is a short step to see that race factors into social position and judgments of merit. As long as we are social creatures, and not just economic or rational ones, racial politics and other socially constituted factors will remain at the core of our lives.

Despite the attention to some of the irrational forces excluded more consistently from analytic traditions, U.S. philosophers in the continental tradition have been no more inclined to address race than have been their analytic counterparts. Perhaps this can be understood in part through a closer examination of the two poles of continental philosophy, on the one side Hegelians and on the other side anti-Hegelians. Those philosophers influenced by Hegel seek to find sources of meaning in some supra-individual social or metaphysical world to which we belong. The antidialectical philosophers, including many of the post-structuralists, focus instead on existential themes of ontological alienation or radical singularity, recently drawing from Kierkegaard or Levinas. While both post-structuralists and dialectical thinkers could contribute to our understanding of racial meanings, the major thrust of both movements has been to favor dimensions of existence that block the social dynamic of race from view. Hegelians draw on larger sources of social meaning to reconcile us to our world, rather than to find its fault lines, its irreconcilable ethical conflicts, or its contemporary struggles. These philosophers emphasize the way in which we draw meaning from social roles and communities, and neglect the ways in which these communities are either torn by unyielding conflict or haunted by past trauma. The confusing sources of contemporary conflict point toward horrors of the past, such as the Middle Passage, that elude all comprehension, only in part because they were not recorded in any written history. The scars will continue to create resentments and inequalities unless we find some means to attend to them. While freedom connotes for the dialectical thinker the overcoming of alienation, the sense of belonging that allows one to feel at home in the world, then where is home for writers in diaspora?

Dialectical themes proliferate in "race writers" such as Toni Morrison, for whom the sense of belonging, the feeling of home, does indeed mark the ideal of freedom. But Morrison's vision of freedom cannot be understood through a dialectic that reconciles us to this world, even as it seeks redemption. The roles, meanings, and communities that history yields are not the ones she would have us seek. For Morrison, home is not a rationalizing of the real that conspires to hide the inevitable struggles among us; it's a vision of a future without humiliation or abandonment. In this vision are those who served as the backdrop for the dramatic rise of Europe and the emergence of nation-states. The lives of these people are haunted by forces larger than any one continent, forces to the other side of reason.

Do post-structuralists come more fully to grips with this other side? If the romance of reason spurs forward dialectical adventures for truth, contemporary post-structuralist ethics attend to the traumatic losses suffered by singular cultures and individuals. The post-structural writers remind us that the real is not inevitably rational, that it is often irrational beyond what we can even recognize as a human passion. Still, the radical breaks in meaning, the obscene passions for the real, the singular decisions made on the edge of madness, do not quite address the historical losses that writers such as Morrison have in mind. The Middle Passage is a story that cannot be told. But this failure is not primarily because the Middle Passage is an evil beyond the capacities of the imagination to convey. The Middle Passage is not retold in the same vein as the Holocaust. This is a story that could have been told, at least in the way that artists have always witnessed pathos, if only accounts had been allowed. The kidnapped of the Middle Passage did not demand respect for singularity so much as a sense of home, or at least this seems to be what Morrison's novels tell us. The prevailing political ethics against slavery, the music of freedom that we know as slave songs, do not evoke incommensurate otherness so much as the pathos of severed bonds and destroyed histories. Morrison's novel *Beloved* presents a haunted discourse on what ruptures and repairs friendships, communities, and families.

Perhaps out of a concern for justice, deeper insights into human meaning, or even a sense of what's cool, continental philosophers over the past decade have turned ever more to the issue of race. Social and political theorists increasingly address race as a major fault line of U.S. politics, and ontological thinkers reflect on the play of race on the horizon of meaning. Du Bois's *The Souls of Black Folk*, with its often-quoted remark on the color line as the problem of the twentieth century, is now part of the canon of philosophy, required reading in doctoral programs such as Emory's.

There is, however, a sense of limits to this progress as well. As a prominent younger generation of New York artists claims to be "post-black," and identity politics generates resentment and reactionary rage rather than a sense of histories to be remembered or debts to be acknowledged, the new racial politics sets in. The new racial politics is not the hot racism that segregates by code or law. Rather, as Collins has observed, the new racial politics coolly contains.[9] While the old racism marked off territories outside of power for race talk, the new racism brings race talk into the regions of power only to tone it down so that race talk subscribes to more dominant concerns.

In politics, the containment of race can be deadly. Our carceral society, to borrow a term from Foucault, is linked with capital in an often-deadly search for profits. Children not normalized through the school system to become "just-in-time" workers for the information age enact rites of passage to maturity in the prison-industrial complex. This containment does not operate through the clean power of what Foucauldians term discipline or the even more sterile biopower of the new hi-tech. Prison means rape, insult, and violation.

We are in fact not merely in the age of discipline and punish, if that phrase serves to best name the normalizing power of the bureaucratic machinery of modern Europe. The neoliberal excesses and the arrogance of what some fear to be the American empire portend variations of a new theme and a new era, an age of hubris. The individualism favored in Anglo-oriented liberalism can provide a blinding ideology that too readily justifies domination over "weaker" cultures, those that lack our own values, if this individualism is not tempered with greater social and historical awareness. This same ideology that celebrates success and power as the reward of individual merit can blind its proud defenders to the political ethics of what we might otherwise trivialize as a matter of social manners, namely, to an assault on social relationships—hubris. If political theorists in the United States lack the categories to explain the so-called liberation of Iraq as the hubris of foreign domination, perhaps this is because modern liberal individualism has narrowed our vision of the social world with its codes of social mores. The very liberalism that we celebrate as our gift to the world can unfortunately blind us to the arrogance of otherwise well-intended social gestures or political acts.

Liberal philosophers foreground the individual and his or her autonomy, consigning our social relationships, and the gestures that partly shape these relationships, into an unfocused horizon of meaning. Social relationships that do emerge into the foreground too often evolve around issues of security, trust, and dependency. The rich and troubling fabric of interdependence that we associate, for example, with the communitarianism of classical tragedies retreats before the insights but also the blindnesses of modern individualism. As a consequence of this modern social minimalism, we contrast autonomy with dependency and weakness, and miss how sociality can be a source of vitality, creativity, adventure, or drama. Moreover, these alternative sources of meaning and identity call into question autonomy as either the sole meaning of freedom or the highest human aim.

The symptoms of liberalism's social minimalism show up in bland portrayals of what I have termed the social Eros of the individual, beginning with the bonds of the family. Traditional philosophers as far back as Aristotle view the mother as supporting the appetites of the child, while more contemporary thinkers have little more to add than that primary caregivers should provide unconditional love as well as the foundations of trust and self-esteem. As I have argued elsewhere, neither conception of maternal nurturing speaks to the kind of power that Frederick Douglass portrays, for example, in his autobiographies, where his mother and grandmother represent the spiritedness that he associates with freedom. Nor do these relatively bland conceptions of nurturing account for how Douglass and other African American writers could envision freedom through the metaphor of home. The social drama of the family—its entangled connection with community and history, and its culture of social manners—is missing from modern liberalism. The absence of this basic understanding of social life distorts contemporary liberal politics.

Liberal philosophers who aim to examine race in social policy may miss its significance for the more profound dimensions of ontology no less than for the fundamental principles of political philosophy. This absence of race in our thought accompanies the relegation of such powerful social bonds and the corresponding valorization of autonomy as our one and only ideal. The libidinal attachments and troubling politics that haunt families no less than nation-states play a more central role in who we are and how we think than we may know. Assuming that individuals do not leave behind social bonds to become freestanding thinkers, philosophers require principles and social cultures to circumscribe their proper due. Race is one of the more troubling but also persistent of our bonds.

NOTES

1. This is true, for example, of Charles Mills's *The Racial Contract* (Ithaca: Cornell University Press, 1997).
2. Michael Walzer, *Spheres of Justice: A Defense of Pluralism and Equality* (Oxford: Blackwell, 1983).
3. Michael Sandel, *Liberalism and the Limits of Justice* (Cambridge: Cambridge University Press, 1982).
4. Patricia Hill Collins, *Black Sexual Politics: African Americans, Gender, and the New Racism* (New York: Routledge, 2004).
5. Kelly Oliver, *Witnessing: Beyond Recognition* (Minneapolis: University of Minnesota Press, 2001).
6. Cynthia Willett, "The Social Element: A Phenomenology of Racialized Space and the Limits of Liberalism," in *Racism in Mind*, ed. Michael P. Levine and Tamas Pataki (Ithaca: Cornell University Press, 2004), 243–60.

7. Judith Butler, Ernesto Laclau, and Slavoj Žižek, *Contingency, Hegemony, Universality: Contemporary Dialogues on the Left* (London: Verso, 2000).

8. Pierre Bourdieu, *Masculine Domination*, trans. Richard Nice (Stanford: Stanford University Press, 2001).

9. Collins, *Black Sexual Politics*.

6

THEORIZING DIFFERENCE:
PHENOMENOLOGY VERSUS POST-STRUCTURALISM

David Couzens Hoy

Ever since Thales, the first philosopher, fell into the well while looking at the stars, the idea of first philosophy has had its critics. To avoid the comedy of Thales' inattention to the mundane, continental philosophy has recently tried to focus less on universal essence and more on difference and particularity. Yet there is a genuine question, raised by Roy Martinez for this volume, whether recent continental philosophy has neglected one of the supposedly most obvious differences between people, namely, race.

A provocative question deserves a provocative answer. The hypothesis this chapter explores is that the tradition of first philosophy, also known as foundationalism, is a crucial factor in the neglect of race. In continental philosophy, traces of this tradition show up insofar as philosophers feel compelled to search for the universal features of human existence, even if they call them transcendental conditions for the possibility of experience, "existentiales," or perceptual constants. Thus the generation of phenomenological philosophers that included Heidegger, Sartre, and Merleau-Ponty attempts to identify the features that all humans share. The thesis I will consider is that insofar as the phenomenological paradigm leads philosophers to theorize what people have in common, they tend to universalize their own situation and to neglect differences in the situations of others.

A corollary thesis to test is that the next paradigm of continental philosophy, post-structuralism, abandons the program of describing the essential features of all human existence and instead becomes an effort to theorize difference. Post-structuralism tries to provide more tools both for making differential phenomena (such as race, class, and gender) accessible to theory, and for opening doors between philosophy and other areas of the humanities and social sciences. The paradigm of post-structural philosophy is not narrowly disciplinary and is receptive to work done under such rubrics as cultural studies, ethnic studies, women's studies, postcolonial studies, and interspecies studies. Further, as continental philosophy moves away from its preoccupation with the universal and the identical, the distinction between "core" and "peripheral" areas of philosophy becomes more difficult to sustain. Because of this decentralization, race becomes as central as any other topic. In fact, the social urgency of race makes it a more important topic than the timeless topics that preoccupied Thales and that standardly are thought to be more properly philosophical.

My approach will be to ask how Pierre Bourdieu, Jean-Paul Sartre, and Michel Foucault provide us with philosophical tools for taking racism apart analytically, although with markedly different styles. Moreover, their contrasting meta-philosophical assumptions lead to differing conclusions about the capacity of philosophy to have effects on social life. Through a comparison of these conclusions I finish with some reflections on whether Sartre's phenomenology or Foucault's genealogy is the better methodology for raising and resolving philosophical issues about race. First, however, let me discuss a major problem analyzed by Bourdieu about the status of philosophy itself, an issue that leads to the neglect of racial issues by mainstream academic philosophy.

Is the "Field" of Philosophy Racist? On Pierre Bourdieu

Race is a difference that ideally should not make a difference. The theorist of race is thus in the difficult rhetorical position of explaining a difference that must be explained away. Whereas this situation would be problematic for the mainstream tradition of philosophy, continental philosophy is already prepared for the difficulty by Max Horkheimer's distinction between traditional theory and critical theory.[1] This distinction in turn draws on the difference between Hume's use of the genealogical method and Nietzsche's, at least as Nietzsche understood that difference. For Nietzsche, the British genealogists tried to dig under psychological phenomena to find the shared features that run through experience. Because genealogy thereby vindicates standard morality, Bernard Williams calls this usage vindicatory genealogy.[2] Nietzsche's genealogy, in contrast, is what Paul Ricoeur identifies as a hermeneutics of suspicion and Bernard Williams describes as an unmasking genealogy. This radical genealogy calls all of morality (and vindicatory genealogy as well) into question.

Critical theory unmasks traditional theory in much the same way. The distinction between traditional theory and critical theory, however, has epistemological as well as moral implications. Briefly, whereas traditional theory assumes a timeless standpoint for its pronouncements, critical theory recognizes that the need for theory arises only in a certain situation and that it can illuminate only that situation. Thus when race is the topic, even if one does not think that race is real under ideal circumstances, one can think that in present society race has real effects. Critical race theory can thus take racial differences in present society seriously even if ideally these differences do not really obtain and should have no normative import.

Critical theory is critical not only of unjust social relations but also of traditional theory for contributing to injustices by neglecting them. Insofar as traditional theorists are preoccupied with timeless truths, they forget the "desert of reality." Critical theory thus wants to call attention to systematic misperceptions of people's situations, and people's own sustained misrecognitions of themselves. One such approach is the reflexive sociology of Pierre Bourdieu. Although he comes later than the Frankfurt School, his accounts of such phenomena as symbolic capital and symbolic violence make him a latter-day critical theorist. He is also important because of his reflexive analyses of the field of philosophy as well as his criticisms of philosophers for ignoring the social conditions of their own theories. I think that the deep question at stake is the following: is there something about the field of philosophy that has prevented philosophers from seeing the issues about race that should be so obvious?

The implicit suggestion that lurks in the shadows of this question is that the *field* of philosophy may be influencing the neglect of racism. How could one go about trying to construct an argument for such a view? Bourdieu's conception of a field and the habitus that occupies it is specifically helpful here. The habitus is made up of dispositions that have been built into the bodily hexis throughout the formative years and are shared by all who belong to a given social group. The field is the background that makes the moves of the habitus intelligible. If the field is the game, the habitus is the feel for the game.

On Bourdieu's model it becomes plausible to think that the traditional aspirations of first philosophy to account for everything and everybody could have resulted in a neglect of particularity and difference, and therefore in a tendency to overlook empirical matters. For instance, he criticizes early analytic philosophy for using the genetic fallacy to dismiss as confused any attempt to bring empirical considerations into logical justifications.[3] Bourdieu calls this indifference to empirical content and practical ends "scholastic reason." Not a recent phenomenon, scholastic reason runs through traditional philosophy from its beginnings in the legend of Thales as told by Plato in the *Theaetetus* to Sartre's magical attitude toward the modern world.⁴ In the tradition of critical theory, Bourdieu wants to uncover the social conditions for scholastic reason and to investigate "philosophers' blindness to their own scholastic blindness," a blindness encouraged by the field of philosophy in that "all its arbitrary content tends to be disguised as timeless, universal self-evidence."⁵

There are at least two ways to interpret Bourdieu's account of the relation of the field and the habitus. One way is to assume that the relation is a causal one, and that an agent's actions are determined by the habitus. Another way to read Bourdieu is to assume that the field and the habitus form a grid of intelligibility that makes some actions seem appropriate and others inappropriate. I prefer to read Bourdieu as offering interpretations of intelligibility rather than causal explanations. On either reading of Bourdieu's terminology, however, it does become possible to say that the field of philosophy leads to a neglect or a marginalization of empirical considerations such as racism. If one also thought that neglecting racism was itself a sign of racism, then the field of philosophy, as well as the tradition of scholastic reason, could be thought to be complicit with the racism in society at large.

What I want to stress at this point is the difference between taking Bourdieu's account of the academic field as a causal one, as opposed to taking it as a grid of intelligibility through which agents' actions become understandable (both to themselves and to other agents).⁶ If Bourdieu's account were a causal one, then the attempt to overcome racism would be futile. If instead he is identifying the conditions that make certain actions intelligible and that preclude other actions, then there is room for choice and interpretation. Within the limits imposed by the presupposed conventions of the background practices (the field) and the agent's dispositions (the habitus), agents have possibilities open to them. Causes cannot be changed, but interpretations can. Thus, even if scholastic reason has led philosophers up to now to think of themselves as overcoming difference and identifying universal conditions, it is possible to reinterpret philosophy so that it can remediate social evil. The grip of an academic field on its practitioners is not that of an iron hand.

Race and Individual Freedom: On Jean-Paul Sartre

Broadening the question and asking how continental philosophers have historically taken a stance on race might stimulate this remediation. Insofar as continental philosophy varies in style, different ways of approaching racism will be tied to different methodologies. This contrast is illustrated aptly by the difference between Jean-Paul Sartre and Michel Foucault on racism, a difference that can be discussed usefully in classrooms. To move from a backward-looking assessment of why continental philosophy has neglected race to a forward-looking remediation, I will compare representative and accessible texts by each philosopher and ask how productive each of these paradigms can be in the critical study of race.

To develop this contrast, I focus first on Sartre's "Portrait of the Anti-Semite." This essay explains the theory behind Sartre's portrayal of the fictional character Lucien Fleurier in his earlier short story "The Childhood of a Leader."[7] Anti-Semitism is clearly just one case of the more general phenomenon of racist hatred. As a case of hate, which is a technical term in *Being and Nothingness*, racism is the hatred of everyone in the other one, or in Sartre's words, "of all Others in one Other."[8] In "Portrait of the Anti-Semite" Sartre insists that anti-Semitism is "an attitude totally and freely self-chosen, a global attitude which is adopted not only in regard to Jews but in regard to men in general, to history and society."[9] Just as all attempts to be at one with oneself fail, hate fails insofar as the other has existed, when the project of hate is to affirm one's freedom by transcending the other. The success of hate is the death of the other, but this death transforms the one who wanted that death irremediably into an object, namely, a bigot.

Racism is thus theorized through the dialectic of freedom, inherited from Hegel. Essential to free self-consciousness is fear, and the anti-Semite is portrayed as a coward. "Coward" is another technical term, and in "Existentialism Is a Humanism" Sartre says that to be a coward is to attempt to hide from total freedom with deterministic excuses. The anti-Semite Lucien wants to be like a rock. His project is to deny his transcendence and to affirm only his facticity. As Sartre says in "Portrait of the Anti-Semite," anti-Semites "are attracted by the durability of stone."[10] They want to become only who they already are, and they nostalgically desire impermeability (i.e., they do not want to be able to change). Thus Lucien thinks that he cannot help his anti-Semitism, and he experiences it as a physical repulsion to Jews. Yet he clearly chooses this hatred and delights in it. There are moments where he is thrilled by letting it overcome him and lead him into a violence that is real in its effects, but which is experienced as a choice. The passion is thus feigned, as all such passion is for Sartre. In Sartre's terms, the passion is *magical*: although at bottom a choice, it is a choice not to recognize itself as a choice, but rather to experience itself as a passion (i.e., as a reaction that one cannot help).

In "Portrait of the Anti-Semite" Sartre illustrates this passion with the example of the French Anglophobe named Jules. Jules was known by his family to hate the English and there was a tacit agreement to avoid any mention of the English when Jules was present. This precaution, says Sartre, gave Jules a "semblance of existence" and it gave the family "an agreeable feeling of taking part in a sacred ceremony."[11] Sartre adds: "And if someone, under certain specific circumstances, after careful deliberation and as it were inadvertently, made an allusion to Great Britain or its Dominions, Uncle Jules pretended to go into a fury and felt himself come to life for a moment. Everyone was happy."[12] This hatred thus gave Jules an identity and he knew that he had a role to play.

Similarly, in "The Childhood of a Leader" Lucien forms his sense of self-identity by becoming an anti-Semite. He initially knows that he is merely pretending to be passionate when he refuses on a particular occasion to shake the hand of a Jew. Immediately afterward he has misgivings and considers apologizing. When he sees that others become afraid of him because of his passionate outbursts, however, he willingly takes on the role of the anti-Semite and becomes a leader of the movement. By becoming known as a rabid bigot, he finds himself liberated and experiences a "rush" that is almost sexual and that Sartre shows to be a form of sadism. Lucien is thus, in Sartre's technical sense, not only a coward but also a *salaud*, that is, someone who thinks that his existence is necessary and that his social role gives him a right to exist. In "Portrait of the Anti-Semite" Sartre concludes that anti-Semitism in particular and racism in general are at bottom fear of one's freedom: "The anti-Semite," writes Sartre, "is the man who wants to be pitiless stone, furious torrent, devastating lightning: in short, everything but a man."[13]

As for racism specifically of whites against blacks, a good indicator of Sartre's approach is his 1948 essay "Black Orpheus," which served as an introduction to an anthology of black poets. Here he begins by employing his analysis of the look in *Being and Nothingness*. There, as an example of the power of the look, Sartre had cited a passage from William Faulkner's novel *Light in August* describing a murder by a group of whites of a black man named Christmas. Sartre quotes the evocative passage from the novel describing the victim at the point of death, whose look will haunt his murderers for the rest of their lives. Faulkner writes of how this look soared into the murderers' memory such that "they are not to lose it, in whatever peaceful valleys, beside whatever placid and reassuring streams of old age, in the mirroring face of whatever children they will contemplate old disasters and newer hopes. *It will be there, musing, quiet, steadfast, not fading and not particularly threatful, but of itself alone serene, of itself alone triumphant.*"[14] In "Black

Orpheus" the look is again that of blacks looking at whites, but now with whites for the first time seeing themselves being seen by blacks. Sartre writes:

> Here are black men standing, looking at us, and I hope that you—like me—will feel the shock of being seen. For three thousand years the white man has enjoyed the privilege of seeing without being seen; he was only a look—the light from his eyes drew each thing out of the shadow of its birth; the whiteness of his skin was another look, condensed light. The white man—white because he was man, white like daylight, white like truth, white like virtue—lighted up the creation like a torch and unveiled the secret white essence of beings. Today, these black men are looking at us, and our gaze comes back to our own eyes; in their turn, black torches light up the world and our white heads are no more than Chinese lanterns swinging in the wind.[15]

Sartre accepts the analysis that black consciousness is divided in a way that white consciousness is not. Black consciousness does not *become* divided from itself. Instead, it *begins* by being already divided from itself and in exile. Moreover, black consciousness is often a "double exile"—both from its origins in Africa and from its displacement in the New World. The colonization of blacks leaves an effect on their use of the language of their colonizers. While not as sophisticated as Jacques Derrida's account whereby language is always already colonized,[16] Sartre's analysis of the relation of blacks to the colonial language is nevertheless effective. "Since the oppressor is present in the very language they speak," writes Sartre of the black poets in this anthology, "they will speak this language in order to destroy it."[17]

But Sartre's tendency to downplay difference and to generalize his own standpoint comes out in his account of these poets of "negritude." Sartre sees them as evangelists who are trying to reveal the black soul and to rediscover the fundamental experience of negritude. Thus black consciousness can emerge only in opposition to white consciousness. Raising black consciousness through increased awareness of negritude is, for Sartre, a necessary feature of the present time. He therefore sees this emphasis on negritude as an "*anti-racist racism.*" It is a form of racism to be overcome insofar as it is only a stepping-stone to the larger struggle of all oppressed peoples. He thinks that heightening black consciousness by looking back at whites and objectifying them is finally only a stage in the dialectic of reaching a final synthesis in the form of universal humanism. In the tradition of Kant and Hegel on universal history, Sartre envisions progress toward "the unity which will come eventually, bringing all oppressed peoples together in the same struggle" and leading to "the abolition of racial differences."[18] Sartre's status in the dominant culture seems to blind him to the suspicion that this universal humanism would be just another name for a disguised assimilation, whereby difference is whitewashed as identity and everyone speaks French.[19]

This meta-philosophical belief in dialectical progress is precisely what Michel Foucault does not share. Foucault rejects both the meta-narrative of the march of history toward a universal humanism as well as the use of that ideal as a measure of the progress of freedom throughout history. There can be no society without power relations, says Foucault, although not all power is domination. For Foucault, while the task of critical philosophy is to minimize domination by thinking differently, it will not overcome all power relations. On Foucault's view, then, difference will persist even if certain differences are transcended. Sartre's dialectical optimism overlooks the particular difference between what Foucault calls ordinary "ethnic" racism, whereby people do not like people who do not resemble them, and the "statist" racism that he sees emerging in the new regime of biopower. Let me therefore now discuss that difference.

When Does Modern Racism Begin? On Michel Foucault

Michel Foucault's best writings on racism have been published only recently and are therefore not well-known, and there are only scattered references to racism in his published works. For instance, the widely read introduction to *The History of Sexuality*, published in 1976, contains some tantalizing remarks about the emergence of what Foucault calls "modern," "biological," or "statist" racism.[20] These remarks cannot be understood without the help of lectures that Foucault was giving at that time. In particular, his lecture course at the Collège de France, published under the title *"Society Must Be Defended,"* is especially illuminating, even if the style is more informal than in the books published in his own lifetime. Delivered in 1975–76, these lively lectures were first published in French in 1997 and in English in 2003. There he spells out the connection of state racism to the emergence of the form of power he calls biopower. To explain this notion of biopower, I need to review Foucault's accounts of other kinds of power.

Power, says Foucault in *"Society Must Be Defended,"* establishes order in two ways. On the one hand, it has the juridical function of obligating and binding people together. On the other hand, much like emotion for Sartre, power is *magical*: it dazzles and immobilizes.²¹ In *Discipline and Punish* Foucault distinguishes further between the power held by the sovereign and a form of power that is more impersonal and systemic, which he calls disciplinary power. The sovereign applied power from the top of society downward, and this power was tied in particular to the sovereign's right to take away the life of his subjects. Hence the power of the sovereign was signified by executions that were not only public but also staged spectacles for the crowd. Disciplinary power works instead from the bottom of society upward, and it forms docile bodies through practices such as are found in prisons, armies, factories, and schools. Subjects submit themselves to these practices, but the subjects are generally not aware of the effects that these practices have in the formation of bodily habits and compliant social attitudes. Unlike Sartre's account, where one could be conscious of one's choice of attitude, for Foucault compliance is molded so gradually over time that it escapes attention.

Thus, in contrast to the political power over subjects exercised by the sovereign, disciplinary power produces the docile bodies of social agents who learn to conform to social norms. Biopower then adds a new dimension to the account of disciplinary power and sovereign power. Both disciplinary power and biopower construct people in ways that do not normally become conscious. Whereas disciplinary power is exercised subliminally through micropractices on individual bodies, biopower involves macroscopic objects, such as populations, that are so large that individuals are not aware of them reflectively. Discipline relates one to one's body in a different way than one's body is related to a population of bodies (where one becomes, for instance, a statistic). The statistic shows that one's freedom is limited to a certain range of constraints of which one may not even be aware. Mortality rate, for instance, is not something that one can freely choose. Government regulations intended to influence mortality rate, however, may affect people's lives significantly. In fact, death is a significantly different factor in biopower than in sovereign power. In contrast to sovereign power, which is the power to take life or let live, biopower is the power to foster life and only to allow, not to cause, death. In the regime of biopower, death becomes something to be hidden away; death even replaces sex as society's greatest biopolitical taboo.²²

At the same time, however, biopower can combine with sovereignty to bring about death on a much more massive scale, through wars, massacres, and genocide. Foucault wants to know how societies get people to die so willingly for such dubious reasons in wars that serve so little purpose. One way they do so is by getting people to hate the enemy. This result is achieved through a form of what he calls state racism. State racism has two functions. The first is to separate out the groups that exist within a population, "to fragment, to create caesuras within the biological continuum addressed by biopower."[23] The second is tied to evolutionary theory (not Darwin's own theory, but social Darwinism). It conjoins the idea of war and the improvement of the race. The average soldier will be motivated to go to war not simply to kill a political adversary, but to destroy an enemy race that poses a biological threat. State racism manifests itself wherever war is played out symbolically through exclusion, rejection, isolation, or any form of political death. In particular, racism develops first through colonization, or specifically through a colonizing genocide that depends on the notion of inferior populations and civilizations.[24]

State racism cannot be understood from the standpoint of sovereign power or of disciplinary power alone. State racism differs from traditional "ethnic" racism, whereby two groups experience mutual distaste for each other.[25] State racism is not based on the race struggle. The race struggle, on which Marx then modeled his idea of the class struggle, supposes two different races, each having different origins. With the addition of a *biologizing* and medicalizing discourse, the notion of race is transformed. Instead of speaking about races in the plural, a new object, race in the singular, appears. Race in this new sense is conceived biologically as the product not of a struggle between two individuals, as in Hegel, but of an evolutionary struggle involving natural selection and the survival of the fittest. Instead of a binary society with racial conflict, the modern state is biologically monist, and its function is to protect and promote the purity of the race.

Modern racism is born, suggests Foucault, when the theme of racial purity supplants that of race struggle. The conflict is no longer a battle for equal *political* rights between competing groups. Instead, the issue is about *social norms*. The task of the state is to make sure that people live up to the norm. Biopolitics does not involve disciplining people's bodies, but instead is a matter of regulating their lives. The normalization that Foucault describes in *Discipline and Punish* becomes even more insidious once the contrast is not simply between the normal and the abnormal, or between groups with different value colorings. Instead, when the discourse includes the power of regularization and the rhetoric of racial purity, with the distinctions between the pure and the impure and the inferior and the superior, it becomes even more dangerous. Because these are *biological* distinctions, they give the state the right to exclude not simply particular individuals but entire populations.

In the regime of biopower, the biological rhetoric of degeneracy can lead readily to genocide.

Today one might hope that the defeat of Nazi- and Soviet-style dictatorships shows that the rhetoric of racial purity is no longer tolerable. But that assessment underestimates the reach of Foucault's vision and minimizes the biopolitical conflicts that persist around the globe (e.g., in the Balkans and in the Middle East). State racism also occurs for people of color in their everyday confrontations with biopower in regulatory mechanisms such as are encountered in housing, health care, employment, education, child care, and most aspects of their highly regulated lives.[26]

Phenomenology and Post-structuralism Compared

Each of the phenomenological and the post-structural paradigms thus provides a powerful example of a trenchant critique of racism. At the same time, the paradigms are strikingly different in both their content and their meta-philosophical stances. Whereas Foucault is concerned with microscopic or macroscopic social patterns that are too small or large for individual consciousness to attend to reflectively, the early Sartre is concerned almost exclusively with subjects and their patterns of consciousness. Although Sartre admirably shows the self-contradiction of the individual racist, all difference in circumstance and historical background melts away in the portrayal of this contradiction. In contrast, Foucault's biopower would remain invisible to the Sartrean, who is preoccupied with individual psychology. Anyone attempting to put either paradigm into practice in the critical study of race should keep in mind the following polemical contrasts.

(1) First, let me clarify a potential ambiguity in the contrast between foundationalism and anti-foundationalism. Sartre's existential phenomenology aims to give a theory of human existence as founded in radical freedom. Does this make it foundationalist or anti-foundationalist? Because of Sartre's emphasis on radical freedom, he argues that there are no foundations for our choices. Thus, in its content and moral message, Sartre's existential account is anti-foundationalist. As a philosophical project to make freedom the fundamental and essential feature of human existence, however, Sartre's phenomenological enterprise echoes the tradition of foundationalist first philosophy. In contrast, Foucault does not attempt to give a theory of human existence, but instead wants to show that there is nothing about human

existence that is not historical. There are no unhistorical essences, incorrigible starting points, or transcendental conditions for the possibility of experience. Even power is not such an essence; power takes different forms at different times, and biopower is only a recent phenomenon.

(2) Sartre's project is to find a priori structures of human existence, in contrast to Foucault's more empirical analyses. Not surprisingly, Sartre tends in his literary works to generalize his own experience and his own psychological propensities. Simone de Beauvoir notes this tendency as well in Sartre's philosophical accounts of sexuality and gender. Sartre seems unaware of how male-oriented his descriptions of sexuality really are. In contrast, Foucault is not describing structures of consciousness that individuals experience directly, and therefore he cannot be accused of universalizing his own particular psychology. Sartre's tendency to extend his own psychology may derive from his impression of what is involved in applying the phenomenological method. Sartre thinks that phenomenology is something anyone can do at any time in a real-world situation. But Husserl's phenomenological method involves bracketing the real world and suspending one's personal interests to discover abstract structures of consciousness *in general*. In contrast to the high level of abstraction in Husserl's philosophy, Sartre's richer and more literary approach has the virtue of being more concrete, though it also tends to infuse the process of describing consciousness in general with the process of generalizing Sartre's own conscious experiences.

(3) Sartre adopts an unhistorical posture and describes modern examples as if they were eternal. Foucault, in contrast, wants to explain how modern structures emerged, not so that we can go back to an earlier mode in which these structures had not emerged, but so that we do not reify them and take them as necessary. Foucault recognizes that the term "modern" is "devoid of meaning,"[27] and he uses it only because there is no other word. Thus he does not privilege the modern, and he is in effect beyond it. He is trying to imagine a standpoint from which we could look back on the present, viewing practices now taken for granted as essential instead as arcane and arbitrary.

(4) Sartre's phenomenology tends to be one-sided. For instance, in his preface on Frantz Fanon he addresses the standpoint of the colonizers more than that of the colonized. He has little to say about Fanon's account of the black experience itself, including the ways in which the body is marked with particularity.[28] Similarly, Sartre does not get deeply inside the experiences of the victims of racism in "The Childhood of a Leader" or "The Respectful Prostitute." This one-sidedness may give the impression that although particular individuals can try not to be racist, as a social phenomenon racism

may be inevitable. The early Sartre does not give a diagnosis that could lead to a society in which the other is not alienated by the look.

(5) This difference points to the major methodological difference between the phenomenological and the post-structural paradigms: Sartre's individualism and Foucault's anti-individualism. Instead of individualism, one could use the term "Cartesianism." For the early Sartre, philosophy must start from the Cartesian standpoint of individual consciousness, even if it rejects a transcendental ego. Foucault, in contrast, does not deny consciousness, but he explains how large social structures shape agency in ways that are not normally available to conscious reflection. These structures are built into the background that makes actions intelligible. Whereas Sartre is a phenomenologist who tries to identify basic features of consciousness, Foucault posits grids of intelligibility that emerge at different points in time and that explain either how similar types of action are in fact incongruous, or how apparently incongruous actions are part of a shared set of social conditions.

These contrasts represent my own sense that for the critical study of race, the post-structural paradigm is potentially more productive than the phenomenological paradigm because of the vestiges of first philosophy in the latter. Undoubtedly, defenders of the early Sartre will take issue with this intentionally provocative portrayal. Perhaps like race itself, however, the difference between phenomenology and post-structuralism would not make so much of a difference in better times. If philosophy abandoned the rhetoric of first philosophy and became thoroughly pragmatic, phenomenology could still be practiced. In fact, this pragmatic spirit could then encourage the use of every possible tool for combating oppression. Such a tool might be a combination tool, like a Swiss Army knife, with phenomenological and post-structural elements, or it could be a new, less eclectic, post-critical approach.[29] As a serious social issue, racism demands that philosophers make every effort to explain it, or to explain it away. In the face of great social evil, a scholastic, meta-philosophical quarrel should not stand in the way of productive critical resistance.

NOTES

1. See the discussion of the distinction between traditional and critical theory in chap. 4 of David Couzens Hoy and Thomas McCarthy, *Critical Theory* (New York: Blackwell, 1994). On the genealogical method see my essay, "Nietzsche, Hume, and the Genealogical Method," in *Nietzsche, Genealogy, Morality: Essays on Nietzsche's "Genealogy of Morals,"* ed. Richard Schacht (Berkeley and Los Angeles: University of California Press, 1994), 251–68.

2. Bernard Williams, *Truth and Truthfulness* (Princeton: Princeton University Press, 2002), 36.

3. Pierre Bourdieu, *Science de la science et réflexivité: Cours du Collège de France, 2000–2001* (Paris: Éditions Raison d'Agir, 2001), 204.

4. Pierre Bourdieu, *Pascalian Meditations*, trans. Richard Nice (Stanford: Stanford University Press, 1997), 13–16, where Bourdieu cites Plato's story in the *Theaetetus* (174a): "While [Thales] was studying the stars and looking upwards, he fell into a pit, and a neat, witty Thracian servant girl jeered at him, they say, because he was so eager to know the things in the sky that he could not see what was there before him at his very feet" (15).

5. Bourdieu, *Pascalian Meditations*, 29.

6. I thank Alexis Shotwell for impressing the importance of this distinction on me. See also Theodore Richard Schatzki, "Overdue Analysis of Bourdieu's Theory of Practice," *Inquiry* 30 (March 1987): 113–35.

7. Jean-Paul Sartre, *The Wall, and Other Stories*, trans. Lloyd Alexander (New York: New Directions, 1948).

8. Jean-Paul Sartre, *Being and Nothingness*, trans. Hazel E. Barnes (New York: Washington Square Press, 1956), 533.

9. Jean-Paul Sartre, "Portrait of the Anti-Semite," in *Existentialism from Dostoevsky to Sartre*, ed. Walter Kaufmann (New York: Meridian, 1975), 332.

10. Ibid., 333.
11. Ibid., 344.
12. Ibid., 344.
13. Ibid., 345.

14. William Faulkner, *Light in August*, as quoted by Sartre, *Being and Nothingness*, 526; italics by Sartre.

15. Jean-Paul Sartre, "Black Orpheus," in *Race*, ed. Robert Bernasconi (Malden, Mass.: Blackwell, 2001), 115.

16. In *Monolingualism of the Other or: The Prosthesis of Origin*, trans. Patrick Mensah (Stanford: Stanford University Press, 1998), Jacques Derrida suggests that every culture is a colony, and that everyone speaks a language that is the other's.

17. Sartre, "Black Orpheus," 122.

18. Ibid., 118. In "Negritude and Modernity or Negritude as a Humanism for the Twentieth Century" (in Bernasconi, *Race*), Léopold Senghor, the editor of the volume of poetry that Sartre is introducing and a self-described "Negritude militant," writes that "Negritude, as a cultural movement is not a racism, not even an 'anti-racist racism,' to use Sartre's formula" (145). Senghor, however, accepts the dream of what Abiola Irélé calls "humanism with a universal scope" (144). For an invaluable summary of the history of this charge against Sartre and of the controversy surrounding the term "negritude," see T. Denean Sharpley-Whiting, "Paulette Nardal, Race Consciousness, and Antillean Letters," in Bernasconi, *Race*, 98–99.

19. Such a charge is implied by Frantz Fanon in *Black Skin, White Masks*, trans. Charles Lam Markmann (New York: Grove Press, 1967), where he expresses his disappointment with Sartre's "Black Orpheus" for being too Hegelian.

20. Michel Foucault, *The History of Sexuality*, vol. 1, *An Introduction*, trans. Robert Hurley (New York: Vintage Books, 1980), 149.

21. Michel Foucault, *"Society Must Be Defended": Lectures at the Collège de France, 1975–76*, trans. David Macey (New York: Picador, 2003), 68.

22. Ibid., 247.
23. Ibid., 255.
24. Ibid., 257.
25. Ibid., 258.
26. Ibid., 251.
27. Ibid., 80.

28. Jerry Miller notes that for Fanon the black body is "a particularity that cannot be universalized." See Jerry Miller, "Fanon's Immoral Body," in his Ph.D. dissertation, "Ethics Without Morality" (University of California, Santa Cruz, 2001), 144.

29. See my discussion of post-critique in David Couzens Hoy, *Critical Resistance: From Poststructuralism to Post-critique* (Cambridge, Mass.: MIT Press, 2004).

7

CONTINENTAL PHILOSOPHY AND THE CONCEPT OF RACE

Georgia Warnke

It might seem that the analytic philosophy of language has cornered the market on questions of race and, consequently, that there is nothing left for continental philosophers to say. In this chapter, I want first to look at the way the analytic philosophy of language helps clarify the problem with race, and then to turn to insights that I think the continental tradition of hermeneutics is best equipped to articulate.

Race and the Analytic Philosophy of Language

According to K. Anthony Appiah, analytic philosophy of language possesses two tools for considering race: an ideational theory and a referential theory of language.[1] Following through on either shows, he thinks, that race makes no sense. According to ideational theories of language, we learn what a word like "race" means when we learn the rules for applying it. Individuals may possess some dissimilar beliefs about a given word, but ideational theories suppose that they share specific criterial beliefs that provide the definition of the word. Those theories that Appiah calls strictly ideational require that all the criterial beliefs be satisfied when the word is correctly applied. The beliefs, in other words, Appiah says, must be individually necessary and jointly sufficient. Accordingly, race will be correctly applied to individuals when it is ascribed in accordance with a specific set of beliefs, such as the beliefs that people with very different skin colors are always of different races and that one's race is determined by the race of one's parents. In the case of racial ascriptions, however, it turns out that neither of these beliefs is necessary: a race can include individuals with different skin colors while a given individual's parents may themselves belong to different so-called races. Nor are the two beliefs sufficient together to define race since they can conflict: one individual's skin may be a different color than that of both his or her parents while another individual's skin may the same color as one's parents although they are defined as belonging to different races.

If "race" cannot be defined by a set of individually necessary and jointly sufficient criteria, will a looser ideational theory work? On this theory, one need not hold all the criterial beliefs about race to know what it means. Instead, one has to hold only "a good number" of them.[2] Hence if we were to divide the elements of race into, say, heritable physical characteristics, shared practices, linked histories and traditions, and, finally, a common site of origin,[3] then knowing what race means requires only that we acknowledge some combination of these when we apply it. As Appiah points out, however, such an account of "race" makes it difficult to distinguish between odd ideas about race and misunderstanding the word. Suppose, for example, that a South African of mostly Dutch ancestry and a South African of mostly Xhosan ancestry share certain heritable physical characteristics. They are both large, possess curly hair, and share certain other morphological features. Further they share a history, although at least some of their ancestors hold different places in that history, and they share a common origin in the region of southern Africa. Is someone mistaken who holds them to belong to the same race? Suppose a pinkish individual shares practices, traditions, and a common site of origin with people whose skin is tawny. Are we mistaken if we think they belong to the same race?

Appiah suggests that a loose ideational theory of race will work only if we accept vagueness and even confusion in what we mean by race. Moreover, he claims that a referential theory of language leads to the same result. On this latter view, race is whatever in the world corresponds to or causes our talk of race. Appiah finds two possible candidates: populations defined as communities of potentially interbreeding individuals at given localities, and groups defined by skin color, hair, and gross morphology, corresponding to the dominant pattern for these characteristics in the major subcontinental regions.[4] Recent research finds some support for the first candidate insofar as it correlates certain short segments of DNA known as markers with broad geographical groups. One problem with that definition, however, is that these groups do not always correspond with the groups that count socially as races. Indeed, Appiah suggests that the Amish as a relatively isolated, interbreeding population might come out as a race on this definition[5] but certainly African Americans would not. Second, if certain markers allow for some distinction among groups, the extent of total genetic variance among individuals within a group socially called a race typically exceeds the variation between "races" themselves.[6] Third, while small population groups such as the Xhosa of South Africa or the Basques of Europe may share more similar gene frequencies with one another than they do with others, their differences from other groups are gradual and shifting rather than the strict separations that might be neatly catalogued as racial divisions.[7] Finally, the long history of population mixing between people from different continents (for conquest and other reasons) means that we need to select a necessarily arbitrary date for linking markers with groups.

The second candidate for a referent for race—namely: groups defined by skin color, hair, and gross morphology—faces problems similar to those encountered by the ideational theory of race: for example, variations in and among skin, hair color, and skull morphology that frustrate attempts to organize groups or individuals into neat categories. W. E. B. Du Bois already found this facet of the concept of race "exasperating": groups vary in color, he wrote, from the "marble-like pallor of the Scandinavian" to the "brown Egyptian"; hair texture and skull size not only differ but are also "exasperatingly intermingled."[8] Those with dark skin may have straight hair like the Chinese, and those with white skin may have curly hair like the Bushman: "Nor does color agree with the breadth of the head, for the yellow Tartar has a broader head than the German."[9] To Du Bois's exasperations we could add those of genetic analysis. The consequence is that, while the racial distinctions we think we understand apply to all individuals, referents for race remain elusive.

Social Construction and Race

What, then, is race? For his part, Appiah gives up on race and turns to the construction of racial identities: races are less entities than processes—namely, processes of what Michal Omi and Howard Winant call racial formations.[10] With regard to the formation of black racial identity this process included: the conquest and colonization of Africa, which took the diverse cultures of Asante, Yoruba, Bakongo, and the like and labeled them indiscriminately as Africans and, later, as Negroes; the Atlantic slave trade and the institution of slavery, which in the United States deliberately separated members of the same ethnicities from one another to break down traditional languages and patterns of leadership for security purposes;[11] and stabilizations of the "color line," which over time strictly distinguished Africans from other indentured servants. Whereas indentured servants once differed only in the length of their servitude, with Africans typically serving somewhat longer than others, various forces and events worked together to enforce African servitude for life and to solidify a white-black divide.¹² The result of all these forces and events was that one's identity at the most fundamental level became one's status as a race; the contemporaneous racialization of "Orientals" and the subsequent racialization of "Hispanics" in the United States followed this same model.

The social formation or construction of racial identity also involves another element: an introjection or appropriation on the part of individuals of their racial label. The combination of ethnic mixing and racial subordination enforced by the institution of slavery meant that slaves needed to forge new kinship systems, new customs, and new forms of religion and expression to retain their health, life, and dignity. These new forms and systems served to draw them together as a group and to forge a consciousness of similarity to one another and dissimilarity to whites.¹³ White consciousness of race followed a similar model: different groups attempted to distinguish themselves from blacks and other "nonwhites" and internalized this racial identity. After the Civil War, this racial consciousness survived through racial ideologies, segregation, discrimination, and the efforts of blacks themselves to redress the inequality in assessments of black and white. Race became and remains a theoretical commitment, according to Appiah, an identity that is so ingrained that it determines life conditions and self-expectations, or what (following sociological practice) Appiah calls scripts.¹⁴

He has reservations about these scripts. We should recall, he says, that "we are not simply black or white or yellow or brown, gay or straight or bisexual, Jewish, Christian, Moslem, Buddhist or Confucian but that we are also brothers and sisters; parents and children, liberals, conservative, and leftists; teachers and lawyers and auto-makers and gardeners; fans of the Padres and the Bruins; amateurs of grunge rock and lovers of Wagner; movie buffs; MTV-holics, mystery readers; surfers and singers; poets and pet-lovers; students and teachers; friends and lovers."¹⁵

While we may possess racial identities as internalized processes of social construction, Appiah's point is that we possess other identities as well, and that part of the solution to the problem of race (and racism) is asserting and affirming these other identities. If we remember that we are not only "blacks" or "whites," but also brothers and sisters, members of different or no religions, chess lovers and baseball players, we can take up a set of crosscutting and interlocking identities. We can take up various allegiances to various others according to both their collective identities, say as members of religions, and their personal identities, say as sports fans. In this way we reduce the tendency of our racial identities to exhaust the options for who we are.

Appiah appears to understand the effect of recognizing our multiple collective and personal identities to be a future in which racial identities can become "recreational,"[16] just as certain ethnic identities have become recreational. Identities as Irish American or Italian American have no social import in the United States any longer; Americans with some amount of Irish or Italian ancestry have the option of taking up their heritage as important parts of and even foundations to their identity, but they may also elect not to. Identities as Irish or Italian Americans no longer determine life scripts in the United States, nor do social practices and institutions construct such identities as socially meaningful. Instead, being Irish American or Italian American is purely personal; it is a potential source of identity that one can lay claim to, take up for certain purposes (such as participating in St. Patrick's Day parades), or ignore entirely.

Might we hope for the day when race is similarly recreational? The history of Irish and Italian identities is a reason for suspicion. Both were at one time considered "problem population[s] at best."[17] In the 1840s, American Anglo-Saxons defined Irish immigrants as a separate race distinguished by dark skin, big hands and feet, broad teeth, bowlegs, potbellies, and pug noses.[18] Beset by a genetic propensity to violence and ignorance, their riotous behavior highlighted their difference from the civilized races. The same racial thinking applied to Italians, eleven of whom were lynched in New Orleans by the White League, a Reconstruction-era group similar to the Ku Klux Klan.[19] The Irish and Italians lost their distinctions as separate races, in large part, as a process of distinguishing other, even more problematic populations. Before the Civil War, the Irish started to become part of the white race as a means of justifying African slavery, and the Italians became white as a means of denying citizenship to Syrians, Turkish, Hindu, Japanese, and others.[20]

These examples suggest that the ground on which certain identities can become recreational is a more basic identity that is not recreational. Indeed, the examples suggest that we can possess recreational ethnic identities in the United States only because racial identities continue to be fundamental: one can be recreationally Irish American or Italian American because and insofar as one remains fundamentally white. One still cannot be recreationally white. In the case of so-called nonwhites, even this degree of recreation is missing. One cannot be recreationally black, nor can one even be recreationally African American; instead one is fundamentally African American because and insofar as one is fundamentally black. The same holds for Asian and Hispanic "races." One cannot be recreationally Chinese American or Japanese American because and insofar as one remains fundamentally Asian and, indeed, foreign. One cannot be recreationally Mexican American or Columbian American because and insofar as one remains fundamentally Hispanic or Latino/a.

Race and Hermeneutics

How might we pursue the possibility of recreational identities without presupposing more fundamental racial identities? How might we conceive of identity so that not only African, Chinese, and Mexican identities become recreational, but also white, black, Hispanic, and Asian? I think the insights of hermeneutics, and particularly of Gadamer's philosophical hermeneutics, can help in this endeavor. To identify individuals as black, white, Hispanic, or Asian is to understand them in a certain way. To this extent race is an interpretation, and our inquiry into it might begin by looking at elements that philosophical hermeneutics identifies in our interpretations of texts. In what follows I look at the (1) multiplicity, (2) contextuality, and (3) historicity of our textual interpretations.

(1) We understand texts to be certain sort of texts (love stories, crime novels, passion plays, and so on) just as we understand people to be certain sorts of people (blacks, whites, Latinos, and so on). Yet in the literary domain, at least outside of religiously ruled societies that insist on the sole validity of one interpretation of canonical texts, we assume that more than one interpretation of a given text is possible. Even when we think that a certain interpretation is a good one, we do not suppose that it is the only way of understanding the text. Instead, we assume that we can focus on different aspects of the text and see the meaning it comprises in different ways. The hermeneutic tradition takes the adequacy of an interpretation to depend on its capacity to unify the parts and whole of a text. The interpretation of the whole is meant to show the significance of each of the parts, while the interpretation of each of the parts is supposed to show the way they contribute to the unified meaning of the whole.[21] Yet the hermeneutic circle of whole and part does not preclude the possibility of unifying whole and part in different ways. We can understand the extent to which the various parts of *Othello* unite to create a story about jealousy, but we can also attend to the way in which the parts create a play about race.

To be sure, we might insist that the play is always and most fundamentally a tragedy. Just as we might insist that it does not matter whether one is Japanese American or Chinese American because one is most fundamentally

Asian, we might insist that it does not matter whether the play is a play about jealousy or a play about race because it is most fundamentally a tragic play. In the literary domain, however, such insistences are usually taken as challenges: What is a tragedy? How are various so-called tragedies the same and different? Is *Othello* best understood as a tragedy at all? Textual interpretations reveal ever-new dimensions of texts as inexhaustible funds of edification and meaning.[22] Nor do we regard one interpretation as more fundamental or basic than any other. *Othello* is not basically a play about race and secondarily a play about jealousy.

The same holds for questions of identity insofar as they are questions of how we understand who we are. We understand people to be certain sorts of people—blacks, whites, Latinos, and so on. Yet if we do not suppose that our textual interpretations are canonical even when we think they are good ones, why should we suppose that our interpretations of people are any more definitive of who they are? Just as we can focus on different aspects of a text and see the meaning it comprises in different ways, we can focus on different aspects of a person or ourselves and see the identity they compose in different ways. We can understand our diffidence, aversion to emotion, and the like in terms of our Anglo-Saxon heritage and understand ourselves in this way, or we can focus on other parts of who we are to compose a different idea of ourselves. We may be Anglo-Saxons, yet we are also professors, siblings, novel readers, and so on. All these accounts of who we are offer ways of understanding ourselves, and it seems odd to suppose that any is more canonical than any other. If we are races, we are not only or most fundamentally races. If *Othello* is no more about race than it is about jealousy, I am no more basically white than I am female, middle-aged, Anglo-American, or a novel reader.

(2) Our different accounts of the meaning of a text belong to different contexts and answer to different concerns. Given one set of concerns, an interpreter may focus on the relation between Othello and Iago; given another set of concerns, another interpreter may focus on Othello's heritage as a Moor. The two interpretations reflect perspectives we bring to the text because of interests we possess. For this reason, the reach of any one interpretation of a text or identity is limited. A Freudian interpretation of *Hamlet* does not exhaust its meaning. Rather, in the literary domain we accept the fact that meaning is infinite, that new dimensions of meaning will appear from different vantage points, and that in relationship to new texts or in different contexts a text can reveal new meanings. If we think of *Hamlet* in Freudian terms, doing so does not invalidate pre- or post-Freudian interpretations. If we try to focus on Ophelia, doing so does not presume to question interpreters

who do not. Rather, dimensions of meaning come in and out of lightness depending on the questions we ask and the concerns we bring to our interpretive projects.

Our understanding of others or ourselves is similarly contextual. Given one set of issues and interests—those related to a history of discrimination or the cultural expectations of loyalty to family, for example—we may understand ourselves as Latinas and be most appropriately understood in this context. This understanding may even be appropriate when we are lecturing on Latina identity (to give a personal dimension to the lecture, say). Yet, given another context and another set of concerns, those related to teaching workload, for example, we are not Latinas but professors. If we are blacks, Latinos, Asians, and whites, we are nevertheless not only or always blacks, Latinos, Asians, and whites. These identities are, at best, only circumscribed ways of understanding who we are, apparent only to certain vantage points and part of only within certain contexts. Racial identities are problematic, on this analysis, not because they are never informative or fitting interpretations of individuals but because they monopolize identity. Race is an oppressive and dogmatic understanding of identity in which individuals are never allowed to be anything other than particular racial identities, even when these identities have no meaning within the context of issue.

Indeed, we might define racism as the claim that individuals are always and only their race. Rather than recognizing identity as contextual, as a matter of who we are within different contexts, racism claims that one context is always appropriate, that blacks or minorities are always blacks or minorities. Perhaps some individuals are blacks or racial minorities in certain contexts, just as they are baseball players or chess enthusiasts in others. Nevertheless, individuals can no more be understood monolithically and always as blacks or minorities than they can be understood monolithically and always as sports fanatics.

(3) If identity is multiple, we are not only or most fundamentally races, and if it is contextual we are not always races. Indeed, as the insights of social construction already highlight, we are races at all only because of the history to which we belong. The way we understand texts is also historically situated, rooted in our traditions of interpretation. For Gadamer, this situatedness is significant, not so much because it shows that meaning is socially constructed, but because it shows that while a given interpretation of a text is contextual and partial, it is not necessarily, for that reason, arbitrary or indiscriminate. We cannot understand texts in just any way we want. Instead, the way that we understand a text is guided by what Gadamer calls its own effective history,[23]

by the way the text has already been taken up, understood, and thought about in the tradition to which we belong. The guide that effective history provides does not require an explicit encounter with all the ways a text has historically been understood. Rather, a text's effective history is already part of the way we approach the text from the start; we cannot return to the time before Bach became classic or before the *Mass in B Minor* became a standard of excellence. Nor can we go back behind our racial history to determine how *Othello* or *The Merchant of Venice* might have been understood without it. Instead, the meaning we understand when we understand a text synthesizes our concerns and interest in it with the ways in which our interpreting predecessors have appropriated it and handed down its meaning in the cultural traditions to which both we and they belong. Gadamer calls this synthesis a "fusion of horizons," but he admits that, to a large degree, the horizon of the text and the horizon of the interpreter are the same.[24] As participants in the tradition for which *Othello* and *The Merchant of Venice* are important framers, we are the heirs of the history they influence; we are their effects. The meaning we understand, then, is less a fusion of two distinct horizons than a development of one horizon that is changed and enriched by its encounter with new circumstances, new questions and relations to new texts and events.

An important aspect of this hermeneutic analysis for an understanding of identity is that it explains the strength of our racial interpretations. The possibilities for our understandings of people are historically rooted in the same way as our understandings of texts. We can understand others and ourselves as blacks, Latinos, Asians, or whites because these categories make sense to us, and they make sense to us because of the developments and experiences of the history of which we are a part. Because of this history, certain aspects of people are important to us for the purposes of determining who they are; we look to their skin color, for example, and not to their eye color. Because of our unidirectional history, we cannot go back behind the Atlantic slave trade, the institution of slavery, or the practices of segregation to understand people in the terms we might have without these events; nor can we decide that race does not matter. Race is a partial and contextual understanding of who we are. Nevertheless, it is also a deeply historical and significant one. Indeed, for some people it will remain the most significant aspect of their identity even if they acknowledge their other identities as well. For some, their identities as parents are most significant; for others, it is their Irish heritage. We can assume that regardless of the strides we make in recreationalizing race, for many people it will reflect that part of themselves in which they take most pride and interest.

No aspect of a hermeneutic concept of race precludes this possibility, just as no aspect of our understanding of a text precludes our interest in one interpretation over others. We should remember, however, that we can reverse the emphasis: if race is significant to us, it is also partial and contextual. From the perspective of pride in our heritages, and especially in the context of struggles for racial equality, we can insist on the significance of racial identities as historically developed understandings of who we are that have continuing effects. Racial interpretations remain important not only to individuals' sense of themselves but also for research and policy purposes, for tracking diseases and treatment options that affect different demographic groups in different ways, for understanding the social, educational, and medical effects of poverty and housing segregation, for devising policies for correcting for centuries of abuse, and so on. It is worth pointing out, however, that racial understandings can also be misleading: looking for sickle-cell anemia only in those who look "black," for example, may fail to find it soon enough in those who do not. Hence, even if racial understandings are appropriate to certain contexts and purposes, no feature of our racial understandings suggests that they are entitled to a monopoly on who we are. Rather, we can be understood in as many different ways as texts are understood.

Problems with a Hermeneutic Analysis

By employing the analytic philosophy of language, Appiah is able to show that the concept of race makes no sense. Under an ideational theory of language, we know what "race" means when we know either the specific criterial beliefs that are individually necessary and jointly sufficient to define it, or a cluster of concepts that we can apply in a looser way. Under a referential theory of language, we know what "race" means when we know what causes our belief in it. Neither theory explains "race." Skin color can conflict with ancestry so that neither is individually necessary or jointly sufficient. Clusters of concepts allow for confusions between odd ideas about race and a failure to understand the concept. Finally, if members of different "races" can share more genes with each other than they do with members of their own "race," it is unclear how a referential theory can work. Accordingly, Appiah replaces the idea of race with that of racial identity and he constructs the latter as the outcome of specific and contingent historical events.

Appiah's brief account of social construction is one influenced primarily by the work of Ian Hacking. If we turn to the use of ideas of social construction in continental philosophy, however, we find an insight that appears to be missing from both the analytic philosophy of language and the hermeneutic account I have just proposed. For crucial to a social constructionist account that takes its bearings from Foucault rather than from Hacking is its dissection of the relation between construction and power. Moreover, from a Foucauldian point of view, what is important about power is the productive use it makes of contradictions. Thus the very contradictions in the concept of race that influence Appiah's skepticism and that influence my own pluralistic and interpretive account serve, from a Foucauldian point of view, as the entry point for race's legal, social, and political institutionalization. Penelope Deutscher's discussion of sexual identities is helpful in suggesting how this process works.[25]

Following Janet Halley's discussion of the 1986 Supreme Court decision in *Bowers v. Hardwick*, Deutscher argues that this now-overturned decision contains two different and contrasting ideas of homosexuality: first, that homosexuality is inborn, and, second, that it is not inborn at all but, instead, a perversion that has the potential to influence or infect heterosexuals. The first claim allows for a strict distinction between homosexuals and heterosexuals on biological grounds; the second claim means that homosexuals have no right to privacy to engage in consensual homosexual acts since such acts may influence or infect the rest of the population. The inconsistencies, however, do not destabilize the idea of homosexuality. Rather, they serve to multiply possibilities for discrimination: if homosexuals cannot be discriminated against on the basis of biology, they can be discriminated against on the basis of their potential influence on others; if they cannot be discriminated against on the basis of their potential influence on others, they can be discriminated against as a separate, minority population.

We can apply the same sort of argument to inconsistencies in the concept of race. If the concept of race is problematic, that characteristic simply provides an opportunity for institutions and practices to impose the concept all the more forcefully. The racial prerequisite cases that Ian F. Haney López has studied make this argument even more impressively than the sodomy cases that Deutscher reviews. From 1790 until 1952, the United States restricted naturalized citizenship to "whites," amending the law in 1870 to include "persons of African nativity and African descent."[26] Consequently district courts, circuit courts, and the United States Supreme Court had to decide who was white, whom the law meant to exclude, and, indeed, what a white person was. If we look at five representative cases decided between 1878 and 1927, we find that they disagreed on these questions. In *Ozawa v. United States* (1922), Takao Ozawa argued for his eligibility for citizenship on the ground of color, insisting, "The Japanese are of lighter color than other Eastern Asiatics, not rarely showing the transparent pink tint which whites assume as their own privilege."²⁷ But the Supreme Court rejected the idea that the words "white person" referred to color: "Manifestly the test afforded by the mere color of the skin of each individual is impracticable as that differs greatly among persons of the same race, even among Anglo-Saxons, ranging by imperceptible gradations from the fair blond to the swarthy brunette, the latter being darker than many of the lighter hued persons of the brown or yellow races. Hence to adopt the color test alone would result in a confused overlapping of races and a gradual merging of one into the other, without any practical line of separation."²⁸

Ozawa, the court concluded, was not white because he was Japanese and the Japanese were, racially speaking, not "Caucasian." In *Ex parte Shahid* (1913) and *United States v. Thind* (1923), however, the Court denied that white meant Caucasian. *Ex parte Shahid*, decided in South Carolina, concerned the question of whether Syrians were white. A 1909 case in Georgia, *In re Najour*, had concluded that Syrians were Caucasian and therefore white; nonetheless, *Ex parte Shahid* said that they were not white because, although they might be Caucasian, they were not European. *United States v. Thind* extended this reasoning. Bhagat Singh Thind relied on *Ozawa* in arguing that he was a high-class Hindu of the Aryan race and that experts from Blumenbach onward had identified Aryans with Caucasians.²⁹ Two 1910 cases decided by the Fifth and Second circuits (*United States v. Dolla* and *United States v. Balsara*) had agreed, deeming "Asian Indians" white, in the first case because of skin color and in the second case because of scientific evidence of belonging to the "Caucasian race."³⁰ Yet three months after rejecting Ozawa for naturalization as a non-Caucasian, the Supreme Court rejected Thind for naturalization as a non-European. Here it wrote that "mere ability on the part of an applicant . . . to establish a line of descent from a Caucasian ancestor will not *ipso facto* and necessarily conclude the inquiry. 'Caucasian' is a conventional word of much flexibility." Moreover, the opinion states, "the Aryan theory as a racial basis seems to be discredited by most" while "the word Caucasian is in scarcely better repute."³¹ One might ask, then, why the Court used it in rejecting Ozawa for naturalization. In any case, in *Thind* the same Court rejected all "scientific classification," basing its decision on the immigrants from the "British Isles and Northwestern Europe" whom the framers "must have had affirmatively in mind," along with the "immigrants from Eastern, Southern, and Middle Europe" who "were received as unquestionably akin to those already here."³²

In these prerequisite cases, white sometimes means Caucasian and sometimes means European; sometimes it has a scientific basis independent of skin color and sometimes it has no scientific basis but refers to the intentions of the framers. Nor did the courts become more consistent after 1927. In twelve cases between 1923 and 1942, numerous ethnicities were dubbed "not white," including Japanese, "Asian Indians," Armenians, Punjabis, Filipinos, Afghanis, and "Arabians." In 1944, however, Arabians became "white." The rationale for the federal court in Michigan calling them not white in 1942 referred to both common knowledge and legal precedent; ironically, so too did the rationale for the federal court in Massachusetts that in 1944 called them white.[33]

Given these peculiarities and inconsistencies in legal reasoning—so that the Supreme Court had to extricate itself from definitions it had made a mere three months earlier, and so that federal courts in different states came to different conclusions (and did so at least once by using exactly the same legal reasoning)—it is not difficult to argue that the courts meant to make no consistent distinctions in determining who could count as "white." Instead, they used the category to designate as nonwhite exactly those people whom they arbitrarily and at least momentarily wanted to designate in this way. "White" can refer to the category of Caucasian, as in *Ozawa v. United States*; or, when this definition fails to accomplish the purposes at hand, it can refer to the geographic area of Europe, as in *United States v. Thind*. When it cannot rely on scientific evidence, the courts can refer to common knowledge, and where they cannot rely on common knowledge, they can refer to scientific evidence. If race is incoherent as a concept, legal and political structures can make efficient use of this incoherence to impose race in just the way they desire.

This entanglement of race and power indicates the limits of an approach to race that relies on the insights of the analytic philosophy of language, inasmuch as that approach fails to see the constructive use that power makes of contradictions in the concept of race. Yet the entanglement of race and power also seems to point to the limits of a hermeneutic approach to race. In this regard, there seems to be an important difference between interpretations of identities and interpretations of texts, for interpretations of identity become institutionalized in a way that textual interpretations do not. To be sure, in a given discipline's hierarchies of power, certain schools and traditions of interpretation will have more status and clout than others.[34] Yet the ascendancy of a certain tradition or school of interpretation does not flow completely free of the interpretive project in the way that the institutions and practices of race do. Illuminating the flaws in a tradition or school of interpretation leads, at least theoretically, to the demise of that school or tradition and to the ascendancy of another. The same is not the case for our traditions of racial interpretation. Instead, the flaws in our understanding of race provide the entry point for the exercises of power that institutionalize it.

Yet it is not clear that this difference between textual and identity interpretations signals the limits of a hermeneutic approach. On the one hand, it is important to recognize the entanglement of race and power. On the other hand, it is precisely a hermeneutic approach that allows us to recognize this entanglement. As noted earlier, the adequacy of a particular interpretation of a text depends on its capacity to synthesize the meaning of the parts of the text with the meaning of the whole. An interpretation may de-emphasize certain parts of the text in favor of others; still, if it must simply ignore large parts of the text, it needs to be able to justify its doing so by showing why these parts are unimportant to the meaning of the whole. For Gadamer, this assumption is less a methodological precept than a point about understanding.[35] We cannot test our understanding of a text against the text itself because we have access to the text only in terms of the very understanding we are trying to test. What we can do, however, is test our understanding against itself or against other parts of itself, assuring ourselves that our understanding is self-consistent and able to account for the text as a whole.

The racial prerequisite cases obviously fail on this standard. In the singular context of assessing the components of a white citizen, courts sometimes refer to the category of Caucasian and sometimes deny its relevance; they sometimes refer to the geographic area of Europe and sometimes do not. Following Deutscher, we can emphasize the way these contradictions open up the space for the exercise of power. Following a hermeneutic analysis we can also locate the reason for the need to employ power at this point. The law, Ronald Dworkin points out, is akin to a chain novel in which different authors create a text serially: the first novelist writes a chapter of the book and hands it on to the second author, who takes up what he or she takes to be its important themes, elaborates and extends them, and then passes the two chapters on to the next author. Each author after the first has both to interpret the unified meaning that the individual chapters compose and to develop the text in their own part or chapter in the way he or she thinks is consistent with that overall interpretation.[36] Similarly, judges take up the law as they find it in a particular area; they interpret the various decisions, statutes, and ideas that compose it, extracting their overall meaning and carrying that meaning on in their disposition of new cases. Hence, to suppose that the Supreme Court can reject Ozawa's application for citizenship because he is not Caucasian and Thind's because the idea of a Caucasian identity is in disrepute is to suppose that a serial novel need possess no overall sense. Either Ozawa, the candidates of *Ex parte Shahid*, Najour, Thind, and Balsara are all white according to "scientific evidence" of belonging to the Caucasian "race" or they are all nonwhite because there is no Caucasian race and the framers did not have them "affirmatively in mind."

A hermeneutic approach, however, goes further. Gadamer insists that if we are to understand the meaning of a text, we must do more than unify its parts and whole. Rather, we must unify part and whole in a way that allows us to see what point the text may have for us. In other words, we must try to understand what the text is saying to which is worth our listening. Again, this requirement, like the requirement for unifying whole and part, is less a methodological precept than a point about understanding. As interpreters, we are the heirs of an effective history that conditions how we approach that which we are trying to understand: we cannot go back before the time for which *Othello* or *The Merchant of Venice* would necessarily raise racial issues for us. But this condition means that a large part of our struggle to understand is to see if and how our tradition may have misled us. Since we are situated in history and traditions, we are compelled to wonder if we can trust them. At the same time, insofar as our history and traditions already orient us to that which we are trying to understand, we can question them only by getting that which we are trying to understand to speak to us. In other words, if we are to do more than simply impose our preconceptions on the text, if we are to test those preconceptions, we must suppose that we can learn from the text and that it can alter our preconceptions. Otherwise, we are less the heirs of our tradition than its apologists.[37]

The same presumably holds for our legal decisions. Dworkin argues that the acceptability of a legal decision depends, first, on its ability to fit that decision into an understanding of a community's legal practice as a whole; still, it depends also on its ability to understand that legal practice in its "best light," or as the best it can be.[38] Dworkin takes seriously the notion that we understand the practice as the best *it* can be; some legal practices may not be very good even when we understand them as the best they can be. Nonetheless, understanding a legal practice in its best light requires that we understand its underlying principles and its development as an attempt to remain true to these principles. In the case of American law, these principles include justice, fairness, and due process. What Dworkin calls "law as integrity" is an understanding of American legal practice that understands it to honor these principles. Moreover, it requires us to employ these principles in adjudicating hard cases and, indeed, mistakes in legal decision making.[39]

On both Gadamer's and Dworkin's account, then, the standard that the hermeneutic circle of whole and part supplies goes beyond mere coherence to include understanding the point of a text or social practice. Not all texts or practices will continue to have one for us. In those cases, although we might be able to understand how the text or practice holds together, we will be unable to make sense out of it on any more substantive level. What is important for our legal tradition, however, is that its underlying point is a set of principles that we continue to take seriously. If we understand our legal practice in terms of a unity of part and whole that includes these principles — in other words, if we understand it in terms of an ideal of integrity — then we must also admit and correct our mistakes so that the whole and part of our legal practice can cohere. Because racial prerequisite laws and the decisions applying them preclude coherence with these principles, we must recognize them as mistakes. They are similar to chapters of a chain novel whose the authors simply failed to understand the narrative's underlying thrust.

To be sure, this conception of law differs from a Foucauldian-inspired account of law as the exercise of arbitrary power. Indeed, it argues that what allows us to see the racial prerequisite cases as exercises of power is just their inability to meet the standards of law as integrity. The hermeneutic unity of whole and part requires more from the courts than that they be consistent in their stipulations of who is to count as white. Unifying the whole of our law with principles of justice, fairness, and due process requires that we jettison race as a consideration for citizenship, a move we finally made in 1952.

Conclusion

The upshot of these reflections is to encourage an understanding of race as partial, contextual, and historical. Race will continue to be an important part of some people's identity. Because of the ongoing effects of the part it has played in our history, it will remain important for medicine, research, and the like. Perhaps, most significantly, race will remain important to struggles to remedy the damage done in its name. Nevertheless, race is only part of who we are, and we need to work to restrict its scope. We need to look forward to the day in which we will need to tell others that we are whites, blacks, Hispanics, or Asians, just as today we need to tell others that we are Italian, novel readers, and backgammon players. Different people will celebrate the different traditions, affiliations, values, and sensibilities to which the centuries of life and struggle in the United States have given rise. Race and racial identity, however, will have a completely individual significance without wider social, political, or economic influence.

NOTES

1. See K. Anthony Appiah "Race, Culture, Identity: Misunderstood Connections," in K. Anthony Appiah and Amy Gutmann, *Color Conscious: The Political Morality of Race* (Princeton, Princeton University Press, 1996), 30–105.
2. Ibid., 36.
3. See Lucius Outlaw, "On W. E. B. Du Bois's 'The Conservation of Races,'" in *Overcoming Racism and Sexism*, ed. Linda Bell and David Blumenfeld (New York: Rowman and Littlefield, 1995), 10111129.
4. Appiah, "Race, Culture, Identity," 72.
5. Ibid., 73.
6. See Stephen Cornell and Douglas Hartmann, *Ethnicity and Race: Making Identities in a Changing World*, (Thousand Oaks, Calif.: Pine Forge Press, 1998), 22–23.
7. See Ian F. Haney López, "The Social Construction of Race: Some Observations on Illusion, Fabrication, and Choice," *Harvard Civil Right-Civil Liberties Law Review* 29, no. 1 (1994): 12–13.
8. W. E. B. Du Bois, "The Conservation of Races," in *The Idea of Race*, ed. Robert Bernasconi and Tommy L. Lott (Indianapolis: Hackett, 2000), 109.
9. Ibid.
10. Michal Omi and Howard Winant, "Racial Formation," in *Race Critical Theories*, ed. Philomena Essed and David Theo Goldberg (Malden, Mass.: Blackwell, 2002), 123–45.
11. Cornell and Hartmann, *Ethnicity and Race*, 103–5.
12. See Ronald Takaki, *A Different Mirror: A History of Multicultural America* (Boston: Little, Brown, 1993), 63–67.
13. Cornell and Hartmann, *Ethnicity and Race*, 105–6.
14. Appiah, "Race, Culture, Identity," 97. See also Robert Gooding-Williams, "Race, Multiculturalism, and Democracy," in *Race*, ed. Robert Bernasconi (Malden, Mass.: Blackwell, 2001), 241–43.
15. Appiah, "Race, Culture, Identity," 103–4.
16. Ibid., 103.
17. Matthew Frye Jacobson, *Whiteness of a Different Color: European Immigrants and the Alchemy of Race* (Cambridge: Harvard University Press, 1998), 57.
18. Ibid., 46.
19. Ibid., 58–59.
20. Ibid., 44.
21. See Wilhelm Dilthey, "The Development of Hermeneutics," in *Dilthey: Selected Writings*, ed. H. Rickman (Cambridge: Cambridge University Press, 1976), esp. 259.
22. See Hans-Georg Gadamer, *Truth and Method*, 2d rev. ed., trans. Joel Weinsheimer and Donald G. Marshall (New York: Continuum, 1994), esp. 296.
23. Ibid., esp. 300–301.
24. Ibid., 299.
25. See Penelope Deutscher, *Yielding Gender: Feminism, Deconstruction, and the History of Philosophy* (New York: Routledge, 1997), 15–19.
26. Ian F. Haney López, *White by Law: The Legal Construction of Race* (New York: New York University Press, 1996), 42–44.

27. Ibid., 81.
28. *Takao Ozawa v. United States*, 260 U.S. 178 (1922). See also López, *White by Law*, app. B, 220.
29. Counsel in *United States v. Bhagat Singh Thind*, 261 U.S. 204 (1923).
30. See López, *White by Law*, app. A, 205.
31. *United States v. Bhagat Singh Thind.* See López, *White by Law*, app. B, 223.
32. *United States v. Bhagat Singh Thind.* See López, *White by Law*, app. B, 224.
33. See López, *White by Law*, app. A, 208.
34. Stanley Fish emphasizes this point in *Professional Correctness: Literary Studies and Political Change* (Oxford: Oxford University Press, 1995).
35. See Gadamer, *Truth and Method*, esp., 293–94.
36. Ronald Dworkin, *Law's Empire* (Cambridge: Harvard University Press, 1986), 229–32.
37. I am not sure that Gadamer would agree with this argument. Nevertheless, it seems to be a legitimate interpretation of what he means by saying that "we cannot stick blindly to out own fore-meaning about the thing if we want to understand the meaning of another. Of course, this does not mean that when we listen to someone or read a book we must forget all our fore-meanings concerning the content and all our own ideas. All that is asked is that we remain open to the meaning of the other person or text. But this openness always includes our situating the other meaning in relation to the whole of our own meanings or ourselves in relation to it" (*Truth and Method*, 268).
38. Dworkin, *Law's Empire*, 227–28.
39. Ibid., 96.

8

PHILOSOPHY IN CHAINS

John Ladd

The question before us is why there is such an underrepresentation of people of color (minorities, so-called) among the faculty and students in prestigious mainline American philosophy departments. This is clearly on many counts a deplorable situation. But I do not want to argue about that. There are many possible explanations for the whiteness of philosophy departments, and many different kinds of programs that have been developed to try to correct it, although they have not been very successful. I shall not consider them here. Instead, I shall focus on what seem to me to be some possible *philosophical reasons* why people of color are turned *down* and are turned *off* by the scholarly state of affairs they encounter in the present-day Anglo-Saxon world of philosophy. This chapter will be about what I see to be some philosophical barriers people of color face when they try to do philosophy in our philosophy departments. I shall call these barriers *philosophical chains*, because in many ways they limit the scope of philosophical inquiry, particularly as regards questions of ethics and political philosophy. As will soon become clear, many of these barriers are encountered by women and radical philosophers of different sorts as well as by philosophers from other traditions.

In short, when I claim that present-day philosophy is in *chains* I mean that the dominant ethos of today's mainstream Anglo-American philosophy imposes restrictions on the right aims of doing philosophy, on the proper sorts of problems to be explored, and on the right ways of dealing with them. As a result it closes off areas of philosophical exploration that an open, inquiring philosopher might want to develop. (Indeed, I would personally put it more strongly and say that philosophers have a duty to explore these verboten areas.)

A quick example will show what I mean. A philosopher might think, as I once did, that there are new and important philosophical problems of ethics that need to be explored through studying the diverse ways of thinking about values in different cultures. To say, "Oh, yes! That's just relativism. Plato took care of it long ago. So why bother us?" is a cheap answer to a serious moral issue, practical and political as well as philosophical.[1] The culturally imperialistic approach that categorizes the ethics of non-Western cultures as "primitive" and so unworthy of philosophical scrutiny is not only theoretically (and empirically) absurd but also immoral and politically dangerous. Such views are based on empirically unfounded fabrications such as those used to defend colonialism.[2] Further, contrary to current practice, it is obvious both for theoretical and political reasons that palpable cross-cultural differences of values can only be understood through a direct study of non-Western approaches to values in the context of their particular culture, language, and supporting beliefs.[3] It should be obvious that we need to learn to listen to people with other points of view instead of attributing ideas to them that we think they believe or ought to believe. Unfortunately, the inbred parochialism of traditional British moral philosophy handed down to us from Hobbes and Locke is still alive today in Anglo-American philosophical circles.

Against that parochialism, I suggest that there is an enormous potential for an insightful and even edifying understanding of basic philosophical problems (e.g., of ethics) to be gained through actually examining what other people from other societies and cultures think. In an increasingly globalizing civilization, ethical studies of that kind will have immense practical importance for intercultural understanding. As I have suggested, the first thing that we will learn is that other people do not always agree with what we take for granted (i.e., Western standards of "rationality"). To find out how other people actually think, we need to listen to them instead of making up what we think they think or ought to think, or else, as we usually do, dismissing them as irrational or, what is even worse, evil.

In this context, indeed, a persistent Socrates might jump in with questions about our own values and their presuppositions that are rooted in Western mentalities. We need to open our minds, and that, as I have said, means to listen! For greater mutual understanding we can look for help by talking with our own colleagues who come from other traditions or who are people of color.

Before proceeding, I must emphasize that it is not my intention in this chapter to offer a full-blown theory on the nature of philosophy. Rather my discussion here will be mostly internalist and critical.[4] I apologize if my "critiques" appear to be exaggerated. They are mainly intended to be speculative and provocative rather than conclusive. My purpose is to raise a few basic questions and to stimulate further discussion of what I take to be prevailing dogmas about what philosophy is and ought to be, and how, as I allege, they block the open consideration of new challenges to our own favorite ethical preconceptions, as well as the consideration of new approaches to old problems of ethics. In other words, it is about how certain philosophical mind-sets act as *chains*! I propose that if there are such chains, they should be examined on their own account and not simply because they conflict with particular preferred alternatives of our own. Everyone is invited to join the debate about philosophy in chains!

Problems for and Problems of Ethics

My late distinguished colleague C. J. Ducasse had a useful way of thinking about philosophical questions. He distinguished between two sorts of questions for a "science," which he called "questions *for*" and "questions *of* "that science. He used the term "science" broadly to include academic disciplines like philosophy and ethics. Let's just call them intellectual disciplines.

Questions for are problems that come from the outside. The discipline may aid in understanding these problems through identifying, clarifying, and sorting out the issues and by pointing out ways of resolving them. Take, for example, a problem for medicine: "How can we deal with this problem (e.g., a complaint such as a pain in the stomach)?"

In contrast, *questions of* are questions that are internal to the discipline itself, such as specialized scientific questions that need to be answered to deal with the other, practical kind of question. These are, for example, questions of physiology (say, anatomy or hematology). They are of direct significance only to professionals, who are the only ones capable of understanding and dealing with them. Of course, such questions can also be studied for their own sake, that is, without any definite practical goal in mind. Medical science is a vast subject.

In philosophy we also have both kinds of questions.[5] To begin with, we have problems *for* philosophy and *for* ethics. These are lived-experienced perplexities (e.g., about justice and happiness). They are perplexities that arise out of human experience in the world and in society. They reflect concerns of ordinary people, including people from other traditions and cultures. Examples might include ethical issues relating to genocide, slavery, ethnicity, human rights, equality, and freedom. Problems like these are problems *for* humanity at large, and are not just problems created by philosophers and of interest only to philosophers.

Let us now turn to questions *of* philosophy (ethics) that arise out of the need to deal with the practical questions, questions *for*, like those just mentioned. This is where ethical theories come in and where the analysis of specific types of ethical problems is required. Of course, philosophy has questions of its own, questions that are specialized within the discipline, such as the problem of the external world, the problem of induction, or the problem of universals. These are obviously questions of philosophy that do not ordinarily interest laypeople. In ethics itself—that is, ethical theory—such questions of philosophy might include puzzles in game theory, the trolley problem, questions about how to define and rank values, and so on. Strictly speaking, they are technical questions of interest only to specialists. They are not perplexities that come from real live experience.

But it is important to observe that, although human problems, questions *for* philosophy, such as those I have mentioned, are not created by philosophers, they are nevertheless problems that really need the help of philosophers to deal with them, to help people to understand them, to provide a diagnosis, and to show how to cope with them. In other words, trained philosophers are needed to help people identify and sort out the issues, and then to show, as far as possible, how to deal with them intelligently and responsibly. Here I have in mind the many urgent human problems facing society that desperately need help from philosophers with their tools of philosophical analysis. In particular, we have many new problems in the United States today that are connected with the intermingling of people from diverse populations, all with diverse loyalties and diverse values.

I mention Ducasse's distinction mainly to remind readers of what most of the great philosophers in the past have taken to be the distinctive character of ethics, namely, its relation to human needs and to social conduct, on the one hand, and to human and social problems. For that reason, Aristotle placed what we now call "ethics" under practical reason and practical wisdom. By the same token, most of the great moral philosophers recognized that ethical problems with which they are concerned come from real life, and that as philosophers they are expected to help society to cope with these problems. There are no better examples of this practical conception of the role of philosophy than the philosophies of Hobbes and of utilitarians like Bentham and Mill.

On the other hand, in contrast to most of classical ethics, a great deal of contemporary academic ethics in the Anglo-Saxon world is preoccupied with what I have called questions *of* ethics, that is, internal technical questions that do not have any obvious tie to real-life problems. The almost-exclusive concern with internal, specialized problems of philosophy might be called *academic scholasticism*. Indeed, many of the contemporary debates among the elite philosophers seem quite like the parody of medieval scholasticism, "How many angels can dance on the head of a pin?" Contemporary scholasticism in philosophy gives preference to questions that can be formulated as technical problems (e.g., puzzles in game theory or in Rawlsian constructions). Combined with a preference for technical problems is the growing scholastic devotion to what might be called *secondhand research*—that is, research that takes the form of critical studies by A of B's paper on C, and so down the line, instead of focusing directly on the identification and analysis of ethical problems themselves.[6] As a consequence of this kind of "inbreeding," new problems are hard to find in the philosophical circle. (It is easy to see why this prevailing scholastic practice erects barriers for people of color who are not in the loop.)

Sidgwick and the Common Sense Syndrome

Let me now return to a more specific scrutiny of the barriers, the "chains," that constrain the scope and character of contemporary ethics. Here it is easiest to begin with Henry Sidgwick,[7] who might be said to have set the stage for the contemporary preferred mode of doing ethics.[8] As Schneewind[9] points out, Sidgwick is an adherent of the "Common Sense school," an approach that Sidgwick seeks to refine by drawing on intuitionism and utilitarianism (he calls them "methods"). These sources set the stage for an ethically conservative approach based on accepted moral opinion. In this vein he apologizes, right at the beginning, for publishing a book "upon a subject so trite as Ethics."[10]

Later he writes that "in seeking a definition of [Justice] we may, so to speak, clip the ragged edge of common usage, but we must not make excision of any considerable portion."[11] It should be pointed out that this view of the methodology of ethics as founded on what might be called "reconstructed common sense" provides the background for Rawls's "reflective equilibrium" and his "constructivism."

The appeal to "received" opinion, regardless of how it is qualified, amounts in the end to basing ethics on the ethical *status quo* and so sanctifies what is essentially *a stay away from difficult issues* approach to ethics.[12] An ethics based on such presumptions is ill-equipped to respond to new social, political, and technological challenges in the modern world and to revolutionary developments generating new sorts of practical questions crying out for philosophical analysis and clarification. Ethical questions relating to colonialism, slavery, and war are not even on the agenda of Victorian philosophy.[13] The excuse, of course, was that such matters pertain only to "primitive people," who being uncivilized are unable to understand and participate appropriately in civilized ethics.[14]

In any case, and apart from all that, Sidgwick states that his immediate object, contra Aristotle, is "not Practice but Knowledge."[15] Again, I would argue that in ethics, theory ("knowledge") and practice cannot be sharply distinguished and separated. They are mutually dependent on each other, conceptually and psychologically.[16]

What is tragic is that this "classical" treatise was composed in the wake of such disasters as the Black Hole of Calcutta and the Crimean War and after the issue of slavery had precipitated the bloody Civil War in the United States. On the other side, it preceded only by a few years the exposures of King Leopold of Belgium's genocidal ventures in the Congo and the coming of World War I. Traditional British Common Sense ethics, I submit, has its limitations as a guide to ethics. Anyway, for purposes of this chapter, we can see how the adoption of Sidgwick's kind of approach to ethics places noteworthy constraints on ways of doing philosophy and contributes a significant link in the chains that I have in mind here.

Let us turn to some other links in the chains preventing creative approaches in contemporary academic philosophical circles.

The "Veil of Ignorance" and the Obsession with Impartiality

To begin with, a significant feature of present-day American-British ethics is its doctrinaire commitment to the problematic dogma that ethics needs to be founded on some notion or other of impartiality, such as, for instance, the "veil of ignorance," the "view from nowhere," and such like. It is taken for granted that the impersonality of ethics is a necessary condition of thinking about ethics in general; it is assumed to define "the moral point of view."

Historically, the notion of impartiality was introduced into eighteenth-century moral philosophy to provide a counter to Hobbesian egoism. Its adherents took the impartiality of a judge as a paradigm, assuming that only if ethics is based on such impartiality can it be objective rather than subjective. There are lots of steps in the analogy that are presupposed here.

It is obvious that some kind of impartiality is a requirement of valid judgments in many institutionalized practices, not only for judges in law courts, but for referees in sports and in competition for prizes, and so on; otherwise, the competitive activity itself would be "unfair" and its purpose would be undermined. But its usefulness in fields such as sport does not warrant its being universalized as a condition of ethics. That is a non sequitur.

Indeed, to assume that an analogous kind of constraint (impartiality) is necessary for a sound ethical discussion is a source of great confusion. It hardly needs to be pointed out that definitions of "impartiality" and its cognates are themselves quite controversial. Indeed, they are miserably obscure and beg many questions. I would maintain that the ethical claims for impartiality are not only ungrounded, but also counterproductive.

Consider, for example, a dispute between two parties with a third party acting as mediator. The job of a mediator is not to decide which party is right (i.e., who should win and who should lose); that is the job of an arbitrator or a judge. In contrast, the job of a mediator is to bring the parties together, to find a peaceful solution to the conflict, an accommodation perhaps. Here we have a lot to learn from the Navajos, where instead of imposing a judicial decision on a defendant as in Western law, the chief Navajo judge sets up a number of reconciliation committees consisting of fellow family and clan members, who, of course, have a vested interest in a peaceful outcome.[17]

What I am arguing here is that the notion of impartiality of ethics is not only incoherent, but it is built on an upside-down conception of ethics itself. Sound ethical judgment does not require limited "input," as the "veil of ignorance" paradigm requires. Rather, judgment requires a maximum of relevant knowledge (and experience), which usually involves shared experience as well as dialogue. To impose a solution on the basis of doctrinaire limitations of knowledge and experience makes any solution arrived at necessarily arbitrary, artificial, and, I might add, usually unjust!

When we are dealing with people of color, who may come from an entirely different background, with different expectations and different kinds of social relations and social experiences, a Procrustean solution of the kind resulting from the "veil of ignorance" is bound to cause unnecessary distress and is liable to provoke antagonistic responses. Further, the use of the artifice of a veil of ignorance smacks of paternalism, with all the troubles that paternalistic colonialism has brought to people from other parts of the world. All this, I contend, lies under the surface of the demand for "impartiality" and the "veil of ignorance"—and, I should add, provides just another link in the chains that keeps mainstream American and British philosophers from taking seriously the philosophical concerns of people of color.

Two Meanings of Personal Identity

Turning now to substantial issues, it is clear that there is a breakdown in communication between the concerns of Anglo-American philosophies and the concerns of people of color over the use of the idea of personal identity. Roughly speaking, for people of color the concept of identity is used to "define" the self in relation to others, especially their own particular group.[18] Thus, for them identity in this sense is basic for understanding and articulating a range of ethical problems that particularly concern them as nonwhites.

For mainstream philosophy, on the other hand, problems relating to identity are primarily metaphysical problems, such as those involved in, say, theories of the self. Here philosophers are perplexed by questions about the identity and continuity of the self over time, a problem that is particularly worrisome for empiricists who have rejected the notion of substance. How do I know that the I of today is the same thing as the I of tomorrow (i.e., is identical to it)? This is particularly troublesome for Humeans, who hold that the self is a bundle of perceptions and yet wish to preserve the kind of ethical standards that presuppose that it is possible for the same selves to be involved in the future as in the present. Hume's theory of promising would make no sense without that kind of presupposition. There is a large literature on this philosophical problem of identity.[19]

It is clear that the concept of identity used by people of color belongs to an entirely different category from that of the concept used in mainline philosophical circles. In fact, their use is actually closer than the philosophical concept to the standard dictionary definition of "identity." For present purposes, we might call the concept in question "psychological," since it was made famous by the psychologist Erik Erickson in his theory of "identity crises." (For purposes of identification, I shall call it *the psychosocial concept of identity*.)

The kinds of problem that involve this psychosocial concept of identity are questions like: "Who am I?" "Where do I fit in a multiracial and multiethnic world?" "Where do I belong?" and so on. Although questions like these may concern whites, they are particularly relevant for people of color as they move into new social environments where they encounter questions about their identify in the face of different social expectations, different social structures, and different sets of social values—especially in regard to what are viewed as different "kinds" of people.

There are many psychological, social, and political questions that arise in connection with problems of identity in this sense, and a good number of them are directly or indirectly ethical. Obviously, for children in American society who are of mixed race the psychological problems of identity are particularly critical. More generally, problems of acceptance and adjustment to new social conditions at all levels have significant ethical implications for all parties in American society.

A full analysis of problems relating to this kind of identity would focus on the close relationship between personal identity and the network of social relationships that contributes to defining one's self-identity.[20] To deal adequately with these issues would lead us to an extended analysis of social relationships as an ethical category.[21]

In addition to such matters, there are a number of theoretical ethical problems connected with the kind of self-identity that I have called psychosocial. How is it to be defined? How does it fit into the body of other ethical and moral psychological concepts? Does it, like the dictionary definition, imply that there are different kinds of people, and, of course, what does that really mean? Here we must be careful with the idea of "a kind of people," so as not to define it in a culturally biased way (e.g., politically or genetically), or in a way that creates the basis for intolerance, racial prejudice, or genocide.

Accordingly, we must always bear in mind that identity in the sense under discussion can be used for evil as well as good purposes (e.g., identifying oneself as a Nazi or a terrorist). Such considerations show that identity is a tricky concept that needs to be carefully qualified if we wish to use it in positive ethical argumentation. In fact, there is a hornet's nest of problems relating to identity. If we wish to bring this kind of identity into accord with an acceptable body of other ethical and moral psychological concepts, the concept needs to be carefully delineated.[22]

It should be obvious, therefore, that to legitimize the concept of identity as it is used here in connection with racial and ethnic identities, we must carefully explain and defend how it is to be used, what it is supposed to cover, and how it relates to other ethically significant concepts. In particular, to avoid its being abused, we must have some clear and plausible way of defining ethically legitimate group identity so as to exclude groups that are nihilistic, destructive, and unethical, like Nazis and other sorts of racist organizations. To do all this, as I have already suggested, requires a lot more reflective philosophical analysis than can be undertaken here.[23]

To continue, even if we have satisfactorily explicated the notion of identity so that it can be used constructively and will be able to play a positive role in moral reflection and ethical dialogue, we still need to ask many other questions: What kind of role should it play? Do we have a duty to respect others' identity? Are human rights connected with identity? Do public institutions like the government need to take racial identity into consideration in their public policies? and so on. In sum, considerations of social, racial, and ethnic identities raise a number of ethical issues that obviously need to be addressed.[24]

One other point that needs to be mentioned here is a philosophical one. There is a close connection between social identities and the self (the ego), at least when they are considered from an ethical point of view. To respect a person's identity is to respect him or her as a person, and its opposite, to "disrespect" a person on account of his or her identity, is ethically objectionable as an attack on his or her personhood. Thus insults and humiliation, which are related, are bad not merely socially but also morally, because they can be viewed as abuses of a person as a person (i.e., as an ego). A few words on this are in order.

We must begin by distinguishing between simply criticizing or reproving another person's conduct for one reason or another and intentionally or even unintentionally abusing a person *as a person*. In this regard, it is especially objectionable to abuse another person simply because he or she is a member of a particular racial or ethnic group. The reason why the latter is so objectionable is that abusing a single person in that way in effect implies that one is abusing the whole group. That, of course, is the essence of racism and of other objectionable forms of discrimination. To put it bluntly, all such misbehaviors must be taken seriously from an ethical point of view, because, whether intentionally or not, they are attacks on persons as persons.

Before going on, I should like to say something more specific about the ethics of *humiliation*, because it has important social and political implications. The dictionary defines "to humiliate" as "to lower the pride or self-esteem of another; to subject another to feelings of inferiority or worthlessness," and so forth. In older times, where honor was prized as both a public and a personal value, to humiliate meant to *dishonor* a person.[25]

Humiliation of another person or group, regardless of whether it is intentional, is ordinarily an intolerable hurt and as such is morally deplorable. More often than not the person who metes out the humiliation comes from a powerful and prestigious upper class (in the case of slavery, the owner), and the right to abuse the other person is regarded by her or him as one of the privileges of their class, power, or ownership. I call attention to the case of humiliation because not only is it immoral per se, but it has numerous repercussions and is especially disruptive socially and politically. A not-uncommon example from the academic world will show what I mean.

A white professor tells an African American student that he cannot expect to pass his course because blacks are not capable of doing satisfactory work in his area (usually a science). How insensitive and counterproductive can remarks like that be? It is especially counterproductive because the uninhibited expression of attitudes like that discourage other African Americans from taking similar courses (in this case, in science).

I conclude this chapter by calling attention once more to the fact that the ethical condemnation of "disrespecting" and "humiliating" another person or group on, say, racist grounds is a topic that is difficult for mainline American moral philosophers to understand because they lack the necessary tools of analysis to address the underlying ethical issues connected with social relationships. Their commitment to an individualistic (atomic) view of human relationships,[26] sometimes called the "billiard ball" concept of social action, makes it impossible for them to deal ethically with the kinds of social situations where, say, one person or group inflicts harm on another person or group. To repeat, they simply lack the conceptual apparatus to deal with social relationships, both positive and negative, as an ethically significant category. Incidentally, I should point out another side of establishment ethics that I have not had time to explore, namely, that its preferred approach focuses on the positive side of ethics, such as what is good and deficiencies of good (i.e., "bad" or "evil"), instead of dealing directly with blatant evils like slavery, genocide, rape, domestic violence, and other evils that as such are not reducible simply to the absence of good. But the question of evil is a wholly different subject that goes beyond the scope of this chapter.

To illustrate concretely what is at issue in this whole matter, let us consider the difference between whites and African Americans over *why* slavery is evil. Mainline whites maintain that slavery is evil because it deprives individuals of the means of securing primary goods. Technically, slavery is bad because of its consequences (i.e., it is "instrumentally" bad). For African Americans, in contrast, particularly those descended from former slaves, slavery as an institution and the mere condition of being a slave—which involves being subject to such degrading behavior as whipping, being sold off, having their womenfolk subject to their owners' lustful desires, and so forth—humiliates them as persons; it degrades them into nonpersons.[27]

What I am concerned with in this chapter is a large subject, of course, and, as I pointed out at the beginning, my contentions about chains are quite speculative and tentative. They are intended to provoke discussion. As far as this last part is concerned all that I can say here is to invite young philosophers to explore the ethics of human relationships as they involve individuals and groups. Particularly important in this regard, as I have just mentioned, is the need to explore the ethical aspects of the widespread disregard of the feelings of others as they are connected with their concept of the self and with associated groups and institutions. The whole subject of the ethics of people's morally significant relationships, as well as the ethical aspects of their connection with social groups and institutions, not to mention reflecting on their evil side, needs to be explored in a way that goes way beyond the present-day restrictions on philosophical inquiry that I have called "chains." Once philosophy is released from its chains, its newfound freedom will enable it to return to its ancient role of helping humankind to understand and cope with the challenges and problems of modern society, which are waiting for help from philosophers with critical insight into understanding and coping with them in an intelligent and rational way—without the present restrictions!

NOTES

1. Philosophical discussions of ethical relativism are to be found in my little collection *Ethical Relativism* (Lanham, Md.: University Press of America, 1985).

2. See Lucien Levy-Bruhl, *La mentalité primitive* (Oxford: Clarendon Press, 1931). Levy-Bruhl argues at some length that the primitive mentality has no place for logic. My own experience proved how completely wrong his arguments are, and in fact he has no empirical evidence to back up his claims. See also John Ladd, "Colonialism and the Moral Philosophers," *Balayi: Culture, Law, and Colonialism* 1 (February 2000): n. 13.

3. As far as I know, my own study of the ethics of the Navajo Indians was the only serious philosophical venture in comparative ethics. Except for courteous acknowledgements of its existence by friends and colleagues, however, the whole idea of the study was ignored by the philosophical world as an eccentric Ladd hobbyhorse. Shortly after its appearance, I received a postcard from my friend John Rawls, saying that my idea of a Navajo ethics was a contradiction of the notion of ethics itself. So much for philosophy and multiculturalism! See John Ladd, *The Structure of a Moral Code: Navaho Ethics* (1957; repr., Eugene, Ore.: Wipf and Stock, 2004).

4. Elsewhere I have distinguished between two different kinds of argument that can be brought against an ethical position one wants to falsify. They might be called *methods of falsification* in ethics. The first kind of argument, which I call *positive (confutation)*, consists of showing that the theory is inconsistent with an accepted position, notably, one's own accepted theory. The second, which I call *negative (refutation)*, tries to show that the theory itself can be dismissed as incoherent, self-contradictory, or absurd on some other account, such as contradicting well-known facts (e.g., of science). The two modes of critique might be called *internalist* and *externalist*, respectively. (The externalist mode bears resemblance to what is called "deconstruction" in current jargon.) The popular method used in philosophical circles today utilizes counterexamples to attack a philosophical theory, including an ethical position. The counterexample technique would be *internalist* (positive) because it presupposes that the counterexample itself is already accepted (or acceptable).

5. When I was a graduate student, a sharp distinction was made between what were called "normative ethics" and "meta-ethics." The first would be concerned with questions *for* ethics (e.g., questions about right and wrong), and the second with questions *of* ethics (e.g., the status of moral judgments, ethical reasoning, etc.). The dogmatic separation of the two kinds of questions came under fire, including in earlier writings of mine. Obviously, the division of questions *for* and questions *of* is only a division of convenience and is in no way absolute.

6. For comments on this problem, I recommend Kant's remarks on this point in his announcement for his lectures in 1764. See John Ladd, "Kant as Teacher," *Teaching Philosophy* 5 (January 1982): 1–9. Needless to say, recent developments of what could be called "applied" ethics, such as medical ethics, business ethics, and engineering ethics, are an exception, since they have been developed in response to the request for philosophical advice on particular problems in the spirit of questions *for* philosophy.

7. Henry Sidgwick, *The Methods of Ethics*, 7th ed. (1907; repr., London: Dover, 1966).

8. John Rawls writes, "Henry Sidgwick, *The Methods of Ethics*, . . . is, I believe, the outstanding achievement of modern moral theory. . . . [It] defined much of the framework of subsequent philosophy." *Collected Papers* (Cambridge: Harvard University Press, 1999), 341.

9. J. B. Schneewind, *Sidgwick's Ethics and Victorian Moral Philosophy* (Oxford: Clarendon Press, 1977).

10. Sidgwick, *Methods of Ethics*.

11. Ibid., 264.

12. Schneewind writes, "There seems to be no indication that Sidgwick was aware of . . . the kind of criticism that a Marxist might give of his assumption that a social consensus is possible in a class society" (*Sidgwick's Ethics*, 193n).

13. See John Ladd, "Colonialism and the Moral Philosophers," *Balayi: Culture, Law, and Colonialism* 1 (February 2000): 115–28. Copies available from the author.

14. See Levy-Bruhl, *La mentalité primitive*.

15. Henry Sidgwick, *The Methods of Ethics*, ed. Emily Elizabeth Constance Jones (New York: Macmillan, 1901), vi.

16. Sidgwick's distinction between practice and knowledge implies a clear-cut bifurcation between the cognitive (knowledge) and the noncognitive (motivational) sides of ethics. As a result of that bifurcation we have the paradoxical consequence that to persuade a person to do his duty, it will be necessary not only to persuade him that it is his duty but also to provide him with a motive (incentive) for doing his duty. A symptom of this difficulty is the fact that Sidgwick himself took pains to create an ethical society, which was an interdisciplinary group of scholars whose aim was to find ways to motivate people to do what is moral. The assumption by the society was that people already *know* what is moral; in addition, however, they also need to be provided with motives to do it. The usual answer was to appeal to religion to provide sanctions. For details, see Henry Sidgwick, *Practical Ethics: A Collection of Addresses and Essays*, ed. Sissela Bok (New York: Oxford University Press, 1998). The papers were originally published in 1898. Here we might ask: Does one, in addition to having a duty, also we need to have a duty to have a motive to do one's duty? Does this not lead to a ladder of duties?

17. The judge's name is the Hon. Robert Yazzie. See his "Life Comes from It: Navajo Justice Concepts," *New Mexico Law Review* 24 (Spring 1994): 175.

18. "To have an identity is in part to be related to others in particular ways and to understand that one is so related." Brian Fay, *Contemporary Philosophy of Social Science* (Oxford: Blackwell, 1996), 46.

19. A useful up-to-date account of problems of identity in the philosophical sense can be found in John Perry, *Identity, Personal Identity, and the Self* (Indianapolis: Hackett, 2002).

20. An illuminating discussion of this whole issue can be found in Fay, *Contemporary Philosophy of Social Science*.

21. See ibid. I have also discussed these concepts in my articles on the idea of community. See John Ladd, "The Idea of Community, an Ethical Exploration, Part II: Community as a System of Social and Moral Interrelationships," *Journal of Value Inquiry* 32 (1998): 153–74. There is a growing philosophical literature on the concepts of social relations and groups related to

them. See, for example, Christine Sistare, Larry May, and Leslie Francis, *Groups and Group Rights* (Lawrence: University Press of Kansas, 2001).

22. Barring such clarification, it is easy to understand why Jews and other groups that were targets of Hitler's genocide take the idea of racial identity itself to be a threatening concept that should be banned.

23. I suggest that the basic logical fallacy underlying Nazi ideology and other objectionable forms of statism is that their basic approach is holistic, so that "social wholes, not their individual human members," are the bedrock of the analysis. For a sociological critique of holism, see Fay, *Contemporary Philosophy of Social Science*, sec. 3.1. For an ethical critique, see part I of "The Idea of Community," *Journal of Value of Value Inquiry* 32 (1998): 3–24.

24. Please remember that here I am concerned only with principles and not with the particularities of legislation and political programs.

25. It may be worthwhile mentioning that Kant, who is so frequently caricatured as a rigid, emotionless Puritan, was in fact explicitly concerned about the sort of personal humiliation to which the lower classes as well as the natives in the colonies were subjected. See Ladd, "Colonialism and the Moral Philosophers."

26. For more on atomism in social theory, see Fay, *Contemporary Philosophy of Social Science*, 30.

27. Whites who have not already done so are urged to read Frederick Douglass's account of the last flogging, which can be found in his *Life and Times of Frederick Douglass* (Hartford, Conn.: Park Publishing, 1881), chap. 17.

CONTRIBUTORS

JOHN D. CAPUTO is the Thomas J. Watson Professor of Religion and Humanities at Syracuse University. He is also David R. Cook Professor Emeritus of Philosophy at Villanova University, where he taught from 1968 until 2004. His most recent publications include *Augustine and Postmodernism: Confessions and Circumfession* (Indiana, 2004); *On Religion* (Routledge, 2001); *More Radical Hermeneutics: On Not Knowing Who We Are* (Indiana, 2000); *The Prayers and Tears of Jacques Derrida: Religion Without Religion* (Indiana, 1997); *Deconstruction in a Nutshell: A Conversation with Jacques Derrida* (Fordham, 1997); and *The Weakness of God: A Theology of the Event* (Indiana, 2006). He also serves as Editor of the Fordham University Press book series Perspectives in Continental Philosophy and Chair of the Board of Editors of the *Journal of Cultural and Religious Theory*.

DAVID COUZENS HOY has taught philosophy at Yale University; Princeton University; Barnard College; Columbia University; University of California, Los Angeles; and University of California, Berkeley. He is currently Distinguished Professor of Philosophy at the University of California, Santa Cruz, where he chaired the department of philosophy for a decade and served several terms as Acting Dean of Humanities. He was awarded the Presidential Chair in Philosophy in 2000 as well as the title of Distinguished Professor of Humanities in 2004. In addition to over sixty essays published in journals and books, he has published *The Critical Circle* (California, 1978) and *Critical Theory* (with Thomas McCarthy, Blackwell, 1996), *Critical Resistance: From Poststructuralism to Post-Critique* (MIT, 2004), as well as the anthology *Foucault: A Critical Reader* (Blackwell, 1984). These works have been translated into many languages, including Italian, French, Japanese, Korean, Spanish, and Chinese. MIT Press published his latest book, *The Time of Our Lives: A Critical History of Temporality*, in 2009.

JOHN LADD is Professor of Philosophy Emeritus at Brown University, where he has been on the faculty since 1950. In addition to Brown University, he has held teaching appointments at Harvard University, the University of Göttingen (Germany), and Smith College. In the early 1950s he made a field trip to New Mexico and conducted a philosophical inquiry into the ethical ideas of the Navajo Indians. The results of this study are set forth in his *Structure of a Moral Code: A Philosophical Analysis of Ethical Discourse Applied to the Ethics of the Navaho Indians* (Harvard, 1956). He was founder and first director of the Brown University Center for the Study of Race and Ethnicity in America. His other published works include the anthologies *Ethical Questions Relating to Life and Death* (Oxford, 1979) and

Ethical Relativism (University Press of America, 1973; 1985); and a translation of *Metaphysical Elements of Justice: Part I of the Metaphysics of Morals by Immanuel Kant*, revised edition (Hackett, 1965; 1998). Ladd's most recent articles include "Philosophical Reflections on Race and Racism," *American Behavioral Scientist* (October 1997); "The Idea of Community: An Ethical Exploration," *Journal of Value Inquiry* (September 1998); and "Colonialism and the Moral Philosophers," which appeared in the February 2000 issue of the journal *Balayi*.

JOSEPH MARGOLIS is Laura H. Carnell Professor of Philosophy at Temple University. His main interests are in the philosophy of the human sciences, the theory of knowledge and interpretation, aesthetics, philosophy of mind, American philosophy, and pragmatism. He serves on the editorial board of many philosophical journals and is completing the third volume in a trilogy of books on contemporary American philosophy. Professor Margolis is currently participating in the Temple philosophy department's Vietnamese Philosophy Exchange. Among his many publications are *Moral Philosophy After 9/11* (Penn State, 2004); *The Unraveling of Scientism: American Philosophy at the End of the Twentieth Century* (Cornell, 2003); *Reinventing Pragmatism: American Philosophy at the End of the Twentieth Century* (Cornell, 2002); *Selves and Other Texts: The Case for Cultural Realism* (Penn State, 2001); and *What, After All, Is a Work of Art: Lectures in the Philosophy of Art* (Penn State, 1999).

ROY MARTINEZ was born in Dangriga, Belize. After studying in the United States, Denmark, and Canada, he received his Ph.D. in Philosophy from l'Université de Montréal. From 1982 to 1984, he served as Principal of Dauphin River School, Dauphin River, Manitoba, Canada, a Saulteaux Indian reservation. Besides articles in *International Philosophical Quarterly*, *Laval théologique et philosophique*, *Philosophy Today*, and several other journals, he has published *Kierkegaard and the Art of Irony* (Humanities Books, 2001) and has edited *The Very Idea of Radical Hermeneutics* (Humanities Press, 1997). His most recent articles include "Acting with Kierkegaard," *International Philosophical Quarterly* (September 2003); and "Figuring Kierkegaard's Religious Individual," *Laval théologique et philosophique* (October 2003). He was Professor of Philosophy and former Chair of the Department of Philosophy (1990–96) and of the Department of Philosophy and Religion (1996–2003) at Spelman College.

LADELLE MCWHORTER is Thomas Professor of Philosophy and Professor of Women, Gender, and Sexuality Studies at the University of Richmond. Her research interests are in feminist theory, twentieth-century French and German philosophy, and political philosophy. She is the author of *Bodies and Pleasures: Foucault and the Politics of Sexual Normalization* (Indiana, 1999), *Racism and Sexual Oppression in Anglo-America: A Genealogy* (Indiana, 2009), and the editor of *Heidegger and the Earth: Essays in Environmental Philosophy* (University of Toronto Press, 2009). Many of her articles, which treat the works of Foucault, Bataille, and Irigaray, have appeared as book chapters and others have been published in the *Journal of Philosophy, Hypatia, Philosophy and Social Criticism, Philosophy Today*, and *International Studies in Philosophy*.

SHANNON SULLIVAN is Head of Philosophy and Professor of Philosophy, Women's Studies, and African and African American Studies at Penn State University. She is the author of *Revealing Whiteness: The Unconscious Habits of Racial Privilege* (Indiana, 2006); and *Living Across and Through Skins: Transactional Bodies, Pragmatism, and Feminism* (Indiana, 2001). She has coedited (with Nancy Tuana) a special issue of *Hypatia* on "Feminist Epistemologies of Ignorance" (Summer 2006), and an anthology on *Race and Epistemologies of Ignorance* (SUNY, 2007).

GEORGIA WARNKE is Distinguished Professor of Philosophy at the University of California, Riverside. She is the author of *Gadamer: Hermeneutics, Tradition, and Reason* (Stanford, 1987); *Justice and Interpretation* (MIT, 1993); *Legitimate Differences: Interpretation in the Abortion Controversy and Other Public Debates* (California, 1999); and *After Identity: Rethinking Race, Sex and Gender* (Cambridge 2007). Her recent articles include "Social Identity as Interpretation" in *Gadamer's Century: Essays in Honor of Hans-Georg Gadamer*, ed. Ulrich Arnswaldt (MIT, 2002); "Rorty's Democratic Hermeneutics," in *Richard Rorty*, ed. Charles Guignon and Richard Riley (Cambridge, 2003); and "Markets, Democracy, and Educational Vouchers," in *Globalization, Culture, and the Limits of the Market: Essays in Economics and Philosophy*, ed. Stephen Cullenberg and Prasanta K. Pattanaik (Oxford, 2004).

CYNTHIA WILLETT is Professor of Philosophy at Emory University. Her research interests include political ethics, moral philosophy, ethics and social theory, race and gender studies, philosophy and literature, new critical theory, and American social thought. She is the author of *Irony in the Age of Empire: Comic Perspectives on Freedom and Democracy* (Indiana, 2008); *The Soul of Justice: Social Bonds and Racial Hubris* (Cornell, 2001); and *Maternal Ethics and Other Slave Moralities* (Routledge, 1995); and the editor of *Theorizing Multiculturalism* (Blackwell, 1998). Her articles have appeared in *Cultural Critique, Philosophy and Literature, Research in Phenomenology*, and the *Journal in Speculative Philosophy*.

INDEX

Note: Page numbers followed by n refer to notes, with note number.

AAUP Bulletin, 32
academic scholasticism, in contemporary ethics, 135–36
academy
 moral failures of, 33
 perception of racism as thing of the past, 41
 perception of scholars of color, 41
 status quo in, white fear of upsetting, 41–42
Adieu to Emmanuel Levinas (Derrida), 11
Adorno, Theodor, approach to racism, 58–59
affirmative action, and notion of fairness, 90–91
Africa, *Weltanschauung* of, 28 n. 34
African Americans. *See* blacks
African philosophy, lack of interest in, 92
Against Ethics (Caputo), 5–6, 12, 20
Agassiz, Louis, 73
AIDS, 8
Allen, Theodore, 64–67, 82 n. 16, 83 n. 17, 85 n. 31
alterity of other
 as invisibility, 8–12
 as visible difference, 12
alternate epistemology, search for, 7–8
American Association of University Professors (AAUP), failure to support free speech, 33
American Philosophical Association, ix
Amos (prophet), 4, 5, 6
analytic philosophy of language
 and definition of race, 114–16, 123–24
 limitations of, 126
anatomo-politics of the human body, 75
ancestral memory, and fear of addressing race issue, xiii–xiv
Anglo America, development of race concept in, 63–69, 71–74
Anglo-American philosophy. *See also* white philosophers
 and ethics of social relationships, failure to address, 142–43
 and evil, failure to adequately address, 142

traditions of: as barriers to inquiry, 55, 132–33; silence on race, xviii
 views on continental philosophy, 55
 views on identity, *vs.* those of people of color, 139–40
antidialectical philosophers, and race issue, 94
Anti-Semite and Jew (Reflexions sur la question juive; Sartre), 57–58, 81 n. 6
anti-Semitism
 as case of racial hatred, 103
 as fear of one's freedom, 104
 Frankfurt School on, 59
 Sartre on, 46–47, 57–58, 81 n. 6, 103–4
Appiah, Kwame Anthony, 26 n. 21, 114–16, 117–18, 123
Aptheker, Herbert, 26 n. 20
Aristotle
 on ethics as practical discipline, 135
 on national instability, 35
artifacts of racism, counterbalancing of, 90–91
Augustine, Saint, xix
The Authoritarian Personality (Adorno et al.), 58–59

Bacon's Rebellion, 65
Banton, Michael, 73
Beauvoir, Simone de, 110
Being and Nothingness (Sartre), 104
Beloved (Morrison), 95
Bentham, Jeremy, 135
Bernasconi, Robert, ix, 38, 51–52, 83 n. 25
biological science
 development of, 70
 and normalization of phenomena, 70
 and race concept, development of, 68–71
biopolitics of the population, 75
biopower
 as antithesis of philosophy, 81
 colonialism and, 76–77, 108
 defined, 75
 efforts to disrupt, 79
 origins of, 74–75
 and state racism, 75–78, 107–9

Black Orpheus (Sartre), 46–47, 104–5
blacks
　anti-black racism, Sartre on, 46–48, 58, 81–82 nn. 4–6, 105–6
　black consciousness, Sartre on, 105
　civility of, in black neighborhoods, 31
　inferiority, origin of concept, 73
　lack of success, causes of, 34
　male, "boy" as term for, 47
　problems of, as product of white domination, 45–46
　racial formation in, 116–17
　students of philosophy, need to recruit, 51–52
bond-laborers
　as *de facto* chattel slaves, 82 n. 17
　rebelliousness of, 64–66
　short life expectancy of, 65, 83 n. 17
Bourdieu, Pierre
　on field and habitus, 101–2
　on foundationalism's failure to address empirical matters, 101–2
　on social status in modern society, 93–94
Bowers v. Hardwick (1986), 124
boy, as term for black males, 47
Brague, Rémi, xii
Burton, Robert, 61
Butler, Judith, 38

Caldwell, Charles, 73
capacitation, American lack of, 34
castration, of slaves, 85 n. 29
Caucasian race, and definition of whiteness, 125–26, 127–28
Chanter, Tina, 38
chattel slavery, in colonial American, prior to black slavery, 82 n. 17
"The Childhood of a Leader" (Sartre), 103–4, 110
Christianity
　American, necessity of profound change in, 35, 36
　conflict with Islam, 36
　and homosexual rights, 8
civility
　of blacks, in black neighborhoods, 31
　impact on racism, 34
　and interracial relations, 31–32, 35
　as key to ending racism, 37
civil rights era, emphasis on colorblind society, 89–90
Civil War, economy of South following, 74
class concept
　complex relationship to race, gender, and nationality, 51
　origin of, xiv
　psychological basis of, xv–xvi
　state racism as response to, 68
Climacus, Johannes, 6
Cody, William "Buffalo Bill," 27 n. 33
Collins, Patricia Hill, 91, 95
colonialism
　and biopower, 76–77, 108
　and development of modern racism, 77
　ethical solipsism in, 27 n. 24
　and language, Sartre on, 105
　and myth of modernity, 44
　reparations owed because of, 44–45
　Third World underdevelopment as legacy of, 43–44
colonialists, as other, 49
colonized people, dependency complex of, 27 n. 24
colorblindness of liberal humanism, as racist, 46–48
colorblind society. *See also* recreational status of racial identity
　as liberal goal, 89–91
　as Sartre's goal, 46–47, 105–6
Common Sense school, as barrier to ethical inquiry, 136–37
comparative ethics
　academy's lack of interest in, 132–33, 143 n. 3
　potential benefits of, 133
compassion, and hospitality, 22–24
concrete realities of life, radical hermeneutics and, 12–13, 21
confession
　as form of this text, xii–xiii, xix
　as unproductive, 42–43
Confessions (Augustine), xix
Conrad, Joseph, 8–9, 16–18, 27 n. 30
containment, politics of
　consequences of, 96
　multiculturalism and, 91
　new racial politics and, 95–96
contextuality of identity, and diffusion of racial identity, 121, 122–23
continental philosophy. *See also* white philosophers
　addressing of racism: boundaries of legitimate philosophy and, 55; and European lack of interest in racism, 57; historical approach, benefits of, 61–62; inability to address racism as structural

problem, 60; increase in, 95; subjectivity in, 59–60; works on race, 57–60
  failure to address race, reasons for, xii, 38–41, 55–57, 89–90, 91, 94, 97, 99
  support of white privilege, necessity of investigating, 49–52
continental tradition
  failure to address race, 91
  and identity, race as force in, 91–95
  racial implications of, 91–92
Cornell, Drucilla, 7
cowardice, Sartre on, 103
Crania Americana (Morton), 73
critical theory, *vs.* traditional theory, 100–101
cultural context of identity, and race, 121, 122–23, 128
cultures of thought, continental, racial implications of, 91–92

"Dark Hearts: Heidegger, Richardson, and Evil" (Caputo), 8–9
darkness
  in Conrad's *Heart of Darkness*, 8–9, 16–18
  of not-knowing, and hospitality toward the other, 22–24
Darwinism, and race concept, 68–69
decolonization, and flight of capital, 44
defensiveness, silence on race as, xiii–xiv
democracy in America, danger of further decline in, 36–37
democracy to come, distance between contemporary democracy and, 5
Demythologizing Heidegger (Caputo), 5–6
Derrida, Jacques
  on accents, significance of, 27 n. 30
  Adieu to Emmanuel Levinas, 11
  on dream of innumerable differences, 13
  on Heidegger, 6
  on inner eyes, construction of, 24
  on *mondialisation*, 15–16
  on monstrous nature of *tout autre*, 15
Descartes, René, 92
Deutscher, Penelope, 124, 127
dialectic, as theme in race writers, 94
Dialect of Enlightenment (Horkheimer and Adorno), 58–59
dignity, depriving others of, as loss of, xvi
disciplinary power, Foucault on, 107
discipline, normalization of, 74–75
Discipline and Punish (Foucault), 107, 108
discipline and punish, age of, 96

dispositif, racism as, 67, 78
diversity, as goal, *vs.* colorblind society, 91
Dooley, Mark, 25 n. 9
Dostoevsky, Fyodor, 8
Douglass, Frederick, 97, 144 n. 27
Du Bois, W. E. B.
  on concept of race, 26 n. 20, 116
  The Souls of Black Folk, 95
  on souls of white folks, 49
Ducasse, C. J., 134
Dworkin, Ronald, 127, 128–29

effective history of text, 121–22
Ellison, Ralph, xvii, 4, 24
Emerson, Ralph Waldo, xvi, xvii, xviii
empirical matters, foundationalism's failure to address, 101–2
England, Saxon racial identity, formation of, 62, 82 n. 13, 82 n. 14
Erikson, Erik, 139
An Essay on the Causes of the Variety of Complexion and Figure in the Human Species (Smith), 72–73
ethical solipsism
  in colonialism, 27 n. 24
  in encounters with the other, 15–18, 19, 23, 27 n. 24
ethical truth, invisibility of, and welcoming of the other, 22–24
ethics
  Common Sense school, as barrier to inquiry, 136–37
  comparative: academy's lack of interest in, 132–33, 143 n. 3; potential benefits of, 133
  contemporary, academic scholasticism in, 135–36
  falsification, methods of, 143 n. 4
  of humiliation, 141–42, 145 n. 25
  impartiality standard, as barrier to inquiry, 137–38
  knowledge *vs.* practice in, 136, 144 n. 16
  non-Western, academy's lack of interest in, 132–33, 143 n. 3
  normative *vs.* meta, 143 n. 5
  as practical discipline, 135, 144 n. 6
ethnocentrism, racism as, 59
etiquette. *See* civility
Europe, belief in European freedom from racism, 40–41
evil, Anglo-American philosophy's failure to address, 142
"Existentialism Is a Humanism" (Sartre), 103

Ex parte Shahid (1913), 125
exploitation of others, as element of human nature, 34–35

face of other
　impossibility of erasing, 17–18
　invisibility of, 8–12
　as visible other, 12
fairness
　and ideal of colorblind society, 90–91
　and procedural republic, 90
falsification, methods of, in ethics, 143 n. 4
Fanon, Frantz
　on colonialism, 27 n. 24, 43–44, 49
　Sartre on, 110
　on Sartre's vision of racelessness, 46–47
　on white condescension, 48
fascism, biopower and, 68, 69
feminist philosophers
　authors addressing race, 38
　failure to address race, reasons for, 38–41
　motives for addressing race, 50–51
　tradition of personal reflection in, 39
feminist theory
　alternate epistemology, search for, 7
　men's relationship to, 50–51
field
　defined, 101
　of philosophy, and neglect of racism, 101–2
first philosophy. *See* foundationalism
Foucault, Michel
　antifoundationalism of, 109–10
　anti-individualism of, 111
　approach to racism, 106–9
　on biopower, 74–78
　death of, 8
　on development of biological science, 70
　Discipline and Punish, 107, 108
　and historical approach to racism, 61–62
　on history of race concept, 62–64, 68–69
　The History of Sexuality, 61–62, 74, 106
　post-structuralism of, 109–11
　on power, 106–7
　rejection of universal humanism as goal, 106
　on response to injustice, 79
　and social construction of racial identity, 124
　Society Must Be Defended, 62, 74, 106–7
foundationalism
　failure to address empirical matters, 101–2
　and neglect of race, 99

　in phenomenological approach, 111
　in Sartre, 99, 109–10
France, belief in French freedom from racism, 40
Frankfurt School
　on anti-Semitism, 59
　on racism, 58–59
Franklin, Benjamin, 64, 83 n. 18
free blacks, reasons for discrimination against, 71–72
Freud, Sigmund
　and continental tradition, 91
　on identity, 93

Gadamer, Hans-Georg
　on adequacy of interpretation, 127
　on effective history of text, 121–22
　and hermeneutics of racial identity, 119
　on interpretation of point, 128, 129, 131 n. 37
gender, complex relationship to race, class, and nationality, 51
genealogical method
　and discovery of new ways of thinking, 80–81
　Hume's *vs.* Nietzsche's use of, 100
Georgia, and slavery, 83 n. 22
Germany, belief in German freedom from racism, 40
Gliddon, George, 73
globalization, as global blanching, 15–16
Goldberg, David Theo, ix
Gooch, William, 71–72, 85 n. 31
Gordon, Lewis, 81 n. 4, 82 n. 7
group identities, Sartre on, 46
guilt. *See* white guilt

habitus, defined, 101
Hacking, Ian, 123–24
Hadot, Pierre, 80
Hale, Grace, 81
Halley, Janet, 124
Hammond, James, xv
Haney López, Ian F., 124–26
Harris, Leonard, ix
Heart of Darkness (Conrad), 8–9, 16–18, 27 n. 30
Hegelians
　on agons for recognition, 93
　and race issue, 94
Heidegger, Martin
　and Conrad's *Heart of Darkness*, 8–9, 16–17

foundationalism in, 99
racial overtones in, 5–6
Hellenistic philosophy, as practice, 80
hermeneutics
  interpretation of laws on race with, 127–29
  interpretation of race with, 119–23
  limitations of interpretation of race, 123–28
historicity of identity, and race, 122–23, 128
The History of Sexuality (Foucault), 61–62, 74, 106
Hitler, Adolf, 40
Hobbes, Thomas, 135
Hoffman, Paul, 26 n. 20
holism, in state racism, 144 n. 23
homosexuality, inconsistencies in constructions of, 124
homosexual rights, as "inventing the good," 7–8
Horkheimer, Max
  approach to racism, 58–59
  on traditional *vs.* critical theory, 100
hospitality toward others
  auto-hospitality as condition of, 21, 23
  as remedy for racism, 20–24
hubris, age of, 96
human nature
  exploitation of others as innate characteristic of, 34–35
  racial hatred as aspect of, 34–35, 61
Hume, David, and genealogical method, 100
humiliation, ethics of, 141–42, 145 n. 25
Huntington, Samuel, 35–36
Husserl, Edmund
  on alterity of other, 10–11
  cognitivism of, 13–14
  on constituting of other, 14
  European prejudice of, 13–14, 16

ideational theory of language, and definition of race, 114–15, 123
identity
  cultural context of, and race, 121, 122–23, 128
  historicity of, and race, 122–23, 128
  multiplicity of, and race, 120
  people of color's perspective on. *See* psychosocial concept of, *below*
  psychosocial concept of: *vs.* philosopher's perspective, 139–40; problems and issues with, 139–41, 144 n. 22
  race as force in: and continental tradition, 91–95; liberal skepticism about, 89–90

racial hatred and, 103–4
social: groups focusing on, 91; liberal skepticism toward, 89–90, 96–97
identity politics
  resentment generated by, 95
  rise of, 91
impartiality in ethics, as barrier to inquiry, 137–38
indentured servants. *See* bond-laborers
individualism
  and blindness toward soical forces, 96–97
  of Sartre, 111
integrity, as standard for law, 128–29
intellectual disciplines, questions *for vs.* questions *of*, 134–36
interracial neighborhoods, Margolis's residence in, 29–32
interracial relations, natural etiquette and, 31–32
The Invention of Race: Black Culture and the Politics of Representation (Lott), ix
The Invention of the White Race (Allen), 64–67
invisibility
  of ethical truth, and welcoming of the other, 21–24
  of racism: in academic status quo, 42; racism's ability to morph and, 34
Iraq war, as hubris of foreign domination, 96
Irish race, white status accorded to, 118
Islam, conflict of Christianity with, 36
Israelites, and slavery, 24 n. 3
Italian race, white status accorded to, 118

Japanese culture, ritual petition of new neighbors for acceptance in, 32
Jefferson, Thomas, 64, 73, 83 n. 18
les juifs, as metonym for innocent victims, 6, 10

Kames, Lord, 85 n. 33
Kant, Immanuel
  on humiliation, 144 n. 25
  as natural historian, 70
  on origin of races, 72–73
  as progenitor of modern concept of race, 83 n. 25
  on race concept, 69
  on racial status of Native Americans, 71, 84 n. 28
Kierkegaard, Søren, 94

knowledge *vs.* practice, in ethics, 136, 144 n. 16
Kristeva, Julia, on racial hatred, 48–49

language
 and colonialism, Sartre on, 105
 philosophy of, and definition of race, 114–16, 123–24
law on race
 hermeneutic analysis of, 127–29
 integrity as standard for, 128–29
 and social construction of racial identity, 124–26
Lawson, Bill, ix
Levinas, Emmanuel
 and Conrad's *Heart of Darkness*, 9
 ethical essentialism of, 12
 on ethical solipsism, 15
 on face of the other, 9–12, 24 n. 3
 on oppressed peoples, 6
 Otherwise Than Being, 10
 and race issue, 94
 tout autre of, 6
Levy-Bruhl, Lucien, 143 n. 2
liberal humanism, racelessness of as racist, 46–48
liberals
 colorblind society as goal of, 89–91
 skepticism toward social identity, 89–90, 96–97
 views on race, 89–90
Linnaeus, Carl, 70, 84 n. 28
look, and alienation, Sartre on, 105, 111
Lott, Tommy, ix
lynching, and psychoanalytic paradigm of United States, 93
Lyotard, Jean-François, on *les juifs*, 6, 10

Mannoni, Dominique O., 27 n. 24
Margolis, Joseph
 house renovation by, 30–31
 ostracizing of, in South Carolina, 32–33
 racially mixed neighborhood of, 29–32
Martín-Alcoff, Linda, 38
Marxism
 philosophical, inability to address racism, 60
 state racism as response to, 68
maternal nurturing, and social Eros of the individual, 97
McGary, Howard, ix
McWhorter, Madelle, 38

Merleau-Ponty, Maurice
 and continental tradition, 91
 foundationalism in, 99
 and politics of flesh, 92
messianisms, concrete *vs.* abstract, 5
Middle Passage, 94, 95
Mill, John Stuart, 135
Mills, Charles W., 26 n. 21
modernity
 myth of, colonialism and, 44
 as white European construct, 15–16
morphological concept of race
 and biopower, 76, 77
 origins of, 71–72, 85 n. 31
Morrison, Toni, 94–95
Morton, Samuel George, 73
motivations, tendency to conceal, xv
mulattoes, reasons for discrimination against, 71–72
multiculturalism
 as goal, *vs.* colorblind society, 91
 and new politics of containment, 91
 philosophical limitations of concept, 91
multiplicity of identities, and diffusion of racial identity, 120
murderousness of freedom, 15–18, 19, 23, 27 n. 24
Murphy, Julien, 58
myth of modernity, colonialism and, 44

Najour, In re (1909), 125
national governments, impotence of to end racism, 33
nationality, complex relationship to race, gender, and class, 51
Native Americans
 as bond-laborers, 65, 83 n. 20
 Kant on race of, 71, 84 n. 28
 as "red" race, 71, 84 n. 28
natural etiquette. *See* civility
natural history, development of biological science from, 70
Nazi Germany, and state racism, 68
negritude
 as anti-racist racism, 105
 controversy surrounding term, 112 n. 18
neoliberalism, and age of hubris, 96
neutral individual, impossibility of, 42
Nietzsche, Friedrich
 and continental tradition, 91
 and genealogical method, 100
 and will to power, 93

non-Western cultures
  ethics of, academy's lack of interest in, 132–33, 143 n. 3
  rationality and, 133, 143 n. 2
normalization
  of discipline, and rise of biopower, 74–75
  of phenomena, biological science and, 70
Nott, Josiah, 73

objectification of others
  and ethical invisibility, 8–12
  and ethical solipsism, 15–18, 27 n. 24
  impossibility of full objectification, xiv
  origin of concept, xiv
Oliver, Kelly, 38
Omi, Michael, 56, 59, 116
On Religion (Caputo), 4
"On the Different Races of Man" (Kant), 84 n. 28
oppression
  addressing of, as *de facto* addressing of racism, 4–7, 24 n. 3, 25 n. 9
  Jews as exemplars of, 6, 10
other
  accepting self as, 18–20
  constituting of, 14
  encounters with: ethical solipsism in, 15–18, 27 n. 24; shock of, 13–18, 48–49
  ethical invisibility of, 8–12
  fear of, 15
  hospitality toward, 20–24
  Husserl on, 10–11
  impossibility of erasing, 17–18
  learning to see, 18–24
  Levinas on, 10–12
  as visible other, 12
  welcoming of inner other, 21, 23
Otherwise than Being (Levinas), 10
Outlaw, Lucius, ix, 26 n. 21
Ozawa, Takao, 124–25
Ozawa v. United States (1922), 124–25, 126, 127–28

Palestinians, as *les juifs*, 6
"A Party Down at the Square" (Ellison), xvii
people of color. *See also* blacks
  awareness of moral evil of white civilization, 43
  perspective on identity: *vs.* perspective of philosophers, 139–40; problems and issues in, 139–41, 144 n. 22

and philosophy, barriers to interest in, 132, 136, 137, 138, 139
  white reparations due to, 45–46
Peyrère, Isaac de, 85 n. 33
phenomenology
  and issue of race, 109–11
  subjectivity and, 59–60
philosophical chains
  as barrier to people of color's interest in philosophy, 132, 136, 137, 138, 139
  defined, 132
philosophy. *See also* Anglo-American philosophy; continental philosophy; feminist philosophers; white philosophers
  barriers to people of color in, 132, 136, 137, 138, 139
  as exploration of new ways of thinking, 80–81
  irrelevance of race to, 89–90
  political perspectives in: necessity of, 42; philosophers' rejection of, 42
  as practice, 80
philosophy profession
  complicity with racism, 102
  need to recruit people of color to, 51–52, 132
  race as challenge to, 89
Plato, scholastic reason in, 101–2
poetics of space, in Merleau-Ponty, 92
political activism, impotence of to end racism, 34
political correctness, perception of critical philosophy of race as, 41
political entropy, and perpetuation of racism, 33–34
politics of recognition, limitations of, 91
polygeny theory, 73–74
population, nation defined as, 75
"Portrait of the Anti-Semite" (Sartre), 103–4
post-structuralism
  openness to peripheral areas of philosophy, 99–100
  and race issue, 94, 95, 109–11
power
  Foucault on, 106–7
  and social construction of racial identity, 124–26
practice *vs.* knowledge, in ethics, 136, 144 n. 16
Pre-Adamite (Peyrère), 85 n. 33
procedural republic, 90
psychoanalytic tradition, on identity, 92–93

psychosocial concept of identity
    as perspective of people of color, 139–40
    problems and issues in, 139–41, 144 n. 22
Puritans, and development of race concept, 62

questions *for* vs. questions *of*, 134–36

race(s)
    complex relationship to gender, class and nationality, 51
    degenerate, and state racism, 76–78
    liberal views on, 89–90
    positive aspects of, 13
    as social construct, 116–17
    as surface phenomenon, 9–13
    un-raced norm, lack of, 16, 18–19, 45
race, biological reality of
    debate on, 26 n. 21, 53 n. 22
    development of concept, 64, 68–71
    irrelevance of, to sociocultural reality, 37, 46, 53 n. 23, 79
    lack of scientific basis for, 13, 26 n. 20, 45
    and morphological concept of race, development of, 71–72, 85 n. 31
    and state racism, 108
race, as concept. *See also* biopower; racial identity; state racism
    biological meaning, development of, 64, 69
    Frankfurt school on, 59
    history of, 60–74
    impossibility of defining, 59, 78, 114–16, 123
    morphological concept: and biopower, 76, 77; origins of, 71–72, 85 n. 31
    origin of races, early theories on, 72–74
    scientific meaning: adaptability of, 79; development of, 68–71; *vs.* state racism, 77–78
    Supreme Court efforts to define, 124–26
race, as topic
    perception of as faddish, 41–42
    perception of as unnecessarily contentious, 41
    sensitivity of, ix, 38–39
racelessness of liberal humanism, as racist, 46–48
race writers, dialectical themes in, 94–95
racial categories
    benign use of, 37, 61, 123, 129
    importance of maintaining: for assessment of white guilt, 45; for remedying damage done, 129
    and positive recognition of people of color, 46–48
racial difference, shock of encounter with, 13–18, 48–49
racial equality, history of approaches to, 89–91
racial formation, 116–17
racial hatred
    depth of, 13
    as element of human nature, 34–35, 61
    impact on hater, 103–4
    Kristeva on, 48–49
    pre-Darwinian concept of racism and, 63
racial identity
    hermeneutics in interpretation of, 119–23
    institutionalization of, 126–27
    internalization of, 117
    problems with hermeneutical interpretation of, 123–28
    recreational status of: as goal, 129–30; possibility of, for non-white races, 118–19, 123; within white groups, 118
    social construction of, 116–17; Foucault and, 124; inconsistencies in, as occasion for discrimination, 124–26
racial politics, new, and containment, 95–96
racial purity. *See* biopower; state racism
racism. *See also* state racism
    ability to morph into invisibility, 34
    anti-black, Sartre on, 46–48, 58, 81–82 nn. 4–6, 105–6
    definition of, 103, 121; in continental philosophy, 59–60; lack of clarity in, 56; personal *vs.* structural views of, 59–60
    and destabilization of U.S., 35–36
    development of concept, 60–74
    as *dispositif*, 67, 78
    ending of: assertion of other identities and, 117; impotence of efforts toward, 33–35; necessary steps toward, 35–36; possibility of, 79, 102
    as fear of one's freedom, 104
    ignoring of, as political act, 42
    persistence of, causes of, 78–79
    scientific: adaptability of, 79; development of, 68–71; *vs.* state racism, 77–78
    as thing of the past: America's false claim of, 37; as excuse for failing to address problem, 39–40, 41

racists
  impact of racial hatred on, xvi–xvii, 103
  psychological pathology of, need for research on, xiv
Radical Hermeneutics (Caputo), 7
radical hermeneutics, and concrete realities of life, 12–13, 21
radical philosophers, traditions of Anglo-American philosophy as barrier to, 132
rationality
  and non-Western cultures, 133, 143 n. 2
  search for alternate epistemology to, 7–8
Rawls, John
  and Common Sense school, 136
  on non-Western ethics, 143 n. 3
  on race-free society, 90
  on Sidgwick, 144 n. 8
reason, as white European construct, 16, 19–20
recapitulation theory
  development of, 71
  as justification for white supremacy, 47–48
recognition, politics of, limitations of, 91
recreational status of racial identity
  as goal, 129–30
  possibility of, for non-white races, 118–19, 123
  within white groups, 118
referential theory of language, and definition of race, 114, 115–16, 123
Reflexions sur la question juive (*Anti-Semite and Jew*; Sartre, Jean-Paul), 57–58, 81 n. 6
religion, prophetic, as summons to address suffering of innocents, 7
religious right, on homosexuality, 8, 25 n. 12
reparations
  colonialism and, 44–45
  fairness and, 90–91
"The Respectful Prostitute" (Sartre), 110
reverse discrimination in academia, 41
Richardson, Bill, 8, 16
Ricoeur, Paul
  on Nietzsche's genealogy, 100
  on pertinence of race issue, xviii
Rorty, Richard, 7
Royal Africa Company, 65

Sandel, Michael, 90
Sartre, Jean-Paul
  on anti-black racism, 46–48, 58, 81–82 nn. 4–6, 105–6

Anti-Semite and Jew, 57–58, 81 n. 6
  on anti-Semitism, 46–47, 57–58, 81 n. 6, 103–4
  approach to racism, 57–58, 102–6
Being and Nothingness, 104
"Black Orpheus," 46–47, 104–5
"The Childhood of a Leader," 103–4, 110
  colorblind society as goal of, 46–47, 105–6
"Existentialism Is a Humanism," 103
  failure to identify solution to racism, 110–11
  foundationalism in, 99, 109–10
  on gender, 110
  on group identities, 46
  individualism of, 111
  on pertinence of race issue, xviii
  phenomenology of, 109–11
  "Portrait of the Anti-Semite," 103–4
  on racial categories, 46–48
  "The Respectful Prostitute," 110
  scholastic reason in, 101–2
  on white guilt, 37, 43
"Sartre on American Racism" (Murphy), 58
Saxon racial identity, formation of, 62, 82 n. 13, 82 n. 14
scars of racism, efforts to heal, 94
scholasticism, academic, in contemporary ethics, 135–36
Schürmann, Reiner, 8
Schutte, Ofelia, 38
scientific racism
  adaptability of, 79
  development of, 68–71
  vs. state racism, 77–78
scripts, racial identity and, 117–18
secondhand research, in contemporary ethics, 136
segregation in Southern U.S., isolation of whites opposed to, 32–33
self
  as other to others, 18–20
  as other to self, 15
  sovereignty of, depriving others of, as self-debasement, xvi–xvii
self-discovery, fear of, silence on race as, xiii–xiv
Sen, Amartya, 34
Senghor, Léopold, 112 n. 18
September 11th terrorist attacks, racial overtones of, xi–xii
Sidgwick, Henry, 136–37, 144 n. 16

silence on race, 3–4
  in American philosophical tradition, xviii
  reasons for, xii–xiv, xviii, 4, 38–41, 55–57, 89–90, 94, 97, 99
  as unacceptable, xiii, xvii
Simon, Paul, 3, 24
Sketches of the History of Man (Kames), 85 n. 33
slavery
  abolition of, 74
  and black racial formation, 116–17
  evil of, as philosophical issue, 142
  inadequacy of legal justifications for, xvi
  in North America, origins of, 65–66, 82 n. 17
  origin of concept, xiv
  rationalizations of, xv–xvi
slaves
  impregnation of, by masters, 73–74
  punishment of, 85 n. 29
slave songs, 95
Smith, Samuel Stanhope, 72–73
social construction of racial identity, 116–17
  Foucault and, 124
  inconsistencies in, as occasion for discrimination, 124–26
Social Darwinism, and race concept, 68–69
social Eros of the individual, 97
social identity
  groups focusing on, 91
  liberal skepticism toward, 89–90, 96–97
social relationships, ethics of, 141–43
Society Must Be Defended (Foucault), 62, 74, 106–7
solipsism, ethical
  in colonialism, 27 n. 24
  in encounters with the other, 15–18, 19, 23, 27 n. 24
The Souls of Black Folk (Du Bois), 95
South Carolina, segregation in, 32–33
sovereignty of self, depriving others of, as self-debasement, xvi–xvii
space, as raced, 92
state racism
  biopower and, 75–78, 107–9
  development of, 68–69
  holism in, 144 n. 23
  vs. scientific racism, 77–78
Stocking, George, 85 n. 33
subjectivity, in continental philosophy, 59–60
superiority, human need for feeling of, xv

Supreme Court, efforts to define race, 124–26, 127–28

teaching of philosophy of race, 103
Thales, 99, 112 n. 4
theory, traditional
  vs. critical theory, 100–101
  critical theory's criticisms of, 101
  failure to address racism, reasons for, 101–2
Thind, Bhagat Singh, 125
Third World
  underdevelopment, as legacy of colonialism, 43–44
  Western reparations due to, 44–45
Thoreau, Henry David, xviii
Thoughts on the Original Unity of the Human Race (Caldwell), 73
Tocqueville, Alexis de, xviii
torture, lack of justification for, xvii
traditional theory
  vs. critical theory, 100–101
  critical theory's criticisms of, 101
  failure to address racism, reasons for, 101–2
truth, accepting relative nature of, 19–20
Tutu, Desmond, 28 n. 34

United Nations, impotence of to end racism, 33
United States
  and culture of hubris, 96
  racist organization of society in, 78
  state racism in, 77
United States v. Balsara (1910), 125
United States v. Dolla (1910), 125
United States v. Thind (1923), 125, 126

veil of ignorance, as barrier to inquiry, 137–38
The Very Rich Hours of Count von Stauffenberg (West), xvii
violence, as central to Western values, 47
Virginia Colony
  Bacon's Rebellion, 65
  development of race concept in, 71–72
  white supremacism in legal code of, 65–66

Walzer, Michael, 90
Webster, Daniel, xvi
West, Paul, xvii
West, Richard, 71

Western values
  collapse of, 43
  as version of Western moral evil, 43
  violence as central element in, 47
  white guilt as form of, 43
white(s)
  American: pride in European heritage, xi; self-satisfaction of, xiv
  as monstrous other to others, 19
  women, self-abnegation of, as tool of white privilege, 51
white civilization, moral evil of, 43
white guilt
  as counterproductive, xii, 42–43, 51
  as form of white moral evil, 43
  racial distribution of guilt and, 45–46
  Sartre on, 37, 43
whiteness
  as generic norm, 16, 18–19, 45
  as mask, 19–20
  reason as construct of, 16, 19–20
  Supreme Court efforts to define, 124–26
white philosophers. *See also* Anglo-American philosophy; continental philosophy
  addressing of race by: analyzing motives for, 50–51; current authors, ix, 38; need for more of, ix; strategies of, 42–43
  failure to address race, 3–4; in American philosophical tradition, xviii; reasons for, xii–xiv, xviii, 4, 38–41, 55–57, 89–90, 94, 97, 99; as unacceptable, xiii, xvii
white privilege
  continental philosophy's support of, importance of investigating, 49–50
  covert functioning of in contemporary society, 45
  invention of concept, 65–68
  as pretense, 19–20
  recapitulation theory as justification for, 47–48
  as source of black problems, 45–46
  white women's self-abnegation as tool of, 51
white race
  groups awarded status as, 118–19
  invention of concept, 64–68
white racial identity, undesirable other required to define, 118
Willett, Cynthia, 38
Williams, Bernard, 100
Winant, Howard, 56, 59, 116
women, white, self-abnegation of as tool of white privilege, 51
women philosophers, and traditions of Anglo-American philosophy, as barrier, 132
The Wretched of the Earth (Fanon), 43–44

Žižek, Slavej, 93

www.ingramcontent.com/pod-product-compliance
Lightning Source LLC
Chambersburg PA
CBHW021406290426
44108CB00010B/416